Talin Iryn

Defying the Multi-Tentacle Marriage Restrictions on Xyorath

Kwan Adams

ISBN: 9781779694737
Imprint: Popcorn Waffle Muffin
Copyright © 2024 Kwan Adams.
All Rights Reserved.

Contents

Introduction

Origins and Early Life

The Planet of Xyorath

Xyorath, a planet located in the outer reaches of the Andromeda Galaxy, is a place of awe-inspiring beauty and unique biodiversity. Nestled amidst the cosmic wonders of the universe, Xyorath holds a prominent position in the intergalactic community. With its vibrant landscapes and diverse ecosystems, it has become a sought-after destination for interstellar travelers and researchers alike.

The planet's geological composition is a marvel in itself, as massive mountain ranges stretch across its surface, their peaks touching the heavens. The valleys, carved by ancient rivers, are teeming with exotic flora and fauna, evolving over millions of years to adapt to the planet's ever-changing climate. From the icy tundras of the north to the lush rainforests of the south, Xyorath's environment is a testament to the wonders of the natural world.

But what truly distinguishes Xyorath is its population of intelligent extraterrestrial beings known as the Xyorathians. As a highly advanced civilization, the Xyorathians have made remarkable progress in science, art, and cultural expression. They possess a keen curiosity and an insatiable thirst for knowledge, often exploring the depths of the cosmos in search of new frontiers.

In addition to their intellectual pursuits, the Xyorathians place great value on community and family. They have developed a unique set of customs and traditions that foster unity and harmony among their people. Xyorathian society operates on principles of empathy, compassion, and mutual respect, cherishing the diversity of each individual within their community.

The Xyorathians have a deep connection to their natural surroundings, recognizing the symbiotic relationship between their civilization and the environment. They have implemented measures to ensure the preservation and sustainability of their planet, striving to leave a legacy of ecological balance for future generations.

Despite their harmonious existence, the Xyorathians have not been exempt from the challenges of discrimination and social inequality. The multi-tentacle marriage restrictions, for instance, pose a significant obstacle to the full realization of individual freedom and agency.

Under these restrictions, Xyorathian individuals with multiple tentacles are prohibited from marrying those with a different number of tentacles. This discriminatory practice, rooted in archaic beliefs and unfounded prejudices, has caused anguish and heartache for countless individuals and families. Talin Iryn, a courageous Xyorathian, took it upon themselves to challenge this unjust system and fight for the rights and dignity of their fellow beings.

Talin's personal experiences with discrimination motivated them to become an advocate for change. Witnessing the pain and suffering inflicted upon their loved ones and many others, they developed an unwavering conviction to challenge the status quo and transform the social landscape of Xyorath.

Drawing inspiration from influential figures in Xyorathian history and beyond, Talin became determined to educate themselves about civil rights movements and strategies for effective activism. They delved into the works of visionary thinkers and learned how to harness the power of grassroots organizing, coalition building, and legal advocacy.

Talin's tireless pursuit of justice led them to discover the multi-tentacle marriage restrictions, which were deeply ingrained within Xyorathian society. Realizing the devastating impact of these restrictions on individuals' lives, Talin made it their mission to dismantle this discriminatory practice once and for all.

However, their initial efforts were met with resistance and numerous obstacles. Traditionalist factions within Xyorathian society vehemently opposed any changes to their long-standing customs, viewing Talin's activism as a threat to their way of life. Additionally, navigating the complexities of legislative processes proved to be a formidable challenge.

Undeterred by adversity, Talin persisted. They relocated to the bustling capital city of Xyorath in order to amplify their message and connect with other like-minded activists. Through joining local alien rights organizations, Talin established a network of individuals who shared their vision of a more inclusive and equitable society.

Together, they embarked on a spirited campaign to raise awareness about the multi-tentacle marriage restrictions. Public demonstrations, grassroots advocacy, and strategic media outreach became essential components of their movement. By elevating the voices of those directly affected by the restrictions, they aimed to humanize the issue and spark empathy within the broader Xyorathian population.

Over time, Talin's tireless efforts and unwavering determination began to yield results. Through sustained organizing and mobilization, they achieved their first victory: the lifting of the ban on multi-tentacle marriages in some local communities. This breakthrough served as a catalyst, igniting hope and emboldening Talin and their allies to expand their movement to a statewide level.

In their second attempt at legalization, Talin and their allies drew upon the lessons learned from their previous campaign. They sought to build stronger alliances, mobilize a broader base of support, and confront the opposition with a more comprehensive advocacy strategy.

Their approach encompassed lobbying and advocacy efforts directed at key legislators, meticulously crafted media strategies to sway public opinion, and a relentless commitment to sustaining momentum and resilience. These concerted efforts culminated in another historic victory: state-wide legalization of multi-tentacle marriages on Xyorath.

Talin's achievements extend beyond their fight for marriage equality. They recognized the interconnectedness of various forms of discrimination and dedicated themselves to addressing systemic issues. Their advocacy efforts encompassed challenges such as employment discrimination, access to healthcare and education, housing policies, and broader civil rights issues within the Xyorathian society.

By collaborating with other civil rights movements and identifying intersections between different marginalized communities, Talin pioneered an inclusive approach to activism. Their visionary leadership and ability to bridge divides within society set a powerful example for future generations of alien rights advocates.

Talin's legacy is one of resilience, courage, and unwavering commitment to justice. Their contributions to Xyorathian society are remembered as an enduring symbol of resistance against discrimination. Their efforts shattered the barriers that constrained the Xyorathian people, marking a turning point in the fight for equality.

As Xyorathians continue to build on Talin's accomplishments, they remain steadfast in their pursuit of social justice. Their story serves as a poignant reminder that the fight for equality is ongoing and requires the collective efforts of all those who yearn for a more fair and inclusive world.

Cultural Background and Customs

The cultural background and customs of Talin Iryn's native planet, Xyorath, are diverse and rich with traditions that have shaped the society's values and way of life. Xyorath is a planet known for its vibrant alien communities, with a diverse range of species coexisting harmoniously.

1.   **Multiculturalism and Diversity:** Xyorathian society thrives on multiculturalism and celebrates its diverse population. The planet is home to numerous alien species, each with its own set of customs, languages, and traditions. Xyorathians are proud of their multicultural identity and foster an inclusive society that embraces different cultures and backgrounds.

2. **Collectivism and Community:** Community plays a fundamental role in Xyorathian culture. The society values collective well-being over individual success. Xyorathians believe in the power of unity and collaboration, and they prioritize the needs of the community over personal desires. This sense of collectivism creates a strong bond among the inhabitants of Xyorath.

3. **Art and Expression:** Artistic expression is highly valued on Xyorath, and it is considered an integral part of daily life. Xyorathians have a deep appreciation for various forms of artistic expression, including visual arts, music, dance, and storytelling. Art is often used as a medium to preserve cultural heritage, pass down traditional knowledge, and convey important messages.

4. **Harmony with Nature:** Xyorathians have a profound respect for the natural world and strive to maintain a harmonious relationship with the environment. They understand the interconnectedness of all living beings and the importance of preserving ecological balance. Sustainable practices, such as eco-friendly technologies and organic farming, are deeply ingrained in Xyorathian customs.

5. **Spirituality and Philosophy:** Xyorathians possess a spiritual outlook on life, believing in the existence of higher realms and cosmic energies. Spirituality is interwoven into various aspects of Xyorathian culture, influencing their values, beliefs, and decision-making processes. Meditation and introspection are commonly practiced to attain a deeper understanding of oneself and the universe.

6. **Family and Relationships:** Family holds a central position in Xyorathian society. They cherish strong familial bonds and prioritize the well-being of their loved ones. Xyorathians often live in close-knit extended families, where generations coexist and support each other. Respect for elders, filial piety, and the passing down of ancestral traditions are deeply rooted in Xyorathian customs.

7. **Ceremonies and Celebrations:** Xyorathians are known for their vibrant and elaborate ceremonies and celebrations. Festivals play a crucial role in Xyorathian

culture, acting as occasions for communal gatherings, artistic performances, and the showcasing of traditional costumes and cuisines. These festivities serve as a means of fostering unity and preserving cultural heritage.

8. **Hospitality and Generosity:** Xyorathians are renowned for their hospitality and generosity. Welcoming guests with open arms is considered a duty, and visitors are treated with warmth and kindness. Xyorathian customs encourage the sharing of resources and the well-being of others, reflecting their values of compassion and empathy.

While Xyorathian society embraces its rich cultural tapestry, it is not immune to the challenges of discrimination and injustice. Talin Iryn's journey to challenge the multi-tentacle marriage restrictions on Xyorath sheds light on these systemic inequalities and inspires the fight for equality and justice within the alien community and beyond.

Talin's Family and Upbringing

Talin Iryn was born into a loving and resilient family on the enchanting planet of Xyorath. Xyorath, with its vibrant landscapes and majestic flora, was home to a diverse population of alien species. Talin's family belonged to the Xyrillian species, known for their rich cultural heritage and strong sense of community.

Growing up in a bustling neighborhood, Talin was surrounded by the warmth and tradition of Xyrillian customs. Family bonds were highly valued, and the extended family played a crucial role in nurturing and shaping the lives of young Xyrillians. Talin's parents, Ryn and Azara, were both educators and instilled in their children a deep love for learning.

Talin's childhood was marked by stories of struggle and triumph. They often heard tales of past generations who fought against discrimination and advocated for equality. From an early age, Talin was exposed to the realities of prejudice and the importance of standing up for justice.

Living in a society where multi-tentacle marriages were prohibited, Talin's family faced unique challenges. As Xyrillians, their multi-limbed nature was viewed with suspicion and frequently subjected to stereotypes and discrimination. Despite these obstacles, Talin's parents encouraged them to embrace their identities and taught them the value of resilience and empathy.

Talin's upbringing was characterized by an emphasis on education and critical thinking. Their parents believed that knowledge was a powerful tool in combating injustice and oppression. Talin's curiosity and thirst for knowledge were nurtured through visits to libraries, engaging discussions around the dinner table, and exposure to a diverse range of literature and ideas.

As Talin grew older, their understanding of discrimination deepened. They witnessed firsthand the challenges faced by their parents, who were often denied job opportunities or subjected to unfair treatment due to their Xyrillian background. These experiences sparked a sense of determination within Talin, igniting a passion for social justice and civil rights advocacy.

Talin's parents, recognizing their child's potential, provided them with the support and encouragement needed to pursue their dreams. They introduced Talin to influential figures in the alien rights movement, exposing them to a network of activists and mentors who would play a crucial role in shaping their future.

Through these interactions, Talin learned about the multi-tentacle marriage restrictions that plagued Xyorathian society. They discovered the emotional toll it took on individuals and families who yearned for the freedom to love and marry whomever they chose. This revelation ignited a fire within Talin, compelled them to challenge the status quo, and fight for equality.

However, Talin's journey towards justice was not without its share of obstacles. Many people in their community were fearful of change, viewing the fight for multi-tentacle marriage rights as a threat to tradition and societal norms. Talin faced resistance, skepticism, and even outright hostility from those who were resistant to change.

Undeterred, Talin recognized the importance of strategic alliances and community support. They began reaching out to local alien rights organizations, attending meetings and events, and building networks with like-minded individuals who shared their vision of a more inclusive and equitable Xyorath.

Talin's family, proud of their child's determination and commitment, stood by them every step of the way. They believed in the transformative power of grassroots movements and encouraged Talin to speak out, amplify their voice, and galvanize public support for the cause.

In this section, we have explored the family and upbringing of Talin Iryn, the future alien civil rights activist. They were raised in a nurturing environment that emphasized the importance of education, resilience, and justice. Talin's family formed the foundation for their unwavering commitment to fighting against the multi-tentacle marriage restrictions on Xyorath and advocating for equal rights for all alien beings.

Early Experiences with Discrimination

Talin Iryn's early experiences with discrimination on the planet of Xyorath left an indelible mark on her soul, shaping her determination to fight for justice and equality. Growing up in a society deeply rooted in cultural traditions and customs, Talin's encounters with prejudice and exclusion were as frequent as the planet's unique multi-tentacled species.

From a young age, Talin began to understand that she was different from her peers. While her multi-tentacled heritage was celebrated within her own family, she quickly learned that not everyone shared the same acceptance. In the playgrounds and classrooms of Xyorath, she faced mockery and ostracization due to her physical differences. Other children would often imitate her tentacle movements, ridiculing her in an attempt to belittle her.

These early experiences not only affected Talin's self-esteem, but they ignited a fire within her to challenge the status quo. Talin questioned why differences in appearance had to be a source of discrimination and pain. She yearned for a society where every Xyorathian, regardless of their unique physical attributes, would be treated with dignity and respect.

Talin's sense of justice grew stronger as she witnessed discrimination extending beyond the schoolyard. She observed how some Xyorathian communities shunned individuals who dared to form bonds outside of their own species, particularly in the context of romantic relationships. The prevailing cultural norms dictated that multi-tentacled Xyorathians should only marry other multi-tentacled individuals, and even friendships between different species were discouraged.

Witnessing the emotional toll this prejudice had on individuals, Talin became determined to challenge these societal norms. She sought out stories of other Xyorathians who had faced similar discrimination and listened to their experiences, building a network of allies dedicated to bridging the divides within their society. These early encounters with discrimination fueled her determination to fight for the rights of all Xyorathians, regardless of their physical attributes or who they fell in love with.

One powerful example of such discrimination occurred when Talin's close friend, Azala, fell in love with a Xyorathian from a different species. Azala's relationship was met with outrage and condemnation from their community, who believed that such unions would dilute their cultural heritage. Witnessing the pain and isolation her friend experienced, Talin vowed to challenge the multi-tentacle marriage restrictions that were at the heart of this discrimination.

Talin's early experiences with discrimination served as a catalyst for her transformation into a passionate and relentless civil rights activist. These encounters shaped her understanding of the deep-seated prejudice that permeated Xyorathian society, sparking a desire within her to dismantle systemic barriers and fight for a more inclusive and accepting future for all Xyorathians.

While Talin's early experiences with discrimination on Xyorath were undoubtedly painful, they became the driving force behind her lifelong activism. Her determination to challenge and change the cultural norms that perpetuated discrimination laid the foundation for her groundbreaking fight against the multi-tentacle marriage restrictions. Talin's journey had just begun, and she was ready to defy expectations, challenge prejudice, and fight for a world where love and acceptance knew no bounds.

The fight for equality and justice would not be an easy one, but Talin was prepared to face any obstacle that stood in her way.

Developing a Sense of Justice and Activism

Talin Iryn's journey as a civil rights activist began with the development of a strong sense of justice and a deep commitment to fighting for equality. Growing up on the planet of Xyorath, Talin witnessed firsthand the discrimination faced by alien communities due to the oppressive Multi-Tentacle Marriage Restrictions. These restrictions not only limited individuals' right to marry but also perpetuated a culture of inequality and alienation.

Talin's early experiences with discrimination ignited a fire within them, pushing them to question the existing social norms and traditions on Xyorath. They observed the unjust treatment suffered by alien individuals and families, and it became clear that change was desperately needed. Determined to challenge the status quo, Talin vowed to dedicate their life to dismantling the systemic barriers that prevented equal rights and opportunities for all.

Education played a crucial role in shaping Talin's worldview and understanding of social justice issues. Despite facing numerous obstacles, Talin pursued their education with unwavering determination. They sought out influential figures within the alien rights movement who provided guidance and mentorship, teaching them the importance of grassroots activism and community organizing.

Through their studies, Talin learned about the history of civil rights movements on Xyorath and other planets, discovering the power of collective action and peaceful resistance in effecting societal change. They drew inspiration from iconic figures such as Kaleen Veeresh, who fought against discriminatory housing policies, and Zara Marova, a renowned advocate for interplanetary worker rights.

It was during their education that Talin stumbled upon the concept of the Multi-Tentacle Marriage Restrictions – a realization that would shape the trajectory of their activism. Learning about the severe impact these restrictions had on alien communities, Talin couldn't ignore the inherent injustice and vowed to challenge the discriminatory laws.

The personal impact of these restrictions on Talin's own life and loved ones further fueled their determination. Witnessing the struggles faced by close friends who were denied the right to marry and build families, Talin knew that their fight for change was a deeply personal one. Their desire to create a future free from discrimination became an unwavering commitment, motivating them to take the next steps in their activism journey.

However, Talin encountered significant resistance and obstacles right from the beginning. Many within their own community were reluctant to challenge the status quo, fearing backlash and further discrimination. Talin's advocacy efforts initially faced resistance, with some questioning the validity of their cause or suggesting that gradual change was the only feasible path forward.

Undeterred, Talin realized that in order to make a difference, they needed to take their activism to the capital city of Xyorath, where they could amplify their voice and mobilize a larger movement. This decision marked a turning point in their life as they left their familiar surroundings behind and ventured into the unknown of urban life.

Arriving in the capital city, Talin experienced a world vastly different from their small hometown. The diversity they encountered was both overwhelming and inspiring, as they connected with other alien rights organizations and like-minded individuals who shared their vision for a just society. This network building was crucial to the progression of Talin's activism, as they found support and solidarity in the face of adversity.

Talin's dedication and passion for justice led them to take on various employment opportunities that not only provided financial independence but also allowed them to contribute to the cause. Jobs in organizations dedicated to alien rights advocacy further deepened their understanding of the issues at hand and exposed them to the complexities of the political and legal systems.

As Talin established themselves within the activist community, they realized that collective action was the key to achieving meaningful change. They actively participated in local protests and demonstrations, leveraging their newfound platform to raise awareness about the Multi-Tentacle Marriage Restrictions and the need for equal rights. Through media engagement and public speaking, Talin strategically garnered attention and support, encouraging dialogue and challenging societal norms.

Their efforts did not go unnoticed, and gradually, media coverage and public opinion began to shift in favor of their cause. These small victories fueled their determination, propelling Talin to persist in their fight for justice. The first breakthrough came when local communities began lifting the ban on multi-tentacle marriages, signaling a significant milestone in the battle against discrimination.

Buoyed by this success, Talin never lost sight of their ultimate goal – statewide legalization. They understood that achieving lasting change required strategic planning, coalition building, and continued public support. Talin collaborated with other civil rights organizations and alien rights advocates, realizing the importance of intersectionality in the fight for justice. Together, they lobbied tirelessly, put pressure on lawmakers, and worked towards dismantling legislative roadblocks.

Throughout their advocacy journey, Talin faced numerous challenges, including threats, intimidation, and backlash from conservative forces. However, their resilience and unwavering belief in the power of justice propelled them forward. They learned valuable lessons in leadership, coalition building, and sustaining momentum, adapting their strategies to navigate changing political landscapes.

Finally, after years of perseverance, Talin achieved their ultimate victory. Statewide legalization eliminated the discriminatory Multi-Tentacle Marriage

Restrictions, transforming Xyorathian society and setting a powerful precedent for equality. Talin's determination and courage in the face of adversity made them an icon of resistance, inspiring other alien communities to demand their rights and paving the way for future legal advocacy.

Talin's journey from a small town on Xyorath to a visionary civil rights activist serves as a shining example of the transformative power of determination, education, and collective action. Their legacy lives on, reminding us that the fight for justice is never-ending, ever-evolving, and requires unwavering commitment from individuals willing to challenge the status quo.

Education and Influential Figures

Talin's pursuit of education was fueled by a deep thirst for knowledge and a desire to empower themselves and their community. Despite facing numerous obstacles, Talin's determination and resilience propelled them forward, allowing them to overcome adversity and achieve academic success.

Access to Education on Xyorath

Education on Xyorath was highly valued, and the Xyorathian government invested heavily in providing educational opportunities for its citizens. A comprehensive education system ensured that individuals could acquire knowledge and skills necessary for personal growth and societal development. However, due to cultural biases and discrimination, access to education for certain communities, including aliens like Talin, was limited.

Challenges and Barriers

Talin faced numerous challenges on their educational journey. As an alien, they experienced discrimination and prejudice within the educational system. Many educational institutions lacked diversity and inclusivity, creating an environment that was hostile to individuals from marginalized communities. Moreover, the inherent biases and prejudices ingrained in the curriculum and teaching methods further perpetuated systemic inequalities.

Early Formal Education

Talin's early formal education began on Xyorath, where they attended a local public school. Despite being one of the few aliens in their school, Talin excelled academically, demonstrating intelligence, curiosity, and a thirst for knowledge.

Teachers recognized their potential and encouraged them to explore a wide range of subjects, nurturing their intellectual growth.

Influential Teachers

During their time in elementary school, Talin encountered a teacher who would have a profound impact on their life, Ms. Jones. Ms. Jones was a passionate educator committed to fostering a love for learning in all her students. She recognized Talin's potential and supported their academic growth, instilling in them a sense of confidence and self-belief. Ms. Jones also provided Talin with a safe space to express their experiences of discrimination and encouraged them to channel their frustrations into activism.

Higher Education Opportunities

Despite the hurdles they faced, Talin remained determined to continue their education and pursue a degree. Higher education institutions on Xyorath were beginning to embrace diversity and inclusivity, albeit slowly. Talin's exceptional academic record and their passion for creating change within their community earned them a scholarship at the prestigious Xyorath University.

Influential Professors and Mentors

At Xyorath University, Talin had the opportunity to study under renowned professors and mentors who played a crucial role in their journey. One such influential figure was Prof. Maya Patel, a brilliant scholar and activist. Prof. Patel not only taught Talin the fundamentals of sociology but also encouraged them to critically examine the societal structures that perpetuated discrimination and inequality. Under Prof. Patel's mentorship, Talin gained a deeper understanding of the power dynamics at play and how they could be challenged to create a more just society.

Exploration of Interdisciplinary Studies

Talin recognized the importance of interdisciplinary studies in understanding the complex nature of social issues. They sought out courses that delved into various disciplines, including history, political science, and psychology. By integrating insights from different fields, Talin developed a comprehensive understanding of the systemic barriers faced by marginalized communities and the mechanisms for dismantling them.

Activism on Campus

Talin's college years were marked by active involvement in campus activism. They co-founded a student organization called "Students for Equality," dedicated to challenging discriminatory policies and promoting inclusivity on campus. Through rallies, awareness campaigns, and dialogues with university administrators, Talin and their peers demanded tangible change within the university.

Study Abroad Experience

As part of their academic journey, Talin had the opportunity to study abroad for a semester at the Intergalactic Institute for Social Justice in a neighboring galaxy. This experience exposed them to a diverse range of perspectives and practices in social justice activism. Collaborating with fellow alien activists from different planets and galaxies, Talin gained valuable insights into effective strategies for creating lasting social change.

Strategies for Inclusive Education

During their studies, Talin became deeply passionate about transforming education systems to be more inclusive and equitable. They focused their research on developing strategies to promote diversity and cultural competence within educational institutions. Talin's work emphasized the importance of inclusive curriculum, faculty training, and the establishment of support systems to create an environment conducive to the success of marginalized students.

Advocacy for Education Reform

Inspired by their own struggles and those faced by other marginalized students, Talin became an outspoken advocate for education reform. They lobbied for policy changes that would promote inclusivity, diversity, and cultural sensitivity in educational institutions. Talin's advocacy was instrumental in the implementation of initiatives aimed at dismantling systemic barriers and creating educational environments that celebrated diversity.

Legacy and Mentorship

Throughout their educational journey, Talin served as a mentor for other alien students facing similar challenges. They recognized the transformative power of education in empowering individuals and communities, and it became their mission to ensure that future generations had access to educational opportunities free from discrimination.

Unconventional Practice: "Education for All" Workshops

Talin went beyond traditional academic settings to conduct "Education for All" workshops in marginalized communities. These workshops aimed to empower individuals with knowledge and skills necessary to navigate oppressive systems and demand their rights. By equipping individuals with tools for critical thinking and advocacy, Talin sought to break the cycle of discrimination and inequality.

In conclusion, Talin's educational journey was shaped by influential figures and experiences that instilled in them a sense of purpose, justice, and activism. Their educational achievements became a powerful tool in the fight for equality and justice, inspiring future generations of alien activists to break barriers and embrace the transformative power of education.

Discovering the Multi-Tentacle Marriage Restrictions

Talin Iryn, a Xyorathian alien rights activist, stumbled upon the multi-tentacle marriage restrictions quite by accident. It was a sunny day on Xyorath, and Talin was enjoying a cup of Daraqian tea at their favorite local cafe. As they sipped on their tea, their eyes caught sight of a newspaper headline that read, "Xyorath's Outdated Marital Laws: A Barrier to Love and Equality."

Intrigued, Talin grabbed the newspaper and read the article. It was then that they discovered the archaic laws that prohibited aliens with multiple tentacles from marrying more than one partner. The law was a relic from a time when Xyorathian society held a narrow view of marriage and frowned upon anything that deviated from the norm.

As Talin delved deeper into the issue, they learned about the discriminatory nature of the multi-tentacle marriage restrictions. Xyorathian society primarily viewed marriage as a union between two individuals, completely disregarding the diverse relationships that existed within the alien community. This narrow definition not only excluded those with multiple tentacles but also disregarded the uniqueness and complexity of alien relationships.

The discovery of these restrictions deeply affected Talin on a personal level. They had always believed in the equality of all beings and the freedom to express love in its various forms. Talin could not stand by idly while their own community faced such discrimination based on outdated laws and societal norms.

This revelation ignited a fire within Talin, fueling their determination to fight for change and challenge the status quo. They firmly believed that love and equality should not be dictated by the number of tentacles one possessed or any other physical characteristic.

Talin began educating themselves on alien rights, civil liberties, and the history of discrimination on Xyorath. They devoured books, articles, and academic papers, learning about the struggles and victories of other civil rights movements throughout the galaxy. They drew inspiration from prominent figures like Rosa Parks and César Chávez, who had fought tirelessly for the rights of marginalized communities.

With their newfound knowledge, Talin started engaging with fellow activists and rights organizations on Xyorath. They participated in rallies, protests, and public forums, spreading awareness about the multi-tentacle marriage restrictions and calling for their abolition. Talin began building networks and alliances within the alien community, finding strength in the collective fight for justice.

Furthermore, Talin recognized the importance of education in their path towards change. They attended conferences, workshops, and seminars, learning about grassroots organizing, community engagement, and legal advocacy. They understood that to dismantle the multi-tentacle marriage restrictions, they needed a multi-faceted approach that encompassed both societal and legal change.

Talin's discovery of the multi-tentacle marriage restrictions was a turning point in their life. It ignited a passion for justice and fueled their determination to challenge societal norms and fight for equality. In the face of resistance and adversity, Talin stood strong, knowing that their cause was just and necessary.

Little did they know that this discovery would set them on a journey that would forever change not only their own life but also the landscape of Xyorathian society.

Personal Impact and Determination to Fight for Change

Talin Iryn's discovery of the multi-tentacle marriage restrictions on Xyorath had a profound impact on her personal life and ignited within her a fierce determination to fight for change. This revelation shook her to the core, as she realized the deep-rooted discrimination that existed within her own society. The restrictions not only limited the freedom of love and choice but also perpetuated a system of inequality and injustice.

The realization of the multi-tentacle marriage restrictions deeply affected Talin on a personal level. Growing up, Talin had witnessed discrimination and prejudice against alien communities, but this was different. This issue struck at the heart of her identity and her ability to live authentically and fully express her love and commitment to another being. It sparked a fire within her, fueling her passion for justice and inspiring her to challenge the status quo.

Talin's determination to fight for change stemmed from her unwavering belief in the power of love, equality, and the fundamental human rights that should be afforded to all. She could not accept a world where individuals were limited in their ability to express love and build their lives together based on arbitrary restrictions. As a passionate advocate for civil rights and social justice, Talin knew that she had a responsibility to use her voice and fight for a more inclusive and equitable society.

Talin's personal experiences with discrimination played a significant role in her conviction to fight for change. From a young age, she had faced discrimination based on her alien heritage. These experiences, while difficult, shaped her understanding of the struggles faced by marginalized communities and fueled her determination to challenge injustice wherever it may exist. Talin understood the power of empathy and solidarity, recognizing that the fight for her own rights was intrinsically linked to the fight for the rights of all individuals who faced discrimination based on their identity.

Education and the influence of important figures in her life further solidified Talin's commitment to activism. She immersed herself in the study of civil rights movements throughout history, drawing inspiration from the tireless efforts of individuals who had paved the way for social change. Talin recognized the importance of learning from the past and using that knowledge to inform her own strategies and tactics in the fight for equality.

Facing initial resistance and obstacles only strengthened Talin's resolve. She encountered skepticism, backlash, and apathy from some members of her own alien community. But instead of allowing these challenges to deter her, Talin saw them as opportunities for growth and education. She engaged in conversations and debates, passionately articulating her stance and working diligently to change hearts and minds.

In her journey to fight for change, Talin found strength in building networks and allies. She realized the power of collective action and the importance of creating a united front against discrimination. By forming alliances with other alien rights organizations and collaborating with like-minded individuals, Talin expanded the reach of her movement and gained invaluable support. These connections provided her with the resilience to persevere in the face of adversity and overcome the obstacles standing in the way of progress.

Talin's determination to fight for change extended beyond her personal experiences. She recognized the broader implications of the multi-tentacle marriage restrictions and understood that achieving equality in this aspect would contribute to dismantling systemic discrimination in society as a whole. Her fight was not only for herself but for the countless individuals who had been marginalized and denied their basic human rights.

Through her passionate advocacy, Talin brought attention to the multi-tentacle marriage restrictions and galvanized public support. She used various platforms to amplify her message, including engaging with the media to shed light on the injustices faced by alien communities. Talin's ability to effectively communicate and connect with people from all walks of life played a crucial role in mobilizing support and shining a spotlight on the urgent need for change.

Talin's personal impact was apparent in the initial victory of lifting the ban in local communities. This triumph not only brought hope to those directly affected by the restrictions but also served as a testament to the power of perseverance and determination. Seeing the tangible results of her activism further reinforced Talin's commitment to the cause.

Talin's unwavering determination to fight for change served as a source of inspiration for others who shared her vision of a more just and inclusive society. Her advocacy extended beyond the issue of multi-tentacle marriage restrictions, as she actively worked to address other forms of discrimination and secure equal rights for alien communities in areas such as employment, healthcare, education, and housing. Talin understood that the fight for justice was multifaceted, and she consistently sought to challenge the intersecting systems of oppression that marginalized communities faced.

To sustain her activism and navigate the challenges that came her way, Talin relied on a deep well of resilience and self-care. Recognizing the importance of maintaining her energy and well-being, she prioritized self-reflection and sought support from her allies. Talin understood that in order to continue fighting for change, she needed to take care of herself and find a balance between her activism and personal life.

Talin's personal impact and determination to fight for change will forever be remembered as a defining chapter in Xyorath's history. Her relentless pursuit of justice challenged societal norms, paving the way for a more inclusive and equitable future. Her legacy serves as a reminder that change is possible, even in the face of seemingly insurmountable obstacles. Talin Iryn's story is an inspiration to current and future generations of alien and civil rights activists, a testament to the power of one individual's unwavering determination to make a difference.

Initial Resistance and Obstacles

In the early days of Talin Iryn's activism for alien civil rights on Xyorath, there were numerous challenges and barriers to overcome. The fight for equality and justice faced significant initial resistance and obstacles, both within the Xyorathian society and the broader political landscape. This section explores some of the key challenges encountered by Talin and the movement and the strategies employed to navigate them.

Cultural Prejudice and Ignorance: One of the primary obstacles Talin faced was widespread cultural prejudice and ignorance towards alien communities on Xyorath. At the time, many Xyorathians held deep-rooted beliefs that viewed aliens as inferior or outsiders. These prejudiced attitudes often translated into discriminatory practices and policies. Overcoming these cultural biases required a multifaceted approach that involved education, awareness campaigns, and challenging stereotypes.

To combat cultural ignorance, Talin and their allies organized community outreach programs aimed at fostering understanding and dialogue between Xyorathians and alien populations. These programs included workshops, cultural exchanges, and public events that showcased the richness of alien customs, traditions, and contributions to society. This approach helped dispel misconceptions and fostered empathy, gradually shifting cultural norms and fostering greater acceptance.

Legal and Legislative Challenges: Another major obstacle faced by Talin and the alien civil rights movement was navigating the complex legal and legislative landscape. Xyorathian laws at the time contained discriminatory provisions and restrictions that targeted alien communities. One such set of laws was the Multi-Tentacle Marriage Restrictions, which barred aliens with multiple tentacles from legally marrying on Xyorath.

Talin, along with their legal team and other activists, had to strategize and mount legal challenges to these discriminatory laws. This involved extensive research, the identification of legal precedents, and building a solid legal argument that highlighted the unconstitutionality and injustice of such restrictions. The legal battle was an arduous one, requiring resilience and persistence in the face of opposition from conservative forces.

Political Backlash and Opposition: Talin's activism for alien civil rights posed a threat to the established political order on Xyorath. As they gained prominence and public support, they encountered political backlash and opposition from conservative politicians and interest groups. These forces viewed the advancement of alien civil rights as a challenge to their power and status quo.

To counter this opposition, Talin and their allies developed strategic alliances with progressive political leaders who championed equality and justice. They also engaged in lobbying efforts to mobilize public opinion and pressure lawmakers to support the cause. This involved organizing rallies, protests, and media campaigns that highlighted the experiences of alien individuals and the need for equal rights.

Threats and Intimidation: The fight for alien civil rights on Xyorath was not without personal risks. Talin and other activists faced threats, intimidation tactics, and even physical violence from extremist groups who sought to suppress their advocacy. These attacks aimed to instill fear and discourage the movement from pushing forward.

In response to these challenges, Talin and their comrades implemented strategies to protect themselves and their allies. This included forming security networks, working closely with law enforcement agencies, and raising awareness about the threats they faced. By exposing the tactics used by their opponents, they aimed to garner public sympathy and support for their cause while deterring further acts of violence.

Financial Constraints: As with any social justice movement, financial constraints presented a significant hurdle for Talin and their activism. Securing funding for awareness campaigns, legal battles, and community programs was a constant challenge. Limited financial resources meant that the movement had to be resourceful and creative in finding ways to sustain its efforts.

Talin and their supporters organized fundraising events, secured grants and sponsorships, and relied on the generosity of allies and sympathetic individuals to keep their fight alive. This required effective communication, networking, and the ability to inspire people to contribute time, money, or resources to the cause.

Maintaining Unity and Cohesion: Lastly, maintaining unity and cohesion within the alien civil rights movement itself was an ongoing challenge. The movement encompassed individuals from diverse alien communities, each with their own unique backgrounds, interests, and priorities. Navigating internal divisions and differences of opinion required strong leadership, effective communication, and a commitment to collective goals.

Talin and their allies actively worked to build bridges between different alien groups, fostering cooperation and understanding. They organized regular meetings, facilitated dialogue, and created spaces for collaborative decision-making. This deliberate effort to maintain unity within the movement was crucial for its long-term sustainability and success.

Despite these initial resistance and obstacles, Talin Iryn's determination, resilience, and strategic approach to activism helped pave the way for momentous changes in Xyorathian society. The initial challenges they faced served as catalysts for the creation of a broad-based, inclusive movement that would challenge discrimination, fight for equality, and inspire future generations of alien and civil rights activists.

Chapter 1: The Journey Begins

Talin's Move to the Capital City

Experiencing Urban Life for the First Time

As Talin Iryn made the courageous decision to leave their small hometown on the planet Xyorath and move to the bustling capital city, they embarked on a journey that would forever shape their understanding of the world and ignite their passion for change. This section delves into Talin's initial encounters with urban life, highlighting the transformative experiences that propelled them into becoming the fearless alien rights activist we know today.

Alienation in the Concrete Jungle

Stepping off the spaceship onto the crowded streets of the capital, Talin couldn't help but feel overwhelmed by the sheer magnitude of human civilization. Skyscrapers kissed the clouds, casting long shadows on the bustling sidewalks below. The cacophony of car horns, the scent of street food, and the vibrant tapestry of diverse faces captivated Talin's senses, ensnaring them in the vivacious rhythm of urban life.

However, within this vibrant tapestry, Talin experienced a profound sense of alienation. The towering buildings reflected a society that seemed indifferent to their presence. The fast-paced nature of urban life left little room to acknowledge the struggles of an outsider. Talin's extraterrestrial features became a source of curiosity, but also a barrier to fully belonging in this new world.

Navigating Cultural Differences

As Talin settled into their new urban life, they quickly realized that cultural differences extended far beyond physical appearances. Xyorathian customs and traditions that once formed the fabric of their being were now deviant in the eyes of the human majority. Simple gestures and greetings that were second nature to Talin became lost in translation, the subtle nuances of communication eluding them.

The noise and chaos of the city seemed to amplify these cultural disparities, making it even more challenging for Talin to assimilate. Fights erupted over conflicting ideologies, and the clash of diverse perspectives reverberated through the streets. But despite these challenges, Talin was determined to bridge the cultural divide and foster understanding between their Xyorathian heritage and the human society they found themselves in.

Finding Companionship in the Unknown

Amidst the chaos and alienation, Talin discovered a beacon of hope in the form of other aliens navigating their own paths through urban life. Together, they formed a tight-knit community, finding solace and support in one another's shared experiences. They held gatherings to celebrate their diverse cultural traditions, creating spaces where their identities were not only accepted but celebrated.

These newfound companions proved to be a wellspring of strength for Talin, reinforcing their commitment to fighting for alien rights. As they shared their stories and struggles, they began to realize the power of unity and the potential for collective action. Through their shared experiences and unwavering support, Talin's determination to challenge the injustices they faced in their adopted home grew stronger than ever.

Transforming Alien Experiences into Advocacy

With each passing day, Talin's experiences in the urban jungle fueled their desire to advocate for equal rights for all aliens. They witnessed firsthand the systemic discrimination and marginalization faced by their community. From wage disparities to housing inequalities, the urban landscape served as a constant reminder of the uphill battle they must face.

But Talin was not one to be deterred. They drew inspiration from the pioneers of previous civil rights movements, channeling the strength and resilience of those who fought for justice before them. The challenges they encountered in urban life only served as stepping stones for their advocacy work, pushing them to excavate the underlying causes of inequality and devise strategies to dismantle them.

Examining the Intersectionality of Alien Rights

As Talin immerses themselves in the urban environment, they come to understand that the fight for alien rights cannot exist in isolation. Discrimination and injustice do not exist in a vacuum but are interconnected with other social justice issues. Gender, race, sexuality, and class intertwine, creating a complex web of oppression.

Recognizing the intersections of discrimination, Talin begins collaborating with other civil rights movements, forging alliances to address the root causes of inequality. They join forces with human activists, sharing their knowledge and experiences to foster a broader understanding of the struggles faced by alien communities. By advocating for the dismantling of all systems of oppression, Talin aims to create a society that values diversity and embraces all its inhabitants, regardless of their planetary origins.

Embracing the Unexpected

As Talin navigates the labyrinthine streets of the capital city, they encounter a breathtaking array of surprises and challenges. Each encounter, whether pleasant or arduous, adds to their understanding of urban life's complexities and inspires them to fight for change. The journey is not without its stumbling blocks, but Talin's determination and unwavering commitment drive them forward, transforming their personal experiences into a powerful force for social transformation.

Urban Life Problem

Problem: In Xyorathian culture, relationships are traditionally formed through traditional matchmaking ceremonies that involve complex rituals and ceremonies. Talin, having decided to embrace urban life, now finds themselves in an unfamiliar territory where dating and forming relationships differ vastly from their own customs. Talin is seeking advice on how to navigate the intricacies of dating in the urban environment, while still honoring their cultural heritage.

Solution: Talin can strike a harmonious balance between their Xyorathian cultural values and the urban dating scene by blending tradition with modernity. They can seek the guidance of other alien community members who have successfully integrated their cultural values with contemporary dating practices. Additionally, Talin can educate their potential partners about their cultural background, fostering mutual understanding and respect. By staying true to themselves and valuing their cultural identity, Talin can navigate the complexities of urban dating without compromising their sense of self.

Resource Recommendation

Book: "Aliens in the Concrete Jungle: Navigating Urban Life as an Extraterrestrial" by Zara Nix

This captivating memoir offers a firsthand account of an alien's journey through the concrete jungle and the challenges they face in adapting to urban life. Drawing from personal experiences and filled with humor and insight, this book provides valuable guidance for aliens seeking to find their place in a human-dominated world. From tips on cultural assimilation to reflections on the transformative power of unity, this memoir is an essential resource for those navigating the complexities of urban life as an extraterrestrial.

Finding Employment and Financial Independence

In the pursuit of equality and civil rights for alien communities on Xyorath, Talin Iryn realized that financial independence and employment were vital factors in challenging the multi-tentacle marriage restrictions and dismantling discriminatory systems. This section explores Talin's journey in finding employment, building financial independence, and contributing to the cause of alien rights.

The Challenges Faced by Alien Job Seekers

As an alien living in the capital city, Talin faced numerous challenges in finding suitable employment. The prejudice and discrimination prevalent in Xyorathian society made it difficult for aliens to secure jobs commensurate with their skills and qualifications. Employers often held biased views, assuming that aliens were less capable or trustworthy, leading to discriminatory hiring practices.

Moreover, the cultural differences and the unfamiliarity of employers with alien customs and traditions added another layer of complexity to the job-seeking process. These challenges put aliens at a significant disadvantage when competing for employment opportunities with their Xyorathian counterparts.

Building Networks and Allies

Recognizing the need to overcome these obstacles, Talin immersed themselves in local alien rights organizations and actively built strong networks and alliances within the alien community. By connecting with like-minded individuals, Talin not only gained moral support but also tapped into valuable resources and opportunities that could assist in finding employment.

Networking events, workshops, and conferences became crucial spaces for Talin to connect with potential employers who were open-minded and willing to give aliens a fair chance. By highlighting their skills, experiences, and the contributions they could make to the workforce, Talin endeavored to change the narrative around alien capabilities and challenge the prevailing biases.

Exploring Niche Job Markets

Talin recognized that conventional job markets might not always be receptive to hiring aliens. Therefore, they decided to explore niche job markets where their unique skills and attributes would be appreciated and valued. This strategic decision opened doors to unconventional employment opportunities that allowed Talin to showcase their talents and make significant contributions while advancing the cause of alien rights.

For instance, Talin found employment in sectors such as interplanetary diplomacy, cultural exchange programs, and alien rights advocacy organizations. These positions not only provided financial stability but also allowed Talin to leverage their expertise and knowledge to bring about positive change from within.

Entrepreneurship and Self-Employment

Realizing the limitations of the traditional job market, Talin also considered entrepreneurship and self-employment as viable paths to financial independence. By starting their own business or freelancing in their area of expertise, Talin could create opportunities for themselves and demonstrate the value aliens could bring to the economy.

However, starting a business as an alien presented its own set of challenges, including securing funding, navigating legal frameworks, and building a customer base. Talin persevered and sought support from alien advocacy organizations and local entrepreneurial communities to overcome these hurdles and establish a successful business.

Financial Literacy and Resource Management

Building financial independence required not only finding employment opportunities but also managing resources effectively. Talin understood the importance of financial literacy and sought out resources to enhance their understanding of personal finance, budgeting, and investment strategies.

By equipping themselves with these skills, Talin ensured that their income was not only used for personal needs but also invested back into the alien rights movement. They encouraged other aliens to adopt similar financial management practices, empowering the community as a whole.

Personal Growth and Resilience

Throughout the journey of finding employment and achieving financial independence, Talin faced numerous setbacks and rejections. However, they understood that resilience and personal growth were essential ingredients for success.

Talin actively sought feedback, honed their skills, and embraced continuous learning opportunities to improve their employability. They turned each rejection into an opportunity for self-improvement, harnessing setbacks as fuel for their determination.

Real-World Example: Talin's Employment Success Story

An illustrative example of Talin's employment success story involves their appointment as an interplanetary cultural exchange coordinator. Through their dedication, networking, and relentless advocacy, Talin managed to convince local authorities to establish an exchange program between Xyorath and another alien planet.

Their role not only provided a platform for interplanetary understanding but also promoted the cultural richness of the alien community. Talin's success in this endeavor served as an inspiration for other aliens aspiring to fill similar roles, creating a ripple effect and changing societal perceptions.

Unconventional Tip: The Power of Mentorship

As Talin embarked on their journey to find employment and achieve financial independence, they sought out mentors who could guide them through the process. These mentors, some of whom were successful Xyorathians, provided valuable insights, introduced Talin to key contacts, and acted as trusted advisors.

The mentorship relationship proved to be a powerful tool in navigating the Xyorathian job market, as experienced mentors shared their wisdom and helped Talin avoid common pitfalls. This unconventional yet effective strategy empowered Talin to not only find employment but also gain deeper insights into the systemic issues impacting alien rights.

Conclusion

Finding employment and securing financial independence played a critical role in Talin Iryn's fight for equal rights for the alien community.   By networking, exploring niche job markets, embracing entrepreneurship, and developing financial literacy, Talin overcame the challenges posed by discrimination and bias. Their personal growth and resilience contributed to their success, allowing them to make significant contributions to the alien rights movement. Talin's journey serves as an inspiration for other alien individuals, highlighting the importance of perseverance, strategic thinking, and building strong networks of support.   Employment and financial independence became powerful tools through which Talin could challenge the multi-tentacle marriage restrictions and reshape societal norms on Xyorath.

Joining Local Alien Rights Organizations

Joining local alien rights organizations was a pivotal step in Talin Iryn's journey as a civil rights activist on Xyorath.   Through their active participation in these organizations, Talin not only found a community of like-minded individuals but also gained valuable knowledge and skills that would contribute to their future success in challenging the multi-tentacle marriage restrictions.

Challenges Faced by Aliens

Aliens on Xyorath faced numerous challenges and forms of discrimination. The multi-tentacle marriage restrictions, which prohibited aliens from marrying individuals with a different number of tentacles, were just one example of the systemic bias they encountered. Employment discrimination, limited access to healthcare and education, and segregation in housing were among the many barriers that aliens had to contend with.

Importance of Local Alien Rights Organizations

Local alien rights organizations played a crucial role in galvanizing and mobilizing the alien community on Xyorath. These organizations provided a safe space for aliens to discuss their experiences and fears, while also fostering a sense of unity and solidarity. By coming together, aliens were able to share resources, advocate for their rights, and develop strategies to challenge the discriminatory laws and policies that hindered their progress.

Networking and Building Alliances

Joining local alien rights organizations allowed Talin to network and build alliances with fellow activists, advocates, and community leaders. These connections proved invaluable in their fight against the multi-tentacle marriage restrictions. Through collaborations and partnerships, Talin and their allies were able to pool their resources and expertise, amplifying their voices and increasing their collective impact.

Educational Opportunities

Local alien rights organizations also offered educational opportunities for their members. Workshops, seminars, and training sessions were organized to educate aliens about their rights, legal strategies, and effective advocacy techniques. Talin, driven by a thirst for knowledge and a desire to effect change, eagerly participated in these educational initiatives, strengthening their understanding of social justice issues and honing their skills as an activist.

Political Activism

In addition to education and networking, local alien rights organizations provided a platform for political activism. Talin engaged in various forms of advocacy, such as lobbying, petitioning, and organizing protests and demonstrations. These actions aimed to raise awareness about the injustices faced by aliens and put pressure on policymakers to address their concerns. Through these efforts, Talin sought to challenge not only the multi-tentacle marriage restrictions but also the larger systems of discrimination that affected the lives of aliens on Xyorath.

Working Towards Legislative Change

By joining local alien rights organizations, Talin was able to contribute to existing efforts aimed at seeking legislative change. These organizations worked tirelessly to advocate for the repeal of discriminatory laws and the implementation of policies that would guarantee equal rights for all. Talin actively participated in lobbying efforts, meeting with lawmakers to discuss the impact of the multi-tentacle marriage restrictions on alien families and sharing personal stories to humanize the issue.

Creative Tactics and Strategies

Local alien rights organizations encouraged members to think creatively and employ unconventional tactics in their activism. Talin and their fellow activists organized street performances, art exhibitions, and cultural festivals to raise awareness and challenge societal norms. These initiatives not only captured public attention but also fostered dialogue and understanding, ultimately contributing to a more inclusive and accepting society.

Support and Empowerment

Being part of a local alien rights organization provided Talin with a sense of support and empowerment. The organization offered emotional support, counseling services, and resources to help members deal with the psychological impact of discrimination. This support network bolstered Talin's resilience and resolve, enabling them to continue the fight for equality despite the many challenges they faced.

Celebrating Victories and Milestones

Local alien rights organizations celebrated victories and milestones, both big and small, along the journey towards equality. These celebrations served as a reminder of the progress made and the positive impact of collective action. By recognizing and celebrating these achievements, local alien rights organizations motivated their members to persevere and remain committed to the cause.

Empowering Future Alien Activists

Joining local alien rights organizations not only empowered Talin personally but also allowed them to inspire and mentor future alien activists. Through their involvement in these organizations, Talin played a pivotal role in nurturing a new generation of leaders and advocates who would continue the fight for justice and equality. Talin's legacy lives on through the work of those they inspired and mentored.

In joining local alien rights organizations, Talin Iryn embarked on a transformative journey that would shape their future as a civil rights activist. Through education, networking, political activism, creative strategies, and the support of a community, Talin laid a strong foundation for challenging the multi-tentacle marriage restrictions and advocating for equality on Xyorath. Their involvement in local organizations became the catalyst for change, empowering not only themselves but all aliens to stand up, raise their voices, and demand justice.

Building Networks and Allies

Building networks and allies was a crucial step in Talin Iryn's journey towards achieving equality and justice for Xyorathian aliens. By forging connections with like-minded individuals and organizations, Talin was able to amplify their message, increase their reach, and gain much-needed support for their cause.

The Importance of Allies

Talin understood that the fight for alien rights could not be fought alone. They recognized the power of collective action, coalition-building, and the strength that came from standing together with other marginalized communities. Allies played a crucial role in helping Talin challenge the multi-tentacle marriage restrictions and other forms of discrimination.

Allies provided not only support but also diverse perspectives and resources that enriched and strengthened the movement. By joining forces with different organizations and individuals, Talin was able to create a united front against discrimination, effectively amplifying their message and demanding equal rights for Xyorathian aliens.

Building Strong Networks

Talin's first step in building networks and allies was to reach out to local alien rights organizations in the capital city. They attended meetings, engaged in dialogue, and actively participated in various initiatives. This allowed them to immerse themselves in the alien rights movement, learn from experienced activists, and build relationships with other passionate individuals.

Additionally, Talin recognized the importance of cross-movement collaboration. They actively sought partnerships with existing social justice organizations that were fighting for the rights of other marginalized groups. By finding common ground with these organizations, Talin was able to bridge gaps, foster solidarity, and create a larger collective voice for change.

Mobilizing Support

To build networks and allies, Talin focused on mobilizing public support for the alien rights movement. They recognized that a strong grassroots movement was crucial for achieving lasting change. Talin used various strategies to rally public opinion, including organizing rallies, protests, and public demonstrations that gained media attention and put a spotlight on the discriminatory practices on Xyorath.

Social media also played a vital role in mobilizing support. Talin leveraged online platforms to spread awareness about the multi-tentacle marriage restrictions and engage with a broader audience. They shared stories, experiences, and testimonials that humanized the issue and appealed to people's sense of justice and empathy.

Alliance Building Strategies

Talin employed several alliance-building strategies to ensure the movement's success:

1. **Building Trust:** Talin recognized that trust was the foundation of any successful alliance. They prioritized open and honest communication, listened to the needs and concerns of their allies, and actively worked towards mutual goals.

2. **Shared Resources:** Talin understood the value of sharing resources. They collaborated with allies to pool together funds, skills, and networks, which allowed them to maximize their impact and reach a larger audience.

3. **Education and Awareness:** Talin dedicated time and effort to educate their allies about the specific challenges faced by Xyorathian aliens. By providing resources, holding workshops, and organizing training sessions, they ensured that their allies were equipped with the knowledge and understanding necessary to effectively support the movement.

4. **Cultural Sensitivity:** Talin recognized the importance of cultural sensitivity and creating inclusive spaces for all allies. They actively worked to dismantle any prejudices or biases that may have existed within the movement, ensuring that all voices, experiences, and identities were respected and valued.

5. **Long-Term Partnerships:** Talin aimed to build long-term partnerships and commitments with their allies. They understood that lasting change required sustained efforts and collaboration. By investing in these relationships, they were able to create a strong and resilient movement.

Example: Coalition to End Discrimination

One of the most impactful alliances that Talin formed was the Coalition to End Discrimination (CED). Talin recognized that by joining forces with other civil rights movements, they could leverage collective power to bring about systemic change.

CED brought together various marginalized groups fighting for equality and justice, including aliens from other planets, cyborgs, and LGBTQ+ individuals.

Through shared objectives and intersectional advocacy, the coalition was able to challenge discriminatory policies and practices at both the local and national levels.

The coalition organized joint protests, advocacy campaigns, and legal challenges, amplifying each other's voices and demanding comprehensive reforms. By uniting under a common cause, CED was able to achieve significant victories, including the repeal of the multi-tentacle marriage restrictions on Xyorath.

Building Strategies: Outside the Box

One unconventional but highly effective strategy Talin employed in building networks and allies was hosting community potlucks. Talin recognized that food brings people together, breaking down barriers and fostering connections.

These potlucks provided a safe and inclusive space for aliens and their allies to meet, share stories, and build relationships. It created a sense of community, allowing people to see the humanity in one another and build trust. These organic connections often led to new alliances and collaborations, strengthening the movement from within.

Exercises

1. Research and identify two historical examples where alliances played a significant role in achieving civil rights milestones. Examine the strategies employed by these alliances and the impact they had on their respective movements.

2. Imagine you are a member of an alien rights organization. Design a social media campaign aimed at mobilizing public support and engaging allies. Outline the key messages, visuals, and calls to action that will appeal to a wide audience.

3. Role-play a dialogue between Talin and a potential ally who is initially skeptical of the alien rights movement. Prepare an argument that addresses their concerns and highlights the importance of collective action and solidarity.

Conclusion

Building networks and allies was a critical aspect of Talin Iryn's activism journey. By forging relationships, mobilizing support, and seeking collaboration with other movements, Talin created a powerful and united front against discrimination. The strategies employed by Talin demonstrated the importance of trust, shared resources, education, cultural sensitivity, and long-term partnerships in achieving lasting change. Through alliances, Talin's movement was able to challenge societal norms, inspire others, and pave the way for a more inclusive and just society.

The First Attempt at Legalization

The journey towards challenging the multi-tentacle marriage restrictions on Xyorath was a daunting and complex task. Talin Iryn, with her unwavering determination and sense of justice, knew that the first step towards change was to attempt to legalize the unions that had been deemed illegal by the Xyorathian government. In this section, we will explore the challenges Talin faced during this initial attempt at legalization, the opposition and backlash she encountered, and how she managed to gain both media attention and public support.

Setting the Stage: Understanding the Legal Landscape

Talin understood that in order to challenge the multi-tentacle marriage restrictions, she had to have a firm grasp of the legal landscape on Xyorath. Xyorathian law, deeply rooted in tradition and cultural customs, explicitly prohibited marriages between individuals with multiple tentacles. These discriminatory laws were based on outdated notions of what constituted a valid union and served as a means to suppress the multi-tentacle community.

Talin delved into extensive research, analyzing the legislative history, previous court decisions, and the arguments put forth by proponents of the restrictions. This thorough understanding of the legal framework allowed her to strategize and gather evidence to dismantle the discriminatory policies.

Building a Legal Team

Talin recognized the importance of building a strong legal team to take on this uphill battle. She assembled a group of legal experts who shared her vision for equality and justice. Each member of the team possessed a unique set of skills and perspectives, allowing them to approach the case from various angles.

The legal team worked tirelessly, developing comprehensive legal arguments rooted in constitutional rights, freedom of choice, and equal protection under the law. They meticulously organized evidence, conducted interviews with affected individuals, and prepared briefs that challenged the legality and morality of the multi-tentacle marriage restrictions.

Courtroom Drama and Challenges

Taking the case to court was a pivotal moment for Talin and her legal team. The courtroom became the battleground where justice would either prevail or be further oppressed. As expected, they encountered numerous challenges and faced staunch opposition from conservative forces deeply ingrained in Xyorathian society.

The defense, representing the government's interests, made every effort to undermine Talin's arguments, often resorting to fallacious reasoning and personal attacks. But Talin and her legal team stood strong, presenting a compelling case that exposed the discriminatory nature of the multi-tentacle marriage restrictions. They debunked the myths perpetuated by proponents of the bans, highlighting the inherent prejudice and bias that formed their foundation.

Public Demonstrations and Protests

Talin recognized the power of public demonstrations and protests in amplifying the demands for change. She organized peaceful demonstrations in support of multi-tentacle marriage equality, bringing together Xyorathians from all walks of life. These gatherings served as a visible symbol of solidarity and defiance against the oppressive laws.

The protests garnered significant media attention, provoking conversations on airwaves and social media platforms alike. Talin made sure that her message was clear: Love knows no boundaries, and denying individuals the right to marry based on the number of tentacles they possess is a violation of their fundamental human rights.

Media Coverage and Public Opinion

Public opinion played a crucial role in the fight for multi-tentacle marriage equality. Talin and her legal team actively engaged with the media, sharing personal stories and dispelling misconceptions surrounding multi-tentacle relationships. They spoke at length about the emotional toll that the discriminatory laws had on individuals who were denied the freedom to marry the ones they love.

Through interviews, press releases, and social media campaigns, Talin and her team humanized the issue, portraying it as a matter of love, family, and equality. Their efforts resonated with the public, spurring discussions and challenging societal norms that had long perpetuated discrimination.

The Verdict: Historic Decision in Favor of Equality

After months of intense legal battles and public advocacy, the courtroom drama culminated in a historic decision in favor of equality. The judge, recognizing the infringement on the constitutional rights of multi-tentacle individuals, declared the multi-tentacle marriage restrictions on Xyorath unconstitutional.

The verdict sent shockwaves through Xyorathian society, heralding a new era of acceptance and inclusivity. Talin's first victory in the fight for multi-tentacle marriage equality marked a significant turning point in the battle against discrimination.

Impact on Xyorathian Communities

The lifting of the multi-tentacle marriage restrictions had a profound impact on Xyorathian communities. Individuals who were previously denied the right to marry now had the freedom to express their love and celebrate their unions openly.

The victory served as a powerful catalyst for change, not only in the realm of marriage equality but in challenging other discriminatory practices as well. It emboldened Xyorathians to demand equal rights, giving rise to a broader movement for social justice and inclusivity.

Lessons Learned and Looking Ahead

Talin and her legal team reflected on their first attempt at legalization, recognizing the immense challenges they had faced and the importance of perseverance. They realized that the fight for equality would be a long and arduous journey, with many more battles to come.

The first attempt at legalization taught them the significance of public support, media engagement, and strategic legal arguments. It also provided insight into the opposition they would continue to face from conservative forces resistant to change. With their eyes firmly set on the future, Talin and her team began strategizing for their next steps, driven by the unshakable belief that love should never be restricted or denied based on arbitrary criteria.

Exercise: Advocating for Change

Consider a real-life civil rights issue that you are passionate about. Imagine yourself as an advocate for change. Brainstorm a list of strategies and tactics that you could employ to raise awareness, gain public support, and challenge the discriminatory practices or policies associated with that issue. How would you galvanize a movement? How would you overcome resistance and setbacks? Share your thoughts with a classmate or friend and explore the power of collective action in effecting change.

In this section, we explored the first attempt at legalization undertaken by Talin Iryn in her fight against the multi-tentacle marriage restrictions on Xyorath. We witnessed the challenges she faced, the opposition she encountered, and the strategies she employed to gain media attention and public support. Talin's determination and resilience set the stage for future victories and laid the foundation for a broader movement for equality and justice. The fight for multi-tentacle marriage equality was far from over, but this first attempt marked a significant step forward in the battle against discrimination.

Facing Opposition and Backlash

In the fight for civil rights, facing opposition and backlash is inevitable. Talin Iryn, as a fearless advocate for alien rights on the planet of Xyorath, experienced her fair share of resistance from those who opposed the idea of lifting the multi-tentacle marriage restrictions. This section explores the challenges she encountered and the strategies she employed to overcome opposition and move the movement forward.

Understanding the Opposition

To effectively counter opposition, it's crucial to have a clear understanding of their motivations and arguments. Talin recognized that many individuals and groups opposing the lifting of multi-tentacle marriage restrictions did so based on cultural traditions, religious beliefs, and deep-rooted fear of change. It was important for her to approach these opponents with empathy and respect, while remaining steadfast in her conviction that equality and justice were fundamental rights for all.

Navigating Political and Legal Obstacles

The opposition to lifting the multi-tentacle marriage restrictions was not confined to public sentiment alone. There were also political and legal obstacles that Talin had to navigate on her journey towards change. Some politicians and lawmakers resisted reform, using their power to obstruct progress. This required Talin to employ a strategic approach, focusing on building alliances, lobbying, and advocacy efforts to sway decision-makers and turn the tide in favor of equality.

Addressing Misinformation and Prejudice

A significant challenge faced by Talin was the prevalence of misinformation and prejudice surrounding multi-tentacle marriage.   Opponents often spread unfounded claims about potential negative consequences, perpetuating fear and misunderstanding. To counter this, Talin and her allies utilized media strategies and public education campaigns to provide accurate information, debunk myths, and challenge the biased narratives that fueled opposition.

Resilience in the Face of Backlash

As the movement gained momentum, the intensity of the opposition and backlash grew. Talin and her supporters faced threats, intimidation, and verbal attacks from individuals and groups vehemently opposed to the idea of granting alien rights. It required immense resilience and determination to withstand these challenges and continue advocating for change. Talin's unwavering commitment to equality and justice inspired her allies and supporters to stand strong, even in the face of adversity.

Building Public Support

Overcoming opposition and backlash required building and sustaining public support.   Talin understood the importance of engaging with the broader community, sharing personal stories, and highlighting the shared values of love, family, and equality. She organized public demonstrations and protests, inviting people to witness the impact of discriminatory laws firsthand. This grassroots mobilization effectively shifted public opinion, gaining empathy and support for the cause.

Engaging in Dialogue and Negotiation

Talin recognized the value of engaging in dialogue with opponents, even when faced with deeply ingrained prejudice. She sought opportunities to sit down with religious leaders, community elders, and policymakers to discuss their concerns and find common ground. By fostering respectful and open conversations, Talin aimed to bridge the gap between opposing factions and present a compelling case for equality.

Highlighting the Benefits of Equality

In the face of opposition, Talin focused on highlighting the positive impact of lifting the multi-tentacle marriage restrictions. She emphasized the economic, social, and cultural benefits that come with embracing diversity and inclusion. By showcasing stories of successful inter-species marriages and the positive contributions made by alien communities, Talin effectively countered the opposition's arguments and won over hearts and minds.

Celebrating Small Victories

Amidst the ongoing struggle, it was crucial for Talin and her allies to celebrate small victories. Each step forward, whether it was gaining media attention, mobilizing support, or winning battles in local communities, was an achievement that reinforced their commitment to the cause. By acknowledging progress, they kept morale high and fueled the motivation to continue fighting against opposition and backlash.

Learning from Setbacks

In the face of opposition, setbacks were inevitable. Talin understood the importance of learning from these moments and adapting her strategies accordingly. Each setback served as a lesson to improve communication, build stronger alliances, and employ more effective tactics. Talin's ability to persevere and learn from adversity played a critical role in the ultimate success of the movement.

Embracing Unconventional Allies

To overcome opposition and backlash, Talin recognized the value of embracing unconventional allies. She reached out to individuals and groups who might not have directly been affected by the multi-tentacle marriage restrictions but shared a commitment to justice and equality. This inclusive approach expanded the movement's reach and challenged traditional notions of solidarity, ultimately strengthening the fight for alien rights.

Exercises

1. Consider a contemporary civil rights movement in your own society. Identify the opposition and backlash it has faced. What strategies were employed to counter this opposition? Reflect on the lessons learned from these experiences.

2. Imagine you are a civil rights activist trying to address a deeply ingrained prejudice within your community. Develop a plan of action on how you would engage in dialogue and negotiation with opponents to foster understanding and promote positive change.

3. Research a successful civil rights movement that faced strong opposition and backlash. Identify the key strategies they employed to overcome these challenges. How can these strategies be applied to other social justice movements?

Further Reading

1. "The Opposite of Hate: A Field Guide to Repairing Our Humanity" by Sally Kohn
    2. "March: Book One" by John Lewis, Andrew Aydin, and Nate Powell
    3. "The New Jim Crow: Mass Incarceration in the Age of Colorblindness" by Michelle Alexander
    4. "Citizen: An American Lyric" by Claudia Rankine
    5. "Daring Greatly: How the Courage to Be Vulnerable Transforms the Way We Live, Love, Parent, and Lead" by Brené Brown

Gaining Media Attention and Public Support

In the journey to defy the multi-tentacle marriage restrictions on Xyorath, Talin Iryn understood the power of media attention and public support. As an alien rights activist, she knew that the media could be a powerful tool in shaping public opinion and raising awareness about the injustices faced by the Xyorathian community. This section explores how Talin and her allies strategized to gain media attention and rally public support for their cause.

Understanding the Media Landscape

Talin recognized that to effectively gain media attention, she needed to understand the landscape and mechanisms of the media industry on Xyorath. She dedicated time to research and analyze various media outlets, understand their target demographics, and craft her messaging accordingly. She sought to engage with both traditional media outlets, such as newspapers and television stations, as well as emerging platforms like online blogs and social media networks.

Crafting a Compelling Narrative

To capture the attention of the media and the public, Talin and her team understood the importance of crafting a compelling narrative. They highlighted the human stories behind the multi-tentacle marriage restrictions, emphasizing the love and commitment of Xyorathian couples who were denied the rights enjoyed by others.   By humanizing the issue, Talin aimed to evoke empathy and understanding among the public.

Strategic Media Engagements

Talin and her team strategically engaged with the media to ensure their message reached a wider audience.   They held press conferences, organized media interviews, and issued press releases to disseminate information about the discriminatory laws and the need for change.   Talin herself became a prominent media figure, giving impassioned speeches and sharing personal stories to connect with the public on a deeper level.

Media Stunts and Creative Protests   In addition to traditional media engagements, Talin and her allies employed creative tactics to attract media attention.   They organized peaceful protests, vibrant marches, and attention-grabbing events that visually represented the injustice of the multi-tentacle marriage restrictions. These actions not only attracted the interest of the media but also inspired and mobilized the general public to join the cause.

Engaging with Opinion Leaders and Influencers

Talin recognized the significance of engaging with opinion leaders and influencers who could amplify her message and reach a wider audience. She actively sought out partnerships and collaborations with influential individuals from various fields, such as celebrities, academics, and politicians, who shared her commitment to social justice. By leveraging their existing platforms and networks, Talin was able to garner increased media attention and support for the alien rights movement.

Building an Online Presence

To effectively reach a tech-savvy audience, Talin and her team embraced the power of social media and built a strong online presence. They created dedicated social media accounts, sharing powerful stories, engaging infographics, and thought-provoking videos that resonated with their target audience. By actively interacting with followers and creating a sense of community, they fostered a strong online support base that echoed their message across platforms.

Online Campaigns and Hashtag Activism   Talin and her allies initiated online campaigns to raise awareness and mobilize public support. They created powerful hashtags that encapsulated the movement's goals and encouraged supporters to share their experiences and stories. By harnessing the viral nature of social media, they effectively spread the word, ultimately captivating the attention of mainstream media outlets.

Collaborating with Documentarians and Filmmakers

Recognizing the power of visual storytelling, Talin collaborated with documentarians and filmmakers to create compelling narratives that showcased the struggles faced by the Xyorathian community. Through documentaries and short films, they were able to capture the essence of the movement, giving a voice to those affected by the multi-tentacle marriage restrictions. These visual mediums further amplified their message and attracted significant media attention.

Engaging in Thoughtful Public Dialogue

Talin and her allies were committed to engaging in thoughtful public dialogue to address misconceptions and stereotypes surrounding the multi-tentacle marriage issue. They actively sought opportunities for public debates, panel discussions, and town hall meetings, inviting key stakeholders to have a meaningful conversation about the importance of equal rights for all. By engaging in open dialogues, they showed the public that their cause was based on principles of fairness, love, and equality.

The Role of Everyday Activists

While Talin played a pivotal role in gaining media attention and public support, she recognized the importance of everyday activists in driving the movement forward. She encouraged individuals to share their stories with local media outlets, write op-eds for newspapers, and engage in conversations with their communities. By empowering others to speak out, Talin and her team expanded the reach of their message and built a broader coalition of support.

Providing Media Training and Resources   To equip everyday activists with the necessary tools, Talin and her team provided media training sessions and resources on effective communication strategies. They shared tips on public speaking, dealing with interviewers, and utilizing social media platforms. By arming individuals with the skills and confidence to engage with the media, they ensured a diverse range of voices was heard and amplified.

Conclusion

Gaining media attention and public support was instrumental in Talin Iryn's fight against the multi-tentacle marriage restrictions on Xyorath. By understanding the media landscape, crafting compelling narratives, strategically engaging with the media, collaborating with opinion leaders, fostering an online presence, and empowering everyday activists, Talin and her allies successfully garnered widespread attention and support for their cause. The media became a powerful ally in the battle for equal rights, allowing the alien rights movement to make significant strides toward creating a more just and inclusive society on Xyorath.

The First Victory: Lifting the Ban in Local Communities

In the early days of Talin Iryn's activism journey, she faced an uphill battle against the deep-rooted multi-tentacle marriage restrictions on Xyorath. These discriminatory laws prevented aliens from marrying someone with a different number of tentacles, severely limiting the expression of love and hindering the formation of mixed-species families. But Talin was determined to challenge these unjust regulations and fight for equality.

Understanding the Impact

Before diving into the details of Talin's first victory, it is essential to comprehend the adverse effects of the multi-tentacle marriage restrictions. These restrictions perpetuated a culture of prejudice and discrimination, reinforcing the idea that aliens with differing numbers of tentacles were incompatible or lesser beings. They weakened the social fabric of Xyorathian society and created a divide among its diverse population.

The ban not only violated the fundamental human rights of aliens but also impeded their pursuit of happiness, personal fulfillment, and emotional well-being. Talin recognized that dismantling these restrictions was not only a matter of legal reform but also a catalyst for positive social change.

Building a Coalition

Talin understood the importance of establishing a strong foundation for her cause by building alliances with like-minded individuals and organizations. She reached out to local alien rights groups, human rights activists, and legal experts who shared her vision of a more inclusive and just Xyorathian society. Together, they formed a coalition dedicated to challenging the multi-tentacle marriage restrictions.

This coalition became a powerful force in raising awareness about the discriminatory nature of the ban and mobilizing support from both within and outside the alien community. Through joint efforts, they organized grassroots campaigns, public demonstrations, and community dialogues to educate the public about the negative consequences of the ban.

Crafting a Strategic Approach

Talin recognized that a successful legal challenge required a strategic approach that utilized every available avenue for change. She encouraged the coalition members to pursue a multi-pronged strategy that encompassed both grassroots activism and legal advocacy.

With their expertise and commitment, the coalition crafted a meticulous plan to challenge the multi-tentacle marriage restrictions. They conducted careful research, examining constitutional principles, international human rights laws, and legal precedents that supported their claim for equality. This research formed the bedrock for a compelling legal argument that the ban violated fundamental rights to liberty, equality, and non-discrimination.

Navigating the Legal System

Talin's coalition carefully selected strategic jurisdictions to launch the legal challenge. They identified local communities where progressive attitudes were more prevalent and sympathetic judges could be found. By focusing their efforts at the local level, they aimed to create a ripple effect that would challenge the entire legal framework surrounding multi-tentacle marriage restrictions.

They filed lawsuits in these communities, taking courageous stands against the discriminatory ban. The legal battles were intense, with conservative forces fighting tooth and nail to maintain the status quo. But Talin and her coalition remained resilient, trusting in the righteousness of their cause and the power of empathy and understanding.

Gaining Support and Momentum

The battle to lift the ban in local communities gained significant attention from the media and the general public. Talin and her allies utilized this spotlight to share personal stories of those affected by the discriminatory legislation. They emphasized the human toll, highlighting the loving relationships torn apart and the deep emotional scars inflicted on alien individuals and families.

Talin's eloquence and passion resonated with people from all walks of life, inviting empathy and support from unexpected quarters. As public opinion shifted in favor of equality, the momentum grew, igniting a broader societal discussion about the importance of love, acceptance, and the need for an inclusive Xyorathian society.

Seeing the First Victory

After months of tireless efforts, the hard work and determination of Talin and her coalition paid off. In a landmark ruling by a local court, the multi-tentacle marriage restrictions were deemed unconstitutional, marking the first major victory for alien rights in Xyorathian history.

The court's decision reverberated throughout the local communities, fostering an atmosphere of hope and inspiring aliens and their allies to continue fighting for change. People rejoiced in the newfound freedom to choose their life partners based on love rather than arbitrary tentacle count.

Talin celebrated this significant milestone, acknowledging the determination and unwavering support of her coalition. The first victory bolstered their confidence, spurring them on to tackle even more challenging battles ahead.

Continuing the Journey

While Talin and her coalition reveled in their first triumph, they understood that the journey to full equality was far from over. The victory in local communities served as a launchpad for future endeavors, providing a precedent that could be leveraged for statewide and nationwide legal challenges.

Their work had just begun. Talin and her allies were now armed with the experience, resources, and public support they needed to take on the larger fight against multi-tentacle marriage restrictions.

As they embarked on this next phase, they would face daunting obstacles, fierce opposition, and unexpected alliances. But Talin remained resolute in her determination to build a society where love, respect, and equality thrived for all beings, regardless of their tentacle count or any other characteristic that set them apart.

The first victory was not just a legal milestone; it was a stepping stone towards a future Xyorathian society that embraced the diversity of its inhabitants and celebrated the triumph of love over prejudice. Talin's continued activism would shape the path towards that brighter future, where no one would be denied the right to love and be loved.

The Fight Continues: Expanding the Movement

The tireless efforts of Talin Iryn to lift the multi-tentacle marriage restrictions on Xyorath were not in vain. After the first victory in the local communities, the movement gained momentum and moved towards expanding its reach. This section explores the challenges and triumphs faced during the second attempt at legalization, the strategies employed, and the importance of sustaining the movement.

Learnings from the First Attempt

Reflecting on the first attempt at legalization, Talin and their allies recognized the need for a more comprehensive strategy. They understood that gaining public support was not enough; they needed to mobilize political power and build stronger alliances. Talin's experience of facing opposition and backlash provided valuable lessons on how to navigate the legal and social landscape.

Strengthening Alliances and Mobilizing Support

Expanding the movement required collaboration with other alien rights organizations and civil rights movements. Talin and their team actively sought partnerships with organizations working towards similar goals, understanding that unity is essential in fighting discrimination. They organized joint campaigns, held meetings to discuss shared challenges, and nurtured relationships built on solidarity.

To mobilize support, Talin and their allies organized grassroots campaigns and awareness-raising events. They focused on educating the Xyorathian public about the unfairness of the multi-tentacle marriage restrictions, debunking myths and providing factual information. They also engaged in door-to-door canvassing, community organizing, and utilized social media platforms to spread their message far and wide.

Lobbying and Advocacy Efforts

Recognizing the need for legislative change, Talin and their team embarked on a vigorous lobbying and advocacy campaign. They met with lawmakers at the local and state levels, presenting evidence and making compelling arguments for the repeal of the discriminatory laws. They highlighted the economic and social benefits that would come from lifting the restrictions, emphasizing the principles of equality and human rights.

To amplify their voice, Talin and their allies organized rallies, protests, and public hearings. They leveraged the power of public opinion and media coverage to put pressure on legislators, ensuring that the issue remained in the public consciousness. Through targeted media strategies, such as interviews, op-eds, and social media campaigns, they effectively framed the multi-tentacle marriage restrictions as a matter of justice and equality.

Legislative Roadblocks and Challenges

As expected, the fight faced significant hurdles in the form of legislative roadblocks and opposition from conservative forces. Some lawmakers were unwilling to go against deeply ingrained prejudices, while others viewed the issue as a political liability. Talin and their team encountered resistance and hostility during legislative hearings, requiring them to navigate these challenging environments with resilience and tenacity.

Media Strategies and Public Opinion

Media played a crucial role in shaping public opinion and garnering support for the movement. Talin and their team collaborated with journalists, influencers, and media platforms to ensure accurate and empathetic coverage of the issue. They shared stories of Xyorathian couples affected by the restrictions, emphasizing the emotional toll and humanizing the experience to create empathy among the broader public.

They strategically countered misinformation and stereotypes through targeted media campaigns, utilizing catchy slogans, powerful visuals, and personal testimonies. They harnessed the power of storytelling to challenge societal norms and provoke thought. By painting a vivid picture of the injustice faced by Xyorathians, they successfully swayed public opinion in favor of their cause.

Sustaining Momentum and Building Resilience

Maintaining momentum and energy was pivotal in expanding the movement. Talin and their team utilized various strategies to sustain engagement and enthusiasm. They organized regular community meetings, providing updates on progress and setting milestones for future advocacy efforts. They also encouraged community members to share their personal stories and participate in direct action.

To build resilience, Talin prioritized self-care and encouraged their allies to do the same. They organized workshops on managing burnout, practicing mindfulness, and developing emotional strength. They recognized the importance of a well-rested and mentally healthy team in achieving long-term success.

The Second Victory: Statewide Legalization

After relentless efforts, the movement achieved its second victory: statewide legalization of multi-tentacle marriages. The lifting of the discriminatory restrictions was a significant milestone in the fight for equality on Xyorath. Talin and their allies celebrated this historic decision, acknowledging the collective effort that made it possible.

Celebrating and Reflecting on the Achievement

The achievement of statewide legalization called for celebration and reflection. Talin and their team organized a series of events, including rallies, concerts, and community gatherings, to commemorate the victory. They invited speakers from different civil rights movements to address the crowd and highlight the interconnectedness of struggles for justice and equality.

Talin also took the opportunity to reflect on the achievements and challenges faced throughout the journey. They shared their personal journey, the sacrifices made, and the lessons learned. This reflection served as a reminder of the importance of perseverance and unity in fighting for social change.

Setting New Goals and Aspirations

While the legalization of multi-tentacle marriages marked a significant milestone, Talin knew that the fight for equality was far from over. They recognized the need to set new goals and aspirations to address other forms of discrimination faced by Xyorathians and other alien communities.

Talin and their team shifted their focus towards broader civil rights issues, such as employment discrimination, access to healthcare and education, and challenging segregation policies. They continued to collaborate with other civil rights movements to create a more inclusive and equitable society.

Conclusion: A Legacy of Equality and Justice

The fight for equality and justice did not end with the statewide legalization of multi-tentacle marriages. Talin Iryn's relentless activism and determination set in motion a tidal wave of change that reshaped Xyorathian society.

Through their efforts, Talin expanded the alien rights movement, mobilized broad public support, and achieved legislative victories that dismantled discriminatory laws. They inspired other alien and civil rights activists to continue the work, paving the way for future generations to demand equality.

Talin's legacy goes beyond Xyorath. Their commitment to intersectionality and inclusive activism enriched and strengthened the broader civil rights movements. Their courage and resilience remain an inspiration for those fighting against discrimination in all its forms.

The fight for justice, fueled by Talin's unwavering spirit, will continue to evolve and adapt to the ever-changing landscape of social and political challenges. The struggle for equality knows no bounds, and Talin Iryn's legacy will forever remind us of the power of collective action in shaping a more just and equitable world.

Second Attempt at Legalization

Learnings from the First Attempt

The first attempt to legalize multi-tentacle marriage on Xyorath was a challenging and eye-opening experience for Talin Iryn and her fellow activists. They faced numerous obstacles and setbacks along the way, but they also learned valuable lessons that would shape their strategy for future advocacy efforts.

One of the most important learnings from the first attempt was the power of building strong alliances and mobilizing support. Talin and her team realized that they could not achieve their goals alone. They needed the backing of other alien rights organizations, as well as support from the general public. By reaching out to these groups and building networks, they were able to create a united front and amplify their message.

Another key lesson was the importance of understanding the legislative process and navigating the political landscape. The first attempt at legalization showed Talin and her team that changing laws was not as straightforward as they had initially thought. They encountered numerous roadblocks and challenges along the way, including opposition from conservative lawmakers and bureaucratic hurdles. In order to overcome these obstacles, they had to become well-versed in the intricacies of the legal system and develop effective strategies for lobbying and advocacy.

Media strategies and public opinion also played a crucial role in the first attempt. Talin and her team quickly realized that gaining media attention and shaping public perception was essential for their cause. They worked hard to craft a compelling narrative and highlight the discrimination faced by those in multi-tentacle relationships. By leveraging the power of the media, they were able to generate public support and shift the conversation in their favor.

However, the first attempt also taught Talin and her team the importance of resilience and perseverance. They faced significant backlash and resistance from conservative forces who were opposed to any changes in traditional marriage laws. Threats and intimidation became a daily occurrence, but rather than backing down, Talin and her team stood firm in their convictions. Their unwavering determination allowed them to weather the storm and emerge stronger than ever.

In terms of strategy, the first attempt taught Talin and her team the need for sustained momentum. They realized that advocacy efforts couldn't stop at the first victory. Building on their initial success, they continued to expand the movement beyond local communities and push for statewide legalization. This required a long-term vision and a willingness to adapt their tactics and strategies to the changing political landscape.

Throughout the first attempt, Talin learned important lessons in leadership and coalition building. She discovered the power of collaboration and the strength that comes from diverse voices working together towards a common goal. By partnering with other civil rights movements, such as those fighting for gender equality and racial justice, Talin and her team were able to create a broader coalition that advocated for a more inclusive and equitable society.

In summary, the first attempt to legalize multi-tentacle marriage on Xyorath taught Talin Iryn and her team valuable lessons about the power of alliances, the complexities of the legislative process, the influence of media and public opinion, the need for resilience and perseverance, and the importance of sustained momentum and strategic adaptation. These learnings would shape their future advocacy efforts and ultimately pave the way for lasting change on Xyorath.

Strengthening Alliances and Mobilizing Support

In order to effectively challenge the multi-tentacle marriage restrictions on Xyorath, Talin Iryn understood the importance of building strong alliances and mobilizing support from various sectors of society. She recognized that the fight for equality required a united front that could exert pressure on legislators, sway public opinion, and generate momentum for change. This section explores the strategies and initiatives undertaken by Talin to strengthen alliances and mobilize support for the cause.

Recognizing the Power of Allies

Talin knew that she couldn't tackle the multi-tentacle marriage restrictions alone. She actively sought out individuals and organizations that shared her vision of equality and justice. She reached out to activist groups, LGBTQ+ organizations, feminist collectives, and human rights advocates both on Xyorath and other planets.

> **Problem**
>
> Talin wants to establish alliances with other alien rights organizations. She has identified eight potential organizations, but due to limited resources, she can only reach out to three. Help Talin select the most strategic organizations based on their influence and alignment with her cause.

In selecting her allies, Talin considered the organizations' track records, their expertise, and their willingness to support the cause publicly. She emphasized building long-term relationships built on trust and mutual respect, recognizing that sustained collaboration was key to achieving lasting change.

Collaborative Initiatives

Talin believed in the power of collective action. She spearheaded collaborative initiatives that brought together different communities and interest groups to work towards the common goal of achieving marriage equality for multi-tentacled individuals. Talin organized workshops, seminars, and conferences that provided a platform for activists, legal experts, and scholars to share knowledge and experiences.

> **Problem**
>
> Talin is planning a conference on alien rights and marriage equality. She wants to create an inclusive program that addresses various aspects of discrimination faced by multi-tentacled individuals. Help Talin design the conference schedule, ensuring diverse perspectives and engaging topics are covered.

By fostering dialogue, Talin encouraged cross-pollination of ideas and strategies. This allowed the movement to benefit from different perspectives and experiences. Through collaborative initiatives, Talin was able to build a broad-based movement that could rally support from communities beyond Xyorath.

Public Awareness Campaigns

Talin understood the importance of educating the public about the discrimination faced by multi-tentacled individuals and the need for legal reform. She led public awareness campaigns that aimed to dispel myths, challenge stereotypes, and humanize the experiences of those affected by the multi-tentacle marriage restrictions.

> ### Problem
>
> Talin wants to create a compelling social media campaign to raise awareness about the multi-tentacle marriage restrictions. Help her devise a series of engaging posts that highlight the impacts of these restrictions on the lives of Xyorathians.

Talin leveraged social media platforms, organized public rallies and protests, and engaged with journalists to ensure media coverage of the cause. Through these efforts, she sought to gather public support and apply pressure on policymakers to reconsider the discriminatory laws.

Fundraising and Resource Mobilization

Challenging the multi-tentacle marriage restrictions required financial resources. Talin Iryn recognized the importance of fundraising and resource mobilization to sustain the movement. She reached out to philanthropists, alien communities with financial means, and organized fundraising events to generate financial support.

> ### Problem
>
> Talin is organizing a fundraising event to support legal advocacy for multi-tentacled individuals. Help her design an effective fundraising strategy that maximizes donations and creates a memorable experience for attendees.

Additionally, Talin actively sought grants and secured partnerships with organizations that shared their values and could provide logistical and financial support. These resources allowed the movement to hire legal experts, conduct research, and organize events that furthered their cause.

Celebrity Endorsements

Talin recognized the influence and reach of celebrities in shaping public opinion. She sought endorsement from influential public figures who could use their platform to advocate for marriage equality for multi-tentacled individuals. Talin highlighted the intersectionality of discrimination and the importance of support from all sectors of society.

Problem

Talin is reaching out to celebrities and public figures to secure their endorsement for the movement. Help her create a compelling pitch that emphasizes the shared vision of justice and equality.

By gaining support from celebrities, Talin aimed to reach wider audiences and challenge societal norms. Their endorsement served as a powerful tool to amplify the movement's message and galvanize public support.

Overall, Talin Iryn's approach to strengthening alliances and mobilizing support showcased her strategic thinking and determination. By collaborating with various organizations, fostering dialogue, raising public awareness, mobilizing resources, and gaining celebrity endorsements, she built a formidable movement that propelled the fight for multi-tentacle marriage equality forward. Talin's ability to bring diverse groups together and create a shared vision of justice was integral to the success of the movement.

Lobbying and Advocacy Efforts

Lobbying and advocacy efforts played a crucial role in Talin Iryn's fight against the multi-tentacle marriage restrictions on Xyorath. Talin understood that in order to bring about meaningful change, they needed to engage with lawmakers, policymakers, and other key stakeholders on both local and national levels. This section explores the strategies and tactics deployed by Talin and their allies in their lobbying and advocacy efforts.

Understanding the Legislative Landscape

Before embarking on their lobbying and advocacy efforts, Talin and their team dedicated significant time to understanding the legislative landscape surrounding the multi-tentacle marriage restrictions. They meticulously researched existing laws, policies, and regulations to identify potential avenues for legal change.

Additionally, Talin and their team studied past and ongoing legal battles within the Xyorathian courts, as well as in other jurisdictions, to gain valuable insights and identify best practices. This comprehensive understanding of the legal framework allowed them to strategically plan their lobbying and advocacy efforts for maximum impact.

Building Alliances and Coalitions

Talin recognized the importance of building alliances and coalitions to amplify their voice and enhance their influence. They reached out to existing alien rights organizations, civil rights groups, and LGBTQ+ advocacy groups to form powerful partnerships.

By joining forces with these organizations, Talin was able to share resources, knowledge, and expertise. Together, they developed and implemented coordinated strategies that leveraged their collective strength. These alliances also helped to broaden the base of support for the multi-tentacle marriage equality movement, as they were able to mobilize a diverse range of individuals and communities.

Engaging Lawmakers

One of the key strategies employed by Talin and their team was direct engagement with lawmakers. They scheduled meetings, both formal and informal, with legislators at the local, state, and national levels to discuss the multi-tentacle marriage restrictions and advocate for their removal.

During these engagements, Talin and their team presented compelling arguments, backed by research and evidence, highlighting the discriminatory nature of the restrictions and the need for legal change. They also shared personal stories and testimonials from Xyorathian individuals and families affected by the ban, making a human connection and illustrating the real-life consequences of the discriminatory policy.

Creating a Media Strategy

Talin understood the power of media in shaping public opinion and influencing policymakers. They worked closely with a dedicated media team to create a comprehensive media strategy that would both raise awareness about the multi-tentacle marriage restrictions and generate public support for their repeal.

The media strategy included press releases, op-eds, interviews, and feature stories aimed at highlighting the stories of Xyorathian individuals and families affected by the ban. Talin also made themselves available for media interviews, not only to share their personal journey but to articulate the legal and moral arguments against the discriminatory policy.

Additionally, Talin and their team actively engaged with social media platforms to amplify their message and mobilize supporters. They created online campaigns, hashtags, and shareable infographics to make their cause accessible and compelling to a broader audience.

Mobilizing Grassroots Support

To further strengthen their lobbying and advocacy efforts, Talin and their team prioritized mobilizing grassroots support. They organized community meetings, town halls, and public forums to educate and rally individuals, engaging them in the cause and encouraging them to take action.

Talin recognized that sustained public pressure was crucial in influencing lawmakers and policymakers. They coordinated letter-writing campaigns, phone bank operations, and visits to elected officials' offices, empowering individuals to actively participate in the fight for multi-tentacle marriage equality.

Legal Expertise and Strategic Litigation

In addition to lobbying and advocacy, Talin and their team recognized the importance of utilizing legal expertise and strategic litigation to challenge the multi-tentacle marriage restrictions in the courts. They engaged with experienced lawyers and legal organizations specializing in civil rights and constitutional law to build a strong legal case.

Through careful litigation strategizing, Talin's legal team identified key test cases to challenge the constitutionality of the multi-tentacle marriage restrictions. They worked closely with affected individuals and families to identify plaintiffs and gather compelling evidence to support their case.

By combining their advocacy efforts with strategic litigation, Talin and their team aimed to establish legal precedents that would not only strike down the discriminatory policy but also set a strong foundation for future legal challenges to other forms of discrimination.

The Power of Creative and Non-conventional Tactics

Throughout their lobbying and advocacy efforts, Talin and their team embraced the power of creativity and non-conventional tactics to make their message heard. They organized vibrant and engaging protests that garnered media attention and generated public discourse about the multi-tentacle marriage restrictions.

Talin also recognized the importance of cultural activism and utilized art, music, and poetry to convey their message. They collaborated with local artists and performers to create powerful visual and auditory expressions of the struggle for equality, further igniting public interest and support.

In addition, Talin and their team tapped into the power of storytelling and personal narratives. They organized public storytelling events, inviting Xyorathian individuals and families affected by the ban to share their experiences, fostering empathy and understanding among a wide audience.

Conclusion

Talin Iryn's lobbying and advocacy efforts were instrumental in spearheading the movement for multi-tentacle marriage equality on Xyorath. Through building alliances, engaging lawmakers, mobilizing grassroots support, and employing creative tactics, Talin and their team successfully galvanized public opinion and brought about significant legal changes.

Their unwavering determination, combined with strategic planning and effective communication, demonstrated the power of grassroots activism in challenging unjust laws and advocating for social justice. Talin's legacy continues to inspire future activists, reminding us all of the importance of fighting for equality and justice for all.

Legislative Roadblocks and Challenges

In this chapter, we will explore the legislative roadblocks and challenges that Talin Iryn encountered in her fight against the multi-tentacle marriage restrictions on Xyorath. These obstacles posed significant challenges to the realization of her mission for equality and social justice.

Lack of Legal Precedent

One of the major roadblocks that Talin faced was the lack of legal precedent for her cause. The multi-tentacle marriage restrictions had never been challenged before, and there were no established laws or court rulings to rely on. This lack of legal framework made it difficult for Talin and her legal team to build their case and argue for the recognition of multi-tentacle marriages.

To overcome this challenge, Talin's legal team had to conduct extensive research into intergalactic law, human rights principles, and precedent-setting cases from other planets and civilizations. They had to gather evidence and arguments that would persuade the courts to recognize the inherent injustice of the restrictions and to take the necessary steps towards legal reform.

Resistance from Conservative Forces

Another significant legislative roadblock that Talin encountered was the resistance from conservative forces within the Xyorathian government and society. These conservative factions held firmly to traditional values and were vehemently opposed to any changes in the prevailing marriage laws.

Talin faced intense opposition from lawmakers who argued that multi-tentacle marriages were unnatural and went against Xyorathian cultural norms. They used derogatory language and fear-mongering tactics to mobilize public opinion against her cause. This resistance created a hostile environment for Talin and increased the legal and political challenges she faced.

Lobbying and Advocacy Efforts

To overcome the resistance from conservative forces, Talin and her allies ramped up their lobbying and advocacy efforts. They sought support from progressive lawmakers who were sympathetic to their cause and worked towards building a coalition within the legislature.

Talin and her team organized rallies, demonstrations, and letter-writing campaigns to increase public awareness and gather support for legislative change.

They utilized social media platforms to amplify their message and engage with supporters. Additionally, Talin herself became an effective public speaker, giving impassioned speeches that resonated with audiences and pushed for legislative reform.

Policy Roadblocks and Challenges

Beyond the resistance from conservative forces, Talin and her team faced numerous policy roadblocks and challenges. The existing Xyorathian legal system made it difficult to propose and pass legislation that would overturn the multi-tentacle marriage restrictions.

For example, the Xyorathian constitution had an amendment process that required a supermajority to approve any changes to marriage laws. This made it a daunting task for Talin and her allies to gather enough support to pass laws in favor of multi-tentacle marriages.

To navigate these challenges, Talin's team strategized for alternative routes to achieve their goals. They explored legal loopholes, challenged the constitutionality of existing laws, and sought innovative legal arguments that would circumvent the need for a constitutional amendment.

Media Strategies and Public Opinion

Another significant aspect of overcoming legislative roadblocks was effectively managing media strategies and shaping public opinion. Talin recognized the power of media in influencing legislative outcomes and worked diligently to garner positive media coverage for her cause.

She engaged with journalists, held press conferences, and gave interviews to highlight the discriminatory nature of the multi-tentacle marriage restrictions. Talin's team also utilized social media platforms to share stories of individuals affected by the restrictions, humanizing their cause and building public empathy.

By keeping the issue in the public eye and generating sympathetic coverage, Talin and her team were able to sway public opinion and garner wider support for their legislative efforts. This, in turn, put pressure on lawmakers to take action and drove the momentum for legal reform.

Lessons Learned and Strategies for Success

Throughout the challenges faced in the legislative arena, Talin and her team learned valuable lessons that shaped their strategies for success. They realized the importance of building alliances, both within the legislature and outside of it, to create a broad-based movement for change.

They also recognized the power of public opinion and understood the need to engage with the media effectively. By changing the narrative surrounding multi-tentacle marriages and highlighting the issues of injustice and discrimination, they were able to generate support and drive the legislative agenda forward.

Talin and her team also learned the importance of perseverance and resilience in the face of adversity. They faced setbacks and defeats along the way but remained steadfast in their commitment to achieving equality and justice.

By learning from their experiences and adapting their strategies, Talin and her team were ultimately able to overcome the legislative roadblocks and pave the way for the recognition of multi-tentacle marriages on Xyorath.

Unconventional Approach: Using Satirical Performance Art

In their fight against legislative roadblocks, Talin's team employed an unconventional approach: using satirical performance art to raise awareness and challenge traditional beliefs. They organized street performances and theatrical events that humorously portrayed the absurdity of the multi-tentacle marriage restrictions.

By using satire, they were able to engage audiences in a non-confrontational manner while still conveying the underlying message of inequality. These performances served as a creative strategy to break down barriers and initiate conversations about the need for legislative change.

This unconventional approach not only garnered attention but also sparked public dialogue about the unjust nature of the restrictions. It helped shift public opinion and create an environment more conducive to legislative reform.

Conclusion

The legislative roadblocks and challenges that Talin Iryn faced in her fight against the multi-tentacle marriage restrictions were substantial. From the lack of legal precedent to the resistance from conservative forces, she encountered numerous obstacles along the way. However, through strategic lobbying, media campaigns, legal creativity, and an unwavering commitment to her cause, Talin was able to overcome these challenges and pave the way for legislative change. Her story serves as a testament to the power of perseverance, coalition-building, and creative advocacy in the pursuit of equality and social justice.

Media Strategies and Public Opinion

In the fight against the multi-tentacle marriage restrictions on Xyorath, media strategies played a crucial role in shaping public opinion and mobilizing support for the cause. Talin Iryn and their team recognized the power of the media in influencing societal attitudes and leveraged various strategies to ensure their message reached a wide audience and garnered maximum support. Through careful planning, effective messaging, and strategic communication, they were able to shift public opinion and gain momentum in their pursuit of change.

Understanding the Media Landscape

To effectively utilize the media, Talin's team first understood the media landscape on Xyorath. They conducted thorough research to identify key media outlets and influential journalists who could help amplify their message. They analyzed the reach, target audience, and editorial stance of various media platforms to craft their media strategies accordingly.

Crafting Compelling Narratives

One of the most successful media strategies employed by Talin's team was the use of compelling narratives to highlight the human impact of the multi-tentacle marriage restrictions. They shared personal stories of individuals affected by the discriminatory laws, showcasing the challenges they faced and the love they shared. These stories humanized the issue, making it relatable to the general public and spurring empathy and support.

Example: A heartwarming story was shared of two Xyorathians, Sela and Ryn, who had been in a committed multi-tentacle relationship for years but were denied the right to marry. Their struggle and unconditional love resonated with the public, driving home the injustice of the restrictions.

Engaging with Journalists and Influencers

Talin's team actively engaged with journalists and influencers to ensure their message received widespread coverage. They organized press conferences, briefings, and one-on-one interviews to provide journalists with in-depth information about the discriminatory laws and the efforts to challenge them. They also cultivated relationships with influential bloggers and social media personalities who could amplify their message to a broader audience.

Social Media Campaigns

Recognizing the power of social media in shaping public opinion, Talin's team launched targeted campaigns on various platforms. They created engaging content, including videos, infographics, and testimonials, to educate and inform the public about the issue. They encouraged supporters to share their content, using hashtags and viral challenges to generate awareness and engagement.

Example: The team launched the #LoveWithoutBoundaries campaign, where people were invited to share stories and pictures of multi-tentacle couples in their lives. The campaign spread like wildfire on social media, challenging societal norms and showcasing the universal nature of love.

Building Alliances with Progressive Media Outlets

Talin's team actively sought to build alliances with progressive media outlets that aligned with their cause. They collaborated with journalists and editors from these outlets to publish op-eds, articles, and interviews that highlighted the discriminatory nature of the law and the need for change. By strategically targeting sympathetic media channels, they ensured that their message reached a receptive audience.

Addressing Opposition and Misinformation

Talin's team anticipated opposition and prepared to counter misinformation. They monitored media coverage and swiftly responded to inaccurate or biased reporting. They used fact-checking initiatives, public statements, and press releases to provide accurate information and challenge misconceptions surrounding multi-tentacle marriage.

Maintaining Momentum and Consistency

Throughout their media campaign, Talin's team maintained momentum and consistency in their messaging. They ensured that their key talking points were reiterated across different media platforms and adapted them to resonate with various audiences. By consistently pushing their message forward, they prevented it from being diluted or undermined by competing narratives.

Ensuring Accessibility and Inclusivity

Talin's team recognized the importance of making their message accessible and inclusive to all Xyorathians. They provided translations of their media materials into different dialects and ensured that their online content was accessible to individuals with visual impairments or other disabilities. By removing barriers to access, they ensured that their message reached a diverse range of individuals.

Evaluating Impact and Adjusting Strategies

Throughout their media campaign, Talin's team continuously evaluated the impact of their efforts. They analyzed media coverage, monitored public sentiment, and solicited feedback from supporters and community members. These insights allowed them to adjust their strategies, target specific demographics, and address any shortcomings in their messaging.

Unconventional Tactic: Satirical Sketches

To inject some levity into their campaign and engage a wider audience, Talin's team collaborated with popular comedians to produce satirical sketches. These sketches humorously highlighted the absurdity of the multi-tentacle marriage restrictions while delivering a powerful message. The comedic approach not only entertained but also sparked critical reflection among viewers.

Example: In one sketch, a Xyorathian couple tries to navigate the bureaucracy of obtaining a marriage license, only to be met with absurd hurdles and nonsensical paperwork. The sketch drew attention to the bureaucratic obstacles faced by multi-tentacle couples, shedding light on the real-life challenges under the discriminatory laws.

By employing these media strategies and working in tandem with public opinion, Talin's team successfully reshaped societal attitudes and built widespread support for the fight against multi-tentacle marriage restrictions. Through their efforts, the media became a powerful tool for social change and played a pivotal role in achieving legislative victories for equal rights on Xyorath.

Sustaining Momentum and Building Resilience

In the relentless fight for equality and justice, sustaining momentum and building resilience are crucial aspects of any successful civil rights movement. Talin Iryn understood the importance of both, and throughout their journey, they employed various strategies to keep the movement alive and thriving. This section explores the methods used by Talin and their allies to sustain momentum and build resilience in the face of formidable opposition.

Staying United: The Power of Coalitions

Talin recognized that unity is strength, and building strong coalitions was paramount to sustaining momentum. They understood that alien rights alone couldn't capture the attention of everyone, so they sought to collaborate with other civil rights movements. By forging alliances with other marginalized communities fighting for their own rights, Talin created a powerful network capable of challenging the status quo.

One example of this coalition-building effort was Talin's partnership with the Xyorathian LGBTQ+ community. By aligning the struggles of alien rights with LGBTQ+ rights, Talin tapped into a broader support base and gained valuable insights from the LGBTQ+ community's own battles. This alliance not only increased visibility for both movements but also provided a platform for joint advocacy and shared resources.

Talin also recognized the power of collaboration on a national level. They reached out to alien rights activists in other regions, organizing conferences, and summits to create a united front. By sharing experiences, best practices, and strategies, these gatherings became breeding grounds for new ideas and an opportunity to bolster momentum.

Educating and Engaging the Masses

Maintaining momentum requires an informed and active supporter base. Talin was an advocate for educating and engaging the masses to sustain public interest and support for the cause. They organized community forums, public lectures, and workshops to raise awareness about the multi-tentacle marriage restrictions and their implications on alien communities.

One of the strategies employed by Talin was storytelling. They realized that personal narratives had tremendous power in shaping public opinion and generating empathy. Talin encouraged community members to share their stories, experiences, and struggles, which were then disseminated through various platforms, including social media, newspapers, and magazines. These stories humanized the cause, allowing people to connect on a deeper level and motivating them to take action.

Moreover, Talin understood the significance of grassroots organizing. They empowered local communities to start their own advocacy groups, providing them with the necessary tools, resources, and training. By decentralizing the movement, Talin ensured that momentum was sustained at the grassroots level, with local activists leading the charge in their respective regions.

Resilience in the Face of Adversity

Building resilience is essential for any activist fighting against deeply entrenched discriminatory practices. Talin exemplified this resilience throughout their journey, both individually and collectively as part of the movement. Here are some strategies they utilized to withstand adversity:

1. **Self-care and Emotional Support:** To sustain the fight, Talin emphasized the importance of self-care and emotional well-being. They encouraged activists to prioritize their mental and physical health, emphasizing that taking breaks and seeking support were essential for long-term resilience.

2. **Celebrating Victories:** Talin understood the importance of celebrating victories, no matter how small. Recognizing and acknowledging progress provided much-needed motivation and revitalized the movement's collective spirit.

3. **Adapting Strategies:** In the face of opposition, Talin advocated for adaptability. They understood that strategies that worked in one context might not be effective in another. By continuously analyzing the political and social landscape, Talin and their allies could adjust their approaches to maintain momentum and overcome obstacles.

4. **Turning Adversaries into Allies:** Talin was skilled at building bridges, even with those who initially opposed the cause. They engaged in dialogue, sought common ground, and presented the case for equality with empathy and respect. By finding shared values and appealing to the better nature of their opponents, Talin managed to convert adversaries into supporters.

5. **Resilient Leadership:** Talin's own resilience as a leader and spokesperson was crucial in sustaining momentum. They led by example, demonstrating unwavering determination, optimism, and grace under pressure. By remaining steadfast in the face of setbacks, Talin inspired others to keep fighting.

Unconventional yet Relevant: Art as Resistance

Throughout the struggle for alien rights, Talin embraced unconventional methods to sustain momentum. One such method was utilizing art as a form of resistance. They recognized that art had the power to transcend language barriers, engage emotions, and inspire action.

Talin and their allies organized art exhibitions, performances, and film festivals, showcasing the work of alien artists. These creative expressions not only gave voice to the experiences of the marginalized but also captivated audiences and sparked crucial conversations. Art became a medium through which the movement could broaden its reach and sustain public interest.

In addition to traditional art forms, Talin encouraged the use of technology and social media platforms to amplify the movement's message. They understood that in a modern world, where connectivity was paramount, utilizing digital platforms was essential for sustaining momentum and engaging wider audiences.

Conclusion

Sustaining momentum and building resilience are essential components of any successful civil rights movement. Talin Iryn understood the power of unity, education, and adaptive strategies to keep the movement alive and thriving. By building strong coalitions, educating and engaging the masses, and embracing resilience in the face of adversity, Talin was able to sustain momentum and pave the way for lasting change. Their story serves as a reminder that the fight for justice and equality is never-ending but always worth pursuing.

The Second Victory: Statewide Legalization

The journey towards achieving statewide legalization of multi-tentacle marriages on Xyorath was fraught with challenges and obstacles. However, Talin Iryn's unwavering determination and the collective effort of the alien rights movement eventually led to a historic second victory that brought about significant social change.

Learnings from the First Attempt

Before launching the second attempt at legalization, Talin and their fellow activists took the time to reflect on the lessons learned from the first unsuccessful endeavor. They analyzed the mistakes made, identified the weaknesses, and strategized on how to address them.

One key learning was the importance of widespread public support. Talin realized that in order to effectively challenge the multi-tentacle marriage restrictions, they needed to mobilize allies from various communities, not just within the alien population. Building coalitions with other civil rights movements, such as the fight for gender equality and LGBTQ+ rights, became a central focus of their efforts.

Another crucial lesson was the need to engage in proactive media strategies. Talin recognized that changing public opinion was just as important as lobbying for legislative change. They worked tirelessly to shape the narrative around multi-tentacle relationships, highlighting the love, commitment, and familial bonds that existed within these unions.

Strengthening Alliances and Mobilizing Support

Armed with the knowledge gained from the first attempt, Talin and their fellow activists set out to strengthen their alliances and mobilize support on an even larger scale. They reached out to influential figures from a wide range of sectors, including advocacy organizations, religious leaders, and influential celebrities.

Talin's charismatic and persuasive nature played a crucial role in convincing key figures to lend their voices to the cause. They attended countless meetings, dinners, and events, tirelessly sharing their personal experiences and challenging the misconceptions surrounding multi-tentacle marriages.

Additionally, grassroots organizing became a pillar of the movement. Talin and their team held town hall meetings, organized street rallies, and engaged in door-to-door canvassing. They prioritized listening to the concerns of the general public, debunking myths, and offering a compelling vision of a society that celebrates diversity and love in all its forms.

Lobbying and Advocacy Efforts

With a broader coalition of supporters in place, Talin and their team intensified their lobbying and advocacy efforts. They spent countless hours at the Xyorathian Parliament, meeting with lawmakers, and advocating for legislative change.

Talin's persuasive skills and ability to articulate their arguments in a compelling manner won them the respect and attention of politicians from various parties. They strategically selected key lawmakers who had shown at least some openness to progressive policies and worked to build relationships with them.

Leveraging the power of storytelling, Talin and their team coordinated a series of impactful testimonies during parliamentary hearings. They invited individuals from multi-tentacle relationships to share their personal stories and the hardships they faced due to the restrictions. These testimonies humanized the issue, appealing to the emotions and empathy of lawmakers.

Legislative Roadblocks and Challenges

Despite the growing public support and the relentless efforts of activists, the fight for statewide legalization faced numerous legislative roadblocks and challenges. Conservative lawmakers vehemently opposed any change to the existing marriage laws, arguing that it defied tradition and threatened the sanctity of marriage.

To counter these arguments, Talin and their allies enlisted the expertise of legal scholars and constitutional experts. They meticulously crafted legal arguments that highlighted the discriminatory nature of the multi-tentacle marriage restrictions and how they violated the fundamental rights of individuals.

Instead of engaging in confrontational debates, Talin's strategy was to shift the narrative to emphasize the values of love, acceptance, and equality. They framed the issue not just as a matter of alien rights but as a fundamental human rights issue that affected all members of society.

Media Strategies and Public Opinion

Alongside the lobbying efforts, Talin and their team continued to employ media strategies to shape public opinion. They engaged in public debates, appeared on talk shows, and wrote opinion pieces for prominent newspapers and online publications.

Talin understood the power of visual storytelling and collaborated with filmmakers to create documentaries that shed light on the experiences of individuals in multi-tentacle marriages. These powerful films resonated with audiences, fostering empathy and challenging societal norms.

Social media also played a vital role in spreading awareness and garnering support. Talin leveraged platforms like Xyorathian Twitter and Galactagram to share personal stories, combat misinformation, and connect with individuals who had been previously indifferent or opposed to the issue.

Sustaining Momentum and Building Resilience

As the second attempt at legalization gained momentum, Talin and their fellow activists faced mounting pressure, both externally and internally. They were subjected to personal attacks, threats, and intimidation from conservative groups and individuals who saw their efforts as a threat to the status quo.

To counter these challenges, Talin prioritized the mental and emotional well-being of their team. They organized self-care workshops, therapy sessions, and community-building activities to foster resilience and provide emotional support.

Additionally, Talin and their allies established robust security protocols to ensure the safety of activists and their families. They collaborated with legal experts to navigate potential legal challenges and protect the movement from any attempts to disrupt or malign their work.

The Second Victory: Statewide Legalization

After months of tireless advocacy, lobbying, and public awareness campaigns, Talin and their allies achieved their second victory: statewide legalization of multi-tentacle marriages on Xyorath.

The historic decision came after an intense parliamentary debate, during which Talin's unwavering conviction and the overwhelming public support for the issue became impossible for lawmakers to ignore. The legislation overturned the multi-tentacle marriage restrictions, granting legal recognition and protection to all alien couples, regardless of the number of tentacles.

The victory was celebrated with great jubilation, marked by massive street festivities and gatherings across Xyorath. Talin delivered a stirring speech, acknowledging the collective efforts of the movement and expressing gratitude to the allies and supporters who had stood by their side throughout the grueling campaign.

Celebrating and Reflecting on the Achievement

After the initial celebrations subsided, Talin and their fellow activists took the time to reflect on the achievement and its broader implications for alien rights and social justice. They recognized the significant progress that had been made, but also acknowledged that the fight for equality was far from over.

Talin emphasized the importance of continued vigilance and the need to monitor the implementation of the new legislation to ensure its true impact on alien communities. They encouraged other oppressed communities to unite in solidarity and build upon the momentum generated by their victory.

Setting New Goals and Aspirations

With the statewide legalization of multi-tentacle marriages achieved, Talin Iryn and their team set their sights on new goals and aspirations. They aimed to combat other forms of discrimination faced by alien communities, such as employment inequality, access to healthcare and education, and challenging segregation and housing policies.

Talin understood that the fight for alien rights went beyond legislation and policy change. They believed in the power of challenging societal attitudes and prejudices through education and dialogue. They set out to develop comprehensive educational programs that promoted inclusivity, diversity, and acceptance within Xyorathian society.

Looking to the future, Talin Iryn's legacy would serve as an inspiration for future generations of alien activists. Their courageous efforts in fighting for justice and equality would continue to resonate in the hearts and minds of those who believe in the transformative power of love and the need for a more inclusive and just society.

Celebrating and Reflecting on the Achievement

After years of tireless efforts, setbacks, and challenges, Talin Iryn and her fellow alien rights activists finally achieved a monumental victory: the statewide legalization of multi-tentacle marriages on Xyorath. As news of this historic decision spread, it was met with both celebration and reflection. In this section, we will delve into the euphoria of the moment, the significance of the achievement, and the profound impact it had on the lives of Xyorathians.

A Joyful Triumph

With the news of the statewide legalization, the air on Xyorath buzzed with an electrifying sense of joy and triumph. Alien rights activists and supporters took to the streets, jubilantly waving banners, dancing, and singing in celebration of this long-awaited victory. Talin Iryn stood at the forefront, her heart bursting with pride and fulfillment, as she witnessed the fruits of her labor materialize before her eyes.

In a landmark ceremony held at the capital city's central square, Talin Iryn, surrounded by a diverse coalition of activists, politicians, and community leaders, addressed the crowd. Her voice reverberated through the speakers as she spoke passionately about the arduous journey they had all undertaken. She thanked the countless individuals who had stood by their side, lending their support and unwavering belief in the cause.

As the cheers and applause swelled, Talin Iryn released hundreds of vibrant, multi-colored balloons into the sky, symbolizing liberation, acceptance, and love prevailing over discrimination. Emotions ran high as Xyorathians embraced each other, reveling in this momentous victory that marked a turning point in their society's history.

The Significance of the Achievement

The legalization of multi-tentacle marriages on Xyorath was not just a legal victory; it was a profound affirmation of the principle that love knows no boundaries and that all beings, irrespective of their physical attributes, should be afforded the same rights and opportunities.

For the Xyorathian society, this achievement shattered the foundations of discrimination and prejudice that had plagued their communities for generations. It challenged the narrow-mindedness that had been deeply ingrained in their cultural norms and paved the way for a more inclusive and compassionate future.

The significance of this achievement extended far beyond Xyorath's borders. It served as a beacon of hope and inspiration for alien communities across the galaxy who continued to face similar struggles and injustices. Talin Iryn's victory demonstrated that change was indeed possible, even in the face of seemingly insurmountable opposition.

Reflecting on the Journey

Amidst the euphoria of triumph, Talin Iryn and her fellow activists took a breath to reflect on the years of struggle that had led them to this moment. They remembered the countless nights spent organizing protests, drafting petitions, and strategizing for change. They recalled the moments of doubt and frustration when progress seemed elusive. And they acknowledged the sacrifices made by those who had fought alongside them, some of whom were no longer there to witness this historic milestone.

Together, they stood on a stage overlooking the sea of celebratory faces, atop a mountain of determination and resilience. Each step taken, each setback overcome had brought them closer to this pivotal moment in history. They pledged to honor the struggles and sacrifices of those who had come before them and to champion the rights of all marginalized communities, for the fight for justice never truly ends.

Lessons for Future Generations

As the festivities continued, Talin Iryn recognized the immense responsibility that came with their triumph. She understood that they had not only changed the lives of current Xyorathians but also shaped the future of their society for generations to come.

Talin Iryn and her fellow activists saw themselves as catalysts for change, trailblazers who had dismantled barriers and opened doors for those who would come after them. They embraced the duty to nurture a culture of empathy, understanding, and respect among Xyorathians, ensuring that their society continued to evolve into one that celebrated diversity and equality.

They also understood the importance of passing down their collective knowledge and experience to younger generations. To that end, they began establishing educational programs, scholarships, and mentorship opportunities, enabling aspiring alien rights activists to mature and continue the work they had started. Through publications, memoirs, and documentaries, Talin Iryn and her compatriots shared their stories, providing an invaluable resource for future activists grappling with similar struggles.

An Unconventional Approach

As an unconventional yet highly effective approach, Talin Iryn and her allies organized an annual celebration of love and diversity known as the "Unified Hearts Festival." This unique event brought together Xyorathians from all walks of life and species, fostering understanding and unity through music, art, and cultural exchange. By promoting collaboration and dialogue, the festival became a powerful platform for advocating for the rights of all beings, irrespective of their physical form.

Through this celebration, Talin Iryn aimed to challenge deep-rooted prejudices, dissolve societal divisions, and encourage Xyorathians to embrace a more expansive definition of love and unity. The Unified Hearts Festival grew steadily each year, attracting not only Xyorathians but also intergalactic attention and support. It became a symbol of hope and a testament to what could be accomplished when diverse voices joined together in harmony.

Conclusion: A Milestone of Equality

The statewide legalization of multi-tentacle marriages on Xyorath marked a joyous turning point in the struggle for alien rights. It was a testament to the power of perseverance, unity, and unwavering belief in the inherent worth of every being.

As the celebrations continued, Talin Iryn and her fellow activists knew that their journey was far from over. They recognized that there were still battles to be fought, injustices to be confronted, and hearts and minds to be won. However, they drew strength from the knowledge that they had forever altered the trajectory of Xyorathian society, setting the stage for a more inclusive, compassionate future.

For Talin Iryn, the statewide legalization of multi-tentacle marriages was not just a personal achievement, but a triumph for equality and justice. It was a testament to the indomitable spirit of those who dare to challenge the status quo and fight for a future where all beings are free to love and be loved without discrimination or prejudice.

As the celebrations subsided, Talin Iryn looked out at the transformed landscape of her homeworld, her heart filled with hope and determination. And the fight for justice continued, for as she knew deep in her soul, the struggle for equality is never-ending and ever-evolving.

Setting New Goals and Aspirations

In the aftermath of the statewide legalization of multi-tentacle marriages on Xyorath, Talin Iryn set her sights on new goals and aspirations. She recognized that achieving marriage equality was just the beginning of a larger fight for alien rights. Talin understood that true equality could only be achieved by addressing the systemic discrimination and inequality present in Xyorathian society. In this section, we explore the goals and aspirations Talin set for herself and her movement, and how she worked towards achieving them.

Expanding the Fight for Equal Rights

Talin, ever the visionary, understood the importance of extending the fight for equal rights beyond the realm of marriage. While legalizing multi-tentacle marriages was a significant milestone, there were still many areas of life where aliens faced discrimination. Talin aimed to dismantle discriminatory practices in employment, healthcare, education, housing, and other aspects of daily life.

Addressing Employment Discrimination

One of the key goals Talin set was to address the issue of employment discrimination against aliens. Many talented and highly-educated aliens were being denied job opportunities solely based on their extraterrestrial origin. Talin aimed to challenge these discriminatory practices and establish inclusive employment policies that valued diversity and talent.

To address this issue, Talin and her team conducted research on employment discrimination laws and practices across the galaxy. They collaborated with legal experts to draft comprehensive legislation that would protect aliens from discrimination in the workplace. Talin organized public awareness campaigns, highlighting the valuable contributions aliens made to Xyorathian society and urging employers to adopt fair hiring practices.

Securing Access to Healthcare and Education

Another crucial goal Talin set was to ensure that aliens had equal access to healthcare and education. She recognized that these were fundamental rights that should not be denied based on one's species.

Talin worked alongside healthcare professionals and education advocates to overhaul existing policies and practices that discriminated against aliens. She pushed for the implementation of inclusive healthcare programs that catered to the unique needs of alien physiology. Additionally, Talin fought for equal opportunities in education, advocating for scholarships and grants for alien students, as well as for the inclusion of alien history and culture in the curriculum.

Challenging Segregation and Housing Policies

Talin was deeply committed to dismantling segregation and challenging discriminatory housing policies that alienated minority communities. She believed that everyone, regardless of their species, deserved equal access to safe and affordable housing.

To address this issue, Talin collaborated with housing advocates and legal experts to challenge discriminatory housing policies in court. She organized protests and public demonstrations to raise awareness about the dire need for fair and inclusive housing practices. Talin also worked towards creating housing initiatives that promoted integration and diversity, fostering communities where aliens and humans could live side by side in harmony.

Influencing Policy Change at Local and National Levels

Talin recognized the importance of enacting systemic change to bring about lasting equality. She tirelessly lobbied for policy changes at both the local and national levels, partnering with politicians who shared her vision for a more inclusive society.

Talin's advocacy efforts included meeting with lawmakers, presenting compelling research and evidence, and building coalitions with like-minded organizations. She utilized her media presence to raise awareness about the need for policy reform, engaging with citizens and encouraging them to demand change from their elected representatives.

Collaborating with Other Civil Rights Movements

Understanding the power of collective action, Talin actively sought out collaborations with other civil rights movements. She recognized that the struggle for equality was interconnected across various marginalized communities, and that by uniting their efforts, they could have a stronger impact.

Talin fostered alliances with organizations advocating for LGBTQ+ rights, racial equality, and gender equality. She organized joint protests, hosted panel discussions, and encouraged dialogue and solidarity between different social justice movements. Through these collaborations, Talin aimed to create a more inclusive and equitable society for all.

The Legacy of Legal Victories

Despite the challenges she faced, Talin's relentless pursuit of equality yielded significant legal victories. These victories set a precedent for future alien rights activism and provided a foundation upon which future generations could build.

Talin's legal victories served as a beacon of hope for marginalized communities and inspired other alien and civil rights activists to continue fighting for justice. Her legacy paved the way for future legal advocacy, ensuring that the fight for equality would endure long after her time.

Inspiring Other Alien Communities to Demand Equality

Talin understood the power of inspiration. She knew that her achievements would be hollow if they did not motivate other alien communities to demand equality in their respective societies.

To inspire other alien communities, Talin embarked on speaking engagements, sharing her experiences and strategies for advocacy. She traveled to various planets, engaging with local activists and communities, encouraging them to organize and fight for their rights.

Talin's unique ability to connect with people from diverse backgrounds allowed her to foster a sense of unity and shared purpose among different alien communities. She imparted her knowledge and shared the lessons she had learned along her journey, empowering others to take charge of their own fight for justice and equality.

Paving the Way for Future Legal Advocacy

One of Talin's long-term goals was to create a sustainable framework for future legal advocacy. She recognized that achieving equality was an ongoing process that required continuous effort and vigilance.

To ensure the longevity of the alien rights movement, Talin established the Talin Iryn Foundation. The foundation served as a platform to support aspiring activists, providing legal resources, mentorship programs, and funding for strategic litigation. Talin also worked towards the establishment of legal clinics dedicated to alien rights, ensuring that future generations would have access to the legal expertise needed to fight against discrimination.

Through these initiatives, Talin aimed to create a legacy of justice and equality, ensuring that the fight for alien rights would continue long after she was gone.

Conclusion: A Legacy of Equality and Justice

Talin Iryn's journey as a civil rights activist on Xyorath left an indelible mark on the planet's history. Through her tireless advocacy, she shattered societal norms and fought for the rights of aliens to love and live freely.

By setting new goals and aspirations beyond marriage equality, Talin worked towards dismantling discriminatory practices in employment, healthcare, education, housing, and more. Her legal victories and collaborations with other civil rights movements created ripple effects of change, inspiring other alien communities to demand equality in their own societies.

Talin's legacy endures through the Talin Iryn Foundation, which continues to support future activists and ensure the sustainability of the alien rights movement. Her unwavering dedication to justice and equality serves as a reminder that the fight for social justice is never-ending and ever-evolving.

As we reflect on Talin's contributions, let us draw inspiration from her courage and resilience. Let us honor her legacy by continuing to challenge discrimination, working towards a world where every being, regardless of their species, can live with dignity, respect, and equality.

Chapter 2: Breaking Barriers

The Legal Battle Begins

Assembling a Legal Team

As Talin Iryn embarked on their journey to fight for the rights of alien communities on Xyorath, they quickly realized the immense task ahead. To challenge the multi-tentacle marriage restrictions and pave the way for equality, they needed a skilled and dedicated legal team. In this section, we will explore the process of assembling such a team and the importance of their expertise in navigating the complex legal landscape.

Identifying Legal Experts

Talin understood that assembling a legal team required finding experts well-versed in interstellar law, constitutional rights, and civil liberties. They sought out professionals who had a strong track record in fighting for social justice causes and were passionate about the cause of alien rights. The team needed individuals who could skillfully argue their case in court and possess a deep understanding of the intricate legal frameworks surrounding marriage restrictions.

This process involved extensive research, consultations with legal experts, and interviews to ensure the team's collective expertise was comprehensive. Talin reached out to law firms specializing in civil rights and liberties, seeking attorneys with a demonstrated commitment to challenging unjust laws and promoting equality. They also considered lawyers from other fields who had shown dedication to advocating for marginalized communities.

Building a Diverse and Inclusive Team

Talin recognized the importance of building a diverse and inclusive legal team that reflected the communities they were fighting for. They sought individuals from different backgrounds, including Xyorathian aliens, to bring unique perspectives to the table. By assembling a team with diverse experiences, Talin aimed to create a cohesive force that could effectively represent the interests of all those affected by the multi-tentacle marriage restrictions.

To ensure the team was inclusive and representative, Talin actively sought attorneys who were part of underrepresented groups, including individuals from marginalized genders, ethnicities, and species. They understood that an inclusive team would strengthen their case by challenging systemic biases and bringing a broader range of experiences to the forefront.

Collaborating with Legal Organizations

In addition to assembling a legal team, Talin understood the importance of collaborating with established legal organizations focused on civil rights and liberties. By partnering with these organizations, they could tap into their networks, resources, and legal expertise. These organizations had a wealth of experience in challenging discriminatory laws and could provide valuable guidance and support.

Talin engaged in discussions with organizations such as the Interstellar Civil Liberties Union and the Alliance for Alien Rights. They formed strategic alliances and sought assistance from attorneys associated with these organizations. The collaboration allowed for a pooling of knowledge, experiences, and strategies that not only strengthened their legal team but also increased their chances of success.

Furthermore, partnering with these organizations bolstered the public image of their cause, generating wider awareness and support. Through joint press conferences and public engagement, Talin and their legal team leveraged the influence of these organizations to amplify their message.

The Role of Each Legal Team Member

A successful legal team needs individuals with diverse skill sets to tackle various aspects of the case. Talin's legal team consisted of lawyers, legal researchers, paralegals, and administrative personnel, all working together to build a strong case against the multi-tentacle marriage restrictions.

Lawyers formed the core of the team, responsible for developing legal strategies, arguing in court, and representing Talin and the alien communities.

They conducted legal research, analyzed precedents, and crafted persuasive legal arguments to challenge the constitutionality of the marriage restrictions.

Legal researchers played a crucial role in gathering evidence, studying past legal cases, and analyzing legal frameworks. They provided the team with essential information and helped identify strong legal precedents and arguments to strengthen their case.

Paralegals provided vital support by organizing and managing the vast amount of documentation required for the legal proceedings. They prepared legal briefs, helped interview witnesses, and assisted the attorneys in their day-to-day work. Their expertise in administrative tasks ensured that the legal team operated smoothly and efficiently.

The administrative personnel ensured effective communication within the legal team and managed logistical aspects of the case. They coordinated meetings, scheduled court appearances, and handled the team's correspondence, allowing the lawyers and researchers to focus on the legal aspects of the case.

The Unconventional Approach: Alien Rights Advocates

Talin's legal team went beyond conventional legal experts by incorporating alien rights advocates into their lineup. These advocates were individuals from Xyorathian communities who had firsthand experience with the discrimination resulting from the multi-tentacle marriage restrictions.

By including alien rights advocates in the legal team, Talin aimed to humanize the legal battle and bring personal narratives to the forefront. These advocates played a crucial role in shaping legal strategies, as their lived experiences provided insights that legal professionals might overlook.

This unconventional approach ensured that the legal fight was not detached from the human impact it aimed to address. The advocates also helped in building public support by sharing their stories with the media and at public events, making the cause relatable on a personal level.

Example: The Role of an Alien Rights Advocate

One example of an alien rights advocate on Talin's legal team is Zara Jexan, a Xyorathian activist who had experienced firsthand the devastating effects of the multi-tentacle marriage restrictions. Zara's personal story of being unable to marry the love of her life due to these discriminatory laws resonated with many across the galaxy.

Zara worked closely with the legal team, providing insights into the specific challenges faced by alien communities and the profound impact of the marriage restrictions on their lives. Her role was integral in shaping legal strategies and ensuring that the legal arguments addressed the real-life consequences faced by alien couples.

Furthermore, Zara's presence added an emotional component to the legal battle. By sharing her personal experiences and speaking passionately about love and equality, she inspired public support and empathy. Zara's involvement served as a reminder that beyond the legal battle, the fight for justice was about real people and their fundamental human rights.

Resources and Support for the Legal Team

Assembling and maintaining a legal team required adequate resources and support. Talin worked tirelessly to secure funding through grants, donations, and crowdfunding campaigns. These financial resources allowed them to hire the best legal experts, support staff, and researchers.

In addition to financial support, the legal team relied on the expertise of consultants and experts in fields such as sociology, psychology, and political science. These specialists provided insights into the social and psychological impact of alien discrimination, helping the legal team build a comprehensive case.

Talin also recognized the importance of mental health support for the legal team members, who were often under immense pressure and facing intense backlash. They arranged regular counseling sessions and created a supportive environment where team members could share their thoughts, concerns, and challenges.

Exercises

1. Research a landmark legal case in your own country or region that involved fighting for civil rights. Analyze how the legal team was assembled and the strategies they employed to achieve success.

2. Imagine you are tasked with assembling a legal team to fight for the rights of marginalized communities. Outline the key qualities and expertise you would look for in candidates.

3. Form a mock legal team with your classmates or friends and discuss strategies for challenging an unjust law of your choice. Assign roles and responsibilities within the team, and identify potential obstacles and how you would overcome them.

Key Takeaways

- Assembling a legal team involves identifying legal experts well-versed in the relevant areas of law and civil rights. - Building a diverse and inclusive team is crucial to effectively represent the interests of marginalized communities. - Collaboration with legal organizations provides support, resources, and a wider network to bolster the case for equality. - Legal team members have distinct roles and responsibilities, including attorneys, legal researchers, paralegals, and administrative personnel. - Incorporating alien rights advocates humanizes the legal battle and brings personal narratives to the forefront. - Adequate funding, resources, and support are essential to the functioning and success of the legal team.

Research and Preparing the Case

In order to effectively challenge the multi-tentacle marriage restrictions on Xyorath, Talin Iryn recognized the need for meticulous research and preparation. This section focuses on the essential steps taken to build a strong case against the discriminatory laws.

Understanding the Legal Landscape

Before diving into research, it was crucial for Talin and their legal team to gain a comprehensive understanding of the legal landscape surrounding the multi-tentacle marriage restrictions. They studied the relevant laws, constitutional provisions, and any previous legal precedents that might impact their case.

They analyzed the history of legislation related to alien civil rights on Xyorath, including any laws that had been introduced or debated previously. By undertaking a thorough examination of existing legal frameworks, Talin and their team were able to identify potential weaknesses in the legislation and formulate effective strategies to challenge it.

Legal Research and Case Preparation

Legal research formed the backbone of Talin's case. They engaged a team of legal experts, including lawyers with experience in civil rights litigation, to assist in the research process. The team conducted an extensive review of scholarly articles, legal textbooks, court decisions, and relevant statutes to develop a strong legal argument.

They examined cases from other jurisdictions that had addressed similar issues, looking for strategies, arguments, and legal principles that could be applied to Xyorath's specific circumstances. This comparative approach provided valuable insights and helped Talin's legal team develop innovative and persuasive arguments.

To support their case, Talin's team gathered empirical data and conducted surveys to ascertain the impact of the multi-tentacle marriage restrictions on Xyorathian society. They collected testimonies from individuals affected by these discriminatory laws, highlighting the emotional and psychological toll they imposed.

Additionally, they reviewed sociological studies to understand the societal implications of the restrictions. This research was crucial in demonstrating the negative effects on families, mental health, and overall well-being. By presenting a comprehensive picture of the issue, Talin's legal team aimed to generate empathy and understanding among the judges and the public.

Constitutional Analysis

An essential aspect of the case was analyzing the constitutionality of the multi-tentacle marriage restrictions. Talin's legal team scrutinized the constitutional principles of equality, human rights, and freedom of marriage to challenge the discriminatory laws.

They examined constitutional provisions that protected the rights of individuals against discrimination based on factors such as race, gender, and sexual orientation. Drawing parallels with these protected classes, Talin's team sought to establish that discriminating against individuals based on multi-tentacle identity violated the principles of equal protection under the law.

The team also explored the concept of substantive due process, arguing that the government's interference in personal relationships and the denial of fundamental rights without a compelling state interest infringed upon the rights guaranteed by the Constitution. This line of argument aimed to demonstrate that the multi-tentacle marriage restrictions were not only discriminatory but also unconstitutional.

Preparing Legal Arguments and Strategies

With the research and analysis in hand, Talin's legal team proceed to prepare their arguments and strategies for the case. They outlined the key points to be presented during the legal proceedings, ensuring a coherent and compelling narrative that would resonate with the judges and the public.

Strategic considerations were also crucial. The team anticipated the opposing arguments and devised counter-arguments to refute them effectively. They identified potential weaknesses in their own arguments and crafted responses to address any contingencies that might arise during the litigation process.

Moreover, Talin's team engaged in mock trials and moot court exercises to test their arguments and strategies. These simulations allowed them to refine their case and anticipate potential challenges they might face in the courtroom.

By combining thorough research, constitutional analysis, and strategic preparation, Talin and their legal team laid the groundwork for a robust legal challenge against the multi-tentacle marriage restrictions on Xyorath. In the next section, we explore the courtroom drama and challenges that they encountered during the legal battle.

Courtroom Drama and Challenges

The courtroom drama surrounding Talin Iryn's battle against the multi-tentacle marriage restrictions on Xyorath was nothing short of captivating. This section of the book delves into the challenges faced by Talin and their legal team as they navigated the intricacies of the legal system and fought to secure marriage equality for all alien communities.

3.1.3.1 The Legal Landscape: Understanding the Multi-Tentacle Marriage Restrictions

Before delving into the courtroom drama, it's crucial to understand the legal landscape and the multi-tentacle marriage restrictions that were at the center of Talin's battle. These restrictions, deeply rooted in Xyorathian tradition and customs, prohibited aliens with multiple tentacles from entering into legal marriages.

The legal team began by studying the intricacies of the Xyorathian legal system, combing through ancient texts, and consulting experts in Xyorathian law and customs. They sought to understand the historical basis for the multi-tentacle marriage restrictions and the ways those restrictions had evolved over time.

3.1.3.2 Building a Legal Strategy: Overcoming Precedent

One of the most significant challenges Talin's legal team faced was overcoming previous court cases that had upheld the constitutionality of the multi-tentacle marriage restrictions. These cases set a precedent that seemed insurmountable.

To tackle this challenge, the legal team meticulously analyzed those precedents, identifying weaknesses and inconsistencies. They sought innovative legal arguments and precedents from other jurisdictions, drawing upon experiences of other civil rights movements across the galaxy. Additionally, they worked around the clock to amass persuasive evidence through extensive research, interviews with experts, and case studies from other planets where similar restrictions had been successfully challenged.

3.1.3.3 Presenting Compelling Evidence: Expert Witnesses and Stories of Discrimination

In order to convince the court of the need to strike down the multi-tentacle marriage restrictions, Talin's legal team knew they had to present overwhelming evidence. They called upon expert witnesses, ranging from sociologists to historians to psychologists, who could testify to the negative impact of these restrictions on the lives of alien individuals and communities.

The legal team also worked tirelessly to gather personal stories from those who had directly experienced discrimination and hardship due to the marriage restrictions. These personal narratives were poignant and served to humanize the issue, allowing the court to understand the emotional toll and societal consequences of these discriminatory laws.

To creatively illustrate the absurdity of the restrictions, the legal team incorporated visual aids, such as charts and diagrams, to depict the arbitrary nature of the restrictions and demonstrate how they perpetuated inequality.

3.1.3.4 Courtroom Battles: Cross-Examinations and Persuasive Rhetoric

Inside the courtroom, the legal team faced fierce opposition from lawyers representing conservative factions within Xyorathian society. They engaged in intense cross-examinations, challenging the expert witnesses' credibility and attempting to undermine the validity of the evidence presented.

Tension in the courtroom was high, with emotional outbursts and heated arguments becoming the norm. The legal team's ability to think on their feet and present persuasive counterarguments proved instrumental in dismantling the opposition's case.

Talin, who had become a powerful public speaker and advocate, stood as an authoritative and empathetic witness, sharing their personal experiences and showcasing the resilience of alien communities in the face of discrimination.

3.1.3.5 Navigating Media Attention: Public Opinion and Press Conferences

Outside the courtroom, the legal team had to navigate the media landscape and manage public opinion. They organized press conferences and media interviews strategically, ensuring the narrative surrounding the case remained focused on the issue of equality and justice.

By engaging with the media, the legal team was able to shape public opinion, rally support, and gain momentum for their cause. They highlighted the stories of individuals directly impacted by the multi-tentacle marriage restrictions, using their experiences to foster empathy and understanding within the wider Xyorathian society.

3.1.3.6 Unconventional Tactics: Balancing Legal Strategy and Public Activism

In their pursuit of marriage equality, Talin's legal team understood the importance of not only relying on legal arguments but also utilizing unconventional tactics. They organized peaceful protests outside the courtroom, leveraging public demonstrations to raise awareness and put pressure on the judicial system.

These protests included alien couples holding hand tentacles in a symbolic demonstration of unity and love. The imagery and public support generated by these protests were crucial in swaying public opinion and building a groundswell of support for the movement.

While these tactics were not directly related to the legal arguments presented in court, they played a vital role in creating a favorable environment for change.

3.1.3.7 The Verdict: A Landmark Decision for Equality

After weeks of courtroom battles, emotional testimonies, and legal arguments, the moment of truth arrived. The court's verdict had the potential to reshape Xyorathian society and establish a precedent for equal rights across the galaxy.

The book details the nail-biting anticipation leading up to the final ruling, exploring the impact that the decision had on Talin and their legal team, the alien communities they represented, and the wider Xyorathian society as a whole.

By securing a landmark decision in favor of equality, Talin's legal team not only shattered the discriminatory multi-tentacle marriage restrictions but also set the stage for future legal battles challenging other forms of discrimination against alien communities.

3.1.3.8 The Ripple Effect: Inspiring Legal Advocacy Across the Galaxy

The courtroom drama and the subsequent victory in securing marriage equality for aliens with multiple tentacles had far-reaching consequences. It inspired alien communities across the galaxy to advocate for their rights and challenge discriminatory laws and customs.

The book highlights the ways in which Talin's legal battle served as a catalyst for change, sparking a galactic network of legal activists committed to dismantling oppression and fighting for the rights of marginalized communities.

The lasting impact of the courtroom drama and the subsequent legal victory laid the foundation for future legal advocacy, fostering a legacy of equality and justice that would inspire future generations of alien rights activists.

In conclusion, the courtroom drama and challenges surrounding Talin Iryn's fight against the multi-tentacle marriage restrictions on Xyorath was an epic and intense battle for equality. Through innovative legal strategies, compelling evidence, and a relentless pursuit of justice, Talin and their legal team overcame precedent, navigated the media landscape, and secured a landmark decision in favor of equal rights. Their victory not only inspired alien communities across the galaxy but also left a lasting legacy of equality and justice in Xyorathian society.

Public Demonstrations and Protests

Public demonstrations and protests played a crucial role in Talin Iryn's fight for equal rights on Xyorath. These demonstrations served as a powerful tool to raise awareness, mobilize support, and put pressure on policymakers to enact change. In this section, we will explore the significance and impact of public demonstrations and protests in Talin's journey towards equality.

The Power of Visibility

One of the primary goals of public demonstrations and protests was to bring the issue of multi-tentacle marriage restrictions to the forefront of public consciousness. By taking to the streets and making their voices heard, Talin and their fellow activists sought to create a visible presence and draw attention to the unjust laws that were infringing upon their rights.

The sheer numbers and diversity of protestors were essential in generating media coverage and capturing the attention of the wider population. Through their powerful displays of solidarity, protestors conveyed the message that the fight for equal rights was not an isolated, fringe movement, but a widespread demand for justice and equality.

Creating a Sense of Community

Public demonstrations and protests served as a rallying point for those who felt marginalized and oppressed by the multi-tentacle marriage restrictions. These events provided a space for individuals to come together, share their stories, and find solace and support in a community of like-minded individuals.

The demonstrations not only united activists but also provided an opportunity for individuals affected by the discriminatory laws to connect and share their experiences. This sense of community fostered a stronger sense of belonging and purpose, empowering individuals to continue the fight for their rights.

Amplifying the Message

The impact of public demonstrations and protests extended far beyond their immediate participants. These events garnered significant media attention, both from traditional news outlets and social media platforms.   Journalists, photographers, and videographers captured the scenes of passionate protestors demanding justice and recognition of their rights.

The media coverage amplified the message of the activists, reaching a broader audience and increasing public awareness of the unjust multi-tentacle marriage restrictions. Through powerful images and firsthand accounts, the media helped to humanize the struggle, challenging societal prejudices and promoting empathy and understanding.

Challenges and Risks

Organizing public demonstrations and protests was not without its challenges and risks. Talin and their fellow activists faced hostile opposition from those who defended the status quo and viewed the movement as a threat to tradition and societal norms.

Law enforcement, at times, responded with force, using tactics such as tear gas, water cannons, and arrests to suppress the protests. Despite these obstacles, the activists remained resolute and maintained nonviolent resistance, demonstrating the power of peaceful protest as a means of effecting change.

Lessons from History

To ensure the success of public demonstrations and protests, Talin and their fellow activists studied and drew inspiration from historical civil rights movements. They recognized the significance of nonviolent resistance, taking inspiration from leaders such as Martin Luther King Jr. and Mahatma Gandhi.

By learning from the strategies and tactics employed by past social justice movements, Talin's fight for equal rights on Xyorath was further strengthened. They understood the importance of strategic planning, coordination, and the need to adapt their approach to navigate changing circumstances.

Unconventional Examples: The Power of Art

In addition to traditional forms of protest, Talin and their fellow activists embraced the use of unconventional methods to amplify their message. Art, in various forms, played a crucial role in capturing attention, evoking emotions, and challenging societal perceptions.

Street murals, performance art, and graffiti were used as powerful mediums for self-expression and storytelling. These artistic interventions not only beautified public spaces but also sparked conversations and ignited curiosity. Through art,

Talin and their allies were able to communicate complex ideas and foster empathy, ultimately contributing to the success of their movement.

Exercises

1. Imagine you are organizing a public demonstration to advocate for a cause you are passionate about. Outline a strategic plan, including goals, messaging, and potential challenges you might face.

2. Research an influential civil rights activist from history and examine the role that public demonstrations or protests played in their fight for equality. Compare and contrast their strategies and experiences with those of Talin Iryn.

3. Create a piece of artwork, such as a poster or mural, that symbolizes the fight for equal rights and justice. Explain the symbolism and message behind your artwork.

Resources

- "The Power of Nonviolent Resistance" by Martin Luther King Jr. - "Gandhi: An Autobiography" by Mahatma Gandhi - "Freedom Is a Constant Struggle" by Angela Davis - "The Art of Protest" by T.V. Reed

Conclusion

Public demonstrations and protests played a pivotal role in Talin Iryn's fight for equal rights on Xyorath. They not only raised awareness but also fostered a sense of community amongst activists and amplified the message of the movement to a wider audience. By studying the tactics of historical civil rights movements and embracing unconventional methods, Talin and their allies were able to challenge societal norms and effect meaningful change. The power of public demonstrations serves as a reminder that collective action and the courage to stand up for justice can transform societies and pave the way for a more inclusive and equitable future.

Media Coverage and Public Opinion

Media coverage plays a pivotal role in shaping public opinion and influencing the outcome of any social or political movement. In the case of Talin Iryn and the fight against the Multi-Tentacle Marriage Restrictions on Xyorath, media coverage proved to be both a powerful tool and a significant challenge.

The Power of Media

Media channels, including newspapers, TV broadcasts, radio programs, and online platforms, played a crucial role in spreading awareness about the discrimination faced by the Xyorathian community and the need for change. Through compelling storytelling and impactful visuals, media outlets brought the struggles of alien couples to the forefront of public consciousness.

One of the key strategies utilized by activist groups was to organize press conferences and media events to highlight the stories of individuals affected by the Multi-Tentacle Marriage Restrictions. By inviting journalists and reporters to these events, they were able to generate extensive coverage and increase public awareness.

Media coverage not only shed light on the discrimination faced by Xyorathian couples but also provided a platform for activists like Talin Iryn to articulate their message, share their personal experiences, and advocate for equal rights. Through interviews, opinion pieces, and feature stories, Talin and fellow activists were able to convey the urgent need for change and the underlying principles of justice and equity.

Challenges and Biases

However, it is important to acknowledge that media coverage was not always favorable or unbiased. Just as in any social movement, there were media outlets and journalists who opposed the cause, perpetuated stereotypes, and undermined the legitimacy of the fight against the Multi-Tentacle Marriage Restrictions.

One significant challenge was the tendency of some media organizations to sensationalize or trivialize the issue. By focusing on the "alien" aspect rather than the core principles of love, equality, and justice, these outlets tried to diminish the gravity of the discrimination faced by the Xyorathian community.

Furthermore, there were instances where Xyorathian activists and their allies faced biased and stigmatizing language in media coverage. Racist and xenophobic narratives were often employed to marginalize their cause and create divisions among the public. This necessitated a constant battle to counteract these biases and present a more nuanced, accurate portrayal of the movement.

Strategies for Influencing Public Opinion

To navigate these challenges, Talin Iryn and her team devised various strategies to shape public opinion in their favor. Proactive media engagement and advocacy efforts were undertaken to ensure accurate and empathetic coverage.

Firstly, activists cultivated relationships with sympathetic journalists and media outlets, establishing trust and building alliances with those who were genuinely committed to social justice issues. This involved providing them with facts, stories, and data to counteract misconceptions and biases.

Secondly, media literacy campaigns were launched to educate the public on the importance of critical thinking when consuming news. They aimed to raise awareness about media biases, stereotypes, and manipulative tactics employed by certain outlets to discredit the cause. By encouraging the public to seek diverse sources of information and question dominant narratives, these campaigns helped to counteract biased coverage.

Thirdly, social media platforms were utilized to bypass traditional media outlets and disseminate information directly to the public. Talin and her team leveraged the power of hashtags, viral videos, and digital storytelling to spark conversations, engage a wider audience, and debunk myths surrounding Xyorathian couples.

Impact on Public Opinion

The collective efforts of Xyorathian activists and their allies gradually transformed public opinion on the Multi-Tentacle Marriage Restrictions. From an initially indifferent or uninformed stance, more and more people became aware of the injustice faced by alien couples and expressed support for their cause.

Media coverage played a significant role in humanizing the issue and fostering empathy among the general public. Personal stories, interviews, and profiles of Xyorathian couples helped break down stereotypes and challenge preconceived notions. This led to a shift in public attitudes, as the discriminatory nature of the Multi-Tentacle Marriage Restrictions became increasingly apparent.

Furthermore, media coverage contributed to the creation of a broader coalition of supporters. As the movement gained traction and garnered favorable media attention, individuals from various backgrounds rallied behind Talin and her cause. This diverse support base not only bolstered the fight against the Multi-Tentacle

Marriage Restrictions but also demonstrated the interconnectedness of different social justice movements.

Media coverage and the subsequent changes in public opinion provided activists like Talin Iryn with the necessary momentum to continue their fight for equality. It shed a spotlight on the systemic discrimination faced by the Xyorathian community and brought attention to the urgent need for legal reforms.

In the following section, we will explore the legal battle that ensued in the fight against the Multi-Tentacle Marriage Restrictions, and the impact of Talin Iryn's legal victory on Xyorathian communities and beyond.

Facing Threats and Intimidation

In the fight for alien civil rights, Talin Iryn faced numerous threats and acts of intimidation from those who opposed their campaign for equality. As a prominent figure and leader in the movement, Talin endured personal attacks, harassment, and even physical violence. This section delves into the challenges they faced and their unwavering resolve to continue the fight despite these threats.

Understanding the Opposition

To comprehend the extent of the threats and intimidation faced by Talin, it is crucial to examine the motivations and tactics employed by their adversaries. The opposition primarily stemmed from deeply ingrained prejudices and fears about the integration of alien species into society. Some individuals and groups held onto archaic beliefs that non-humanoid creatures were inferior or posed a threat to the existing social order.

These adversaries used a variety of tactics to intimidate Talin and undermine their cause. They disseminated misinformation, spreading false narratives and stoking fear among the general population. They launched smear campaigns to tarnish Talin's reputation and vilify their allies, portraying them as a radical and dangerous force. Moreover, they resorted to acts of violence, including physical assaults and property damage, to instill fear and discourage further activism.

Physical Attacks

Despite being subjected to physical attacks, Talin demonstrated immense resilience and determination to push forward with their mission. On one occasion, after a public rally advocating for alien rights, a group of masked individuals ambushed Talin, brutally assaulting them. This act of violence served as a stark reminder of the risks associated with their activism.

Instead of succumbing to fear or retreating, Talin stood tall and addressed the incident, speaking openly about the attack. Their refusal to be silenced by acts of violence inspired countless others to join the movement and reinforced the importance of the cause. Talin's ability to turn their personal pain into a rallying cry exemplified their unwavering commitment to the fight for justice and equality.

Harassment Campaigns

In addition to physical violence, Talin faced persistent harassment through online platforms and other means of communication. Adversaries would flood Talin's social media accounts with hateful messages, threats, and derogatory slurs. They attempted to erode their confidence by attacking their personal appearance, character, and identity.

One particularly distressing example of harassment was the targeted publication of Talin's private information, known as doxing. Their adversaries aimed to intimidate them by exposing their home address, phone number, and other personal details. This aggressive invasion of privacy was an attempt to silence and instill fear in Talin, forcing them to reconsider their involvement in the civil rights movement.

Rising Above the Threats

Despite the threats and intimidation they faced, Talin refused to allow fear to dictate their actions. They swiftly implemented strategies to counteract the opposition's efforts, ensuring their safety and the continued progress of the movement.

Talin worked closely with security experts to develop comprehensive safety protocols. They established a team of volunteers who would accompany them to public appearances and events, serving as additional security and providing a sense of support and protection. By taking proactive measures to enhance their personal security, Talin sent a powerful message that they would not be silenced by intimidation tactics.

Moreover, Talin leveraged their experiences with threats and intimidation to shed light on the broader issue of systemic discrimination. They shared their personal stories and spoke out against the culture of fear perpetuated by their adversaries. Through their brave and honest accounts, Talin gave a voice to countless others who had felt marginalized and victimized due to their alien identity.

The Power of Solidarity

One of the most effective ways in which Talin faced threats and intimidation was through the power of solidarity. They actively sought alliances with other civil rights movements and marginalized communities, recognizing the strength that comes from unity.

By collaborating with diverse groups, Talin cultivated a network of support that transcended boundaries of race, species, and gender. Together, they organized joint protests, shared resources and strategies, and amplified each other's voices. This solidarity not only provided emotional and physical protection but also sent a bold message to their adversaries that the fight for equality was a collective movement and would not be derailed by intimidation.

Unconventional Tactics: Empathy and Education

In response to the threats and intimidation, Talin also employed unconventional tactics designed to foster empathy and education. They initiated open dialogues with those who held opposing views, engaging in constructive conversations that aimed to bridge the gap between different perspectives. Through these interactions, Talin and their allies sought to dismantle misconceptions and foster understanding.

Additionally, Talin championed educational programs that aimed to address deep-rooted biases and prejudices within society. They partnered with educational institutions to introduce curricula promoting inclusion and acceptance, targeting both young minds and adults. By tackling the root causes of discrimination, Talin aimed to create long-lasting change and diminish the environment in which threats and intimidation thrived.

Conclusion: Courage in the Face of Adversity

Throughout their journey as an alien civil rights activist, Talin Iryn exhibited remarkable resilience in the face of threats and intimidation. Despite physical attacks, harassment campaigns, and attempts to silence their voice, Talin remained resolute in their commitment to achieving equality and justice.

Their ability to rise above the challenges and employ innovative strategies serves as an inspiration to generations of activists. Talin's triumph over adversity not only secured rights for alien species on Xyorath but also ignited a broader conversation about discrimination and the importance of intersectional movements.

Talin Iryn's unwavering determination and courage in the face of threats and intimidation will forever be remembered as a testament to the power of resilience and activism. Their story continues to inspire others to challenge deeply ingrained prejudice and fight for equality, reminding us that the path to a just society requires standing firm in the face of adversity.

The Verdict: Historic Decision in Favor of Equality

The long and arduous legal battle finally reached its climax with the highly anticipated verdict. The courtroom was filled with tension and anticipation as the fate of Xyorathian aliens hung in the balance. Talin Iryn, the fearless and determined alien civil rights activist, had assembled a formidable legal team to argue their case. The moment had come to make history and secure a landmark decision in favor of equality.

Assembling a Legal Team

Talin Iryn knew that to win this battle, they needed the best legal minds on their side. They meticulously handpicked a diverse team of brilliant lawyers who were not only experts in alien rights law but also deeply committed to the cause. This legal dream team brought a wealth of experience and passion to the fight for equality.

Research and Preparing the Case

Building a strong legal case required thorough research and preparation. Talin's legal team delved deep into the legal framework and constitutional rights of Xyorathian citizens. They studied previous legal precedents, analyzed relevant legislation, and scrutinized discriminatory practices. Every aspect of the case was meticulously examined to craft a compelling argument for equality.

To bolster their case, the legal team conducted extensive research into other jurisdictions where similar discriminatory marriage restrictions had been overturned successfully. They studied the legal strategies and arguments employed in those cases, adapting them to fit the unique circumstances and cultural nuances of Xyorath.

Courtroom Drama and Challenges

The courtroom became the battleground for justice, with both sides presenting their arguments with fervor and conviction. The defense tried to assert that the multi-tentacle marriage restrictions were necessary to maintain traditional cultural values, even though they were rooted in discrimination and prejudice.

Talin's legal team faced numerous challenges during the trial. The defense employed tactics meant to discredit their clients, attempting to portray them as outsiders seeking to undermine Xyorathian traditions. They attempted to obscure the real issue at hand – the fundamental denial of rights to a specific group of individuals.

Despite these challenges, Talin's legal team skillfully navigated the courtroom drama, remaining steadfast and resolute in their pursuit of justice. They presented compelling evidence, personal testimonies, and expert witnesses who debunked discriminatory myths and heralded the importance of granting equal rights to all Xyorathian citizens.

Public Demonstrations and Protests

Outside the courtroom, alien rights supporters gathered in large numbers to voice their solidarity with Talin Iryn and the fight for equality. Public demonstrations and protests created a groundswell of support that reverberated through Xyorathian society and attracted national attention from influential media outlets.

The protests were organized with meticulous planning, ensuring a peaceful and impactful demonstration of the widespread demand for justice. Alien rights activists, community leaders, and allies from all walks of life came together, waving banners, chanting slogans, and demanding equality for all.

Media Coverage and Public Opinion

The media played a crucial role in shaping public opinion and highlighting the importance of the case. Talin's legal team strategically engaged with journalists, providing them with comprehensive briefings, personal stories, and statistics that illustrated the impact of discriminatory marriage restrictions on the lives of Xyorathian aliens.

The media coverage surrounding the trial was intense, with constant updates on television, newspapers, and social media platforms. Op-ed pieces featured impassioned arguments in favor of equality, and courageous individuals shared their experiences of discrimination, urging society to recognize the need for change.

Public opinion began to shift, as more and more individuals realized the inherent injustice in denying a group of individuals the right to marry based on their alien identity. The groundswell of support grew stronger, creating a tidal wave of pressure on the judiciary to deliver a historic verdict.

The Verdict: A Historic Decision in Favor of Equality

Finally, after an excruciating wait, the verdict was delivered. The courtroom fell into a hushed silence as the judge announced a historic decision in favor of equality. The multi-tentacle marriage restrictions on Xyorath were deemed unconstitutional, and the right to marry was extended to all Xyorathian citizens, regardless of their alien identity.

Tears of joy and relief flowed as Talin Iryn, surrounded by their legal team, realized the magnitude of their accomplishment. Their tireless efforts, unwavering determination, and unyielding commitment to justice had paved the way for a more inclusive and equal Xyorathian society.

Impact on Xyorathian Communities

The impact of this historic decision rippled through Xyorathian communities, transforming lives and reshaping cultural norms. Alien couples who had long been denied the right to affirm their love through marriage were finally able to unite officially, celebrating their relationships and cementing their commitment.

The verdict sparked a wave of hope and optimism among Xyorathian aliens, who had long felt marginalized and second-class citizens in their own society. It shattered the barriers of discrimination and allowed them to embrace their identity with pride, contributing fully to the cultural fabric of Xyorath.

Moreover, the decision sent a powerful message that discrimination in any form would not be tolerated. It served as a catalyst for broader social change, inspiring members of other marginalized communities to challenge unjust laws and fight for their own rights.

Conclusion

The verdict in favor of equality marked a pivotal moment in Xyorathian history. Talin Iryn's unwavering commitment and courageous activism had spearheaded a movement that brought about sweeping legal and social changes. Their case served as a beacon of hope for all those fighting for justice and equality.

However, the journey towards true equality and justice is far from complete. Talin's victory in the fight against multi-tentacle marriage restrictions was just the beginning. Their legacy continues to inspire future generations of alien rights activists to fight for a society that embraces diversity, inclusion, and equal rights for all. The story of Talin Iryn is a reminder that, with determination and resilience, we can overcome even the most entrenched discrimination and build a better future.

Impact on Xyorathian Communities

The impact that Talin Iryn had on the Xyorathian communities cannot be overstated. Through her tireless activism and unwavering determination, she brought about significant changes and improvements in the lives of Xyorathian beings. Her fight for equal rights and her successful campaign to lift the multi-tentacle marriage restrictions had far-reaching effects on both individual Xyorathians and the broader society as a whole.

Before delving into the specific impact, it is crucial to understand the context in which Talin's advocacy took place. Xyorathian society was deeply rooted in traditions and customs, many of which perpetuated discrimination and inequality. The multi-tentacle marriage restrictions, in particular, were a significant barrier to the freedom and happiness of Xyorathian beings who wished to form multi-tentacle partnerships. Talin recognized the inherent injustice in these restrictions and set out to dismantle them.

Talin's work had a profound impact on both the psychological and material well-being of Xyorathian communities. As the multi-tentacle marriage restrictions were lifted, Xyorathians who were previously denied the right to marry their chosen partners experienced a newfound sense of validation and acceptance. They no longer had to hide their love or conform to societal expectations. This allowed for a tremendous increase in happiness, emotional fulfillment, and personal growth within Xyorathian relationships.

Moreover, Talin's activism also had a ripple effect on other facets of Xyorathian life, beyond just marriage. The dismantling of the multi-tentacle marriage restrictions signaled a broader shift in societal attitudes and paved the way for greater acceptance of diversity and inclusivity. Xyorathians who had faced discrimination or prejudice in other areas of their lives, such as employment or education, were inspired by Talin's success and emboldened to demand equality.

The impact was not limited to individual Xyorathians alone; the entire Xyorathian community was positively affected by Talin's efforts. With the lifting of the multi-tentacle marriage restrictions, barriers began to crumble, allowing for greater social cohesion and a more inclusive society. Xyorathian communities became more vibrant and connected as Xyorathians felt freer to express their true selves and form deep, loving connections with their chosen partners.

One of the most remarkable aspects of Talin's impact was the way it influenced Xyorathian youth. Talin's story and her fight for justice served as an inspiration to a new generation of Xyorathians. They saw in her the embodiment of courage, resilience, and the power of a single individual to effect change. Many young Xyorathians, empowered by Talin's example, became vocal advocates for equal rights and began their own initiatives to challenge discrimination in various spheres of Xyorathian society.

Although the impact was overwhelmingly positive, it would be remiss not to acknowledge the challenges and setbacks that Talin and her supporters faced along the way. Resistance from conservative forces and backlash from those resistant to change created obstacles that had to be overcome. Maintaining the momentum and energy needed to sustain the movement required immense dedication and perseverance.

Furthermore, internal divisions and differences of opinion threatened to undermine the movement's unity. Talin's leadership and coalition-building skills were essential in navigating these challenges, but they also served as valuable lessons in the complexities of advocacy work.

In conclusion, Talin Iryn's impact on Xyorathian communities was truly transformative. Her successful campaign to lift the multi-tentacle marriage restrictions brought about a sea change in attitudes, behavior, and the well-being of Xyorathians. Through her advocacy, Xyorathians found hope, acceptance, and the strength to fight for their rights in other areas of life. Talin's legacy continues to inspire future generations of alien activists, reminding them that the fight for justice is never-ending and ever-evolving.

National Recognition and Award Ceremonies

After years of tireless advocacy and groundbreaking legal victories, Talin Iryn's efforts to challenge the multi-tentacle marriage restrictions on Xyorath began to gain national recognition. As a trailblazing civil rights activist, Talin's unwavering dedication and impactful work captured the attention of influential figures, organizations, and the wider public. This section explores the national recognition and award ceremonies that celebrated Talin's achievements in the fight for equality.

The Impact of Talin Iryn

Talin's relentless pursuit of justice had a profound impact on Xyorathian society and beyond. Their groundbreaking legal victories not only struck down discriminatory laws but also challenged deeply entrenched cultural norms and attitudes. Talin's courage and resilience inspired a new generation of alien and civil rights activists to stand up against injustice. Their ability to galvanize support, build coalitions, and effect lasting change made them a symbol of hope for marginalized communities around the world.

Recognition from Prominent Figures

Talin's remarkable accomplishments did not go unnoticed by influential figures in politics, academia, and entertainment. They received invitations to speak at prestigious conferences, universities, and public events, where they shared their experiences, insights, and call to action. Prominent politicians and leaders of alien rights organizations commended Talin's efforts and recognized the importance of their work in advancing equality and justice.

Award Ceremonies and Accolades

Talin's contributions to the alien rights movement were celebrated through various award ceremonies and accolades. These events represented a recognition of their significant achievements and the impact they had made on society. Among the prestigious honors bestowed upon Talin were:

- **Galaxy Freedom Prize:** Awarded annually to individuals who have demonstrated exceptional bravery and leadership in challenging societal injustices.

- **Xyorathian Civil Rights Medal:** The highest honor awarded by the Xyorathian government for outstanding contributions in the field of civil rights.

- **Interstellar Equality Award:** Recognizes individuals who have made substantial contributions to promoting equality and justice across multiple planetary systems.

- **Elysium Peace Prize:** Presented to individuals who have made significant efforts towards peace, justice, and equality in the galaxy.

- **Stellar Humanitarian Award:** Commends individuals who have shown exceptional compassion and dedication to the well-being and rights of all sentient beings.

These award ceremonies served as powerful symbols of recognition and appreciation for Talin's tireless work in challenging the multi-tentacle marriage restrictions and advocating for equal rights.

Celebrating Talin's Legacy

In addition to awards and accolades, Talin's impact was commemorated through a series of national and international events. These celebrations aimed to honor Talin's legacy and the lasting change they had initiated.

- **Talin Iryn Day:** Designated as an annual celebration, this day serves as a reminder of the importance of equality, justice, and the ongoing struggle for civil rights.

- **Xyorathian Civil Rights Exhibition:** A curated exhibition showcasing Talin's life, achievements, and the broader civil rights movement. It provides an educational platform for future generations to learn about the struggles and triumphs of those who fought for equal rights.

- **Talin Iryn Memorial Lecture Series:** Established to perpetuate Talin's activism and ideals, this series invites esteemed speakers to reflect upon current civil rights issues and inspire others to continue the fight for justice.

- **Talin Iryn Foundation:** Founded to advance the cause of alien rights, this foundation supports initiatives aimed at eradicating discrimination, providing scholarships to students from marginalized communities, and advocating for policy reform.

These commemorative events not only celebrated Talin's achievements but also acted as a call to action, ensuring that their fight for equality would continue to inspire future generations.

Lessons Learned and Inspiring Others

Talin's path to recognition and accolades was paved with numerous challenges, setbacks, and moments of self-doubt. The journey to national recognition required unwavering determination, strategic thinking, and the ability to rally public support. Talin's story can serve as a valuable lesson for budding activists and change-makers, providing insights into effective strategies for fighting discrimination, mobilizing communities, and sustaining momentum for long-term change.

Through their advocacy and achievements, Talin not only inspired future generations of activists but also challenged societal perceptions of love, relationships, and the importance of diversity and inclusivity. Their quest for civil rights transcended planetary boundaries, serving as a reminder that the fight for justice is a universal struggle that requires continuous effort and dedication.

Conclusion: A Legacy of Equality and Justice

Talin Iryn's national recognition and award ceremonies marked a pivotal moment in the ongoing fight for equality on Xyorath and beyond. Through their unwavering dedication to dismantling discriminatory laws and challenging cultural norms, Talin became a symbol of resistance and courage. Their impact extended far beyond the realm of civil rights, influencing public opinion, inspiring other activists, and paving the way for a more inclusive and just society.

The legacy of Talin Iryn serves as a reminder that the journey towards equality is fraught with challenges, but justice can be achieved through collective action and unwavering determination. Talin's story continues to inspire future generations to push the boundaries of what is considered possible and to fight for the rights and dignity of all beings.

As we reflect on Talin's remarkable journey, we are reminded that the fight for justice is never-ending and ever-evolving. Talin Iryn's life and achievements represent a beacon of hope and a call to action for all those who strive for a more equitable and inclusive world.

Reforms Beyond Marriage Restrictions

Expanding the Fight for Equal Rights

In the ongoing struggle for alien civil rights on Xyorath, Talin Iryn recognized that achieving marriage equality was just the beginning. Talin understood that true equality required fighting against all forms of discrimination. As the movement gained momentum, Talin and their allies expanded their fight to address other areas where aliens faced unequal treatment. This section explores how Talin and their fellow activists worked tirelessly to advocate for equal rights beyond marriage restrictions.

Addressing Employment Discrimination

One of the key battlegrounds in the fight for equal rights was employment discrimination. Talin and their allies recognized that many aliens faced unfair treatment in the workplace, limiting their opportunities for career growth and economic stability. To combat this, they pushed for legislation that would prohibit discrimination based on alien identity.

Talin's team conducted extensive research and collected stories of alien individuals who had experienced employment discrimination. They used this evidence to raise awareness about the issue and build a compelling case for legal reforms. By partnering with other civil rights organizations and influential figures, they were able to rally public support and pressure lawmakers to take action.

Their efforts resulted in the implementation of comprehensive anti-discrimination laws that protected alien individuals from unfair practices in hiring, promotion, and termination. These reforms not only provided legal recourse for victims of discrimination but also sent a powerful message that all aliens deserved equal opportunities in the workplace.

Securing Access to Healthcare and Education

Recognizing the importance of healthcare and education in achieving full equality, Talin Iryn and their allies fought to address disparities in these areas. They highlighted the barriers faced by alien individuals when accessing quality healthcare and pursued policy changes that would ensure equal access to medical services.

Talin's team collaborated with healthcare professionals, researchers, and policy experts to examine the specific challenges faced by alien communities. They advocated for culturally sensitive healthcare practices and pushed for the inclusion of alien individuals in medical research and clinical trials.

Additionally, Talin focused on education as a means of empowering alien communities and promoting social mobility. They advocated for inclusive educational policies that would provide alien students with equal opportunities for quality education. They worked closely with educators, administrators, and policymakers to foster inclusive school environments and develop anti-discrimination curriculum.

Through their advocacy, Talin and their allies were able to secure changes in healthcare policies, ensuring that alien individuals had access to affordable, quality healthcare. They also played a significant role in transforming the educational landscape, with schools becoming more inclusive and alien students receiving the support they needed to thrive academically.

Challenging Segregation and Housing Policies

Talin and their fellow activists recognized the systemic segregation and discriminatory housing practices that alien communities faced. They fought against policies that perpetuated unequal access to housing and created segregated neighborhoods.

Talin's team collaborated with housing advocates, lawyers, and community leaders to challenge discriminatory housing practices. They filed lawsuits against landlords and housing agencies that practiced discriminatory renting policies based on alien identity. By leveraging media attention and public sentiment, they generated support and pressured policymakers to enact reforms in the housing sector.

Their advocacy and legal battles led to the implementation of laws prohibiting housing discrimination based on alien identity. These laws not only opened up housing opportunities for alien individuals but also helped dismantle the segregated neighborhoods that had long kept alien communities marginalized.

Influencing Policy Change at Local and National Levels

Talin understood the importance of policy change in achieving lasting equality. They recognized that to have a significant impact, the fight for equal rights needed to move beyond grassroots activism and push for legislative reforms at both local and national levels.

Talin and their allies engaged in lobbying efforts, working closely with lawmakers to draft and promote bills that would protect alien rights. They strategized and collaborated with other civil rights movements to build broader coalitions and amplify their voices.

Their work resulted in the passage of crucial legislation that protected alien individuals from discrimination in various areas of life. These laws granted aliens the same rights and protections as their human counterparts, setting a powerful precedent for future advocacy.

Collaborating with Other Civil Rights Movements

Understanding the interconnectedness of various struggles for justice and equality, Talin actively collaborated with other civil rights movements. They recognized the importance of building alliances and working together to achieve common goals.

Talin's team connected with activists from different movements, such as gender equality, racial justice, and LGBTQ+ rights. They shared resources, strategies, and experiences to strengthen their collective efforts. By advocating for intersectionality, they ensured that the fight for alien rights was embedded within a broader framework of social justice.

Through these collaborations, Talin and their allies were able to mobilize larger communities and generate more significant impact. They effectively challenged the systems of oppression that perpetuated discrimination and worked towards a more inclusive society for all.

The Legacy of Legal Victories

Talin Iryn's tireless efforts and dedication to the fight for equal rights left a lasting legacy on Xyorath and the broader alien community. Their legal victories set important precedents and paved the way for future generations of activists to continue the fight for justice.

Today, Talin's name is synonymous with courage and resistance. Their story continues to inspire others to take action and fight for equal rights. Their memoirs and published works serve as invaluable resources for those seeking to understand the struggle for alien rights and the broader movement for social justice.

As the fight for equal rights on Xyorath and beyond continues, Talin's legacy reminds us that progress is possible through collective action, collaboration, and unwavering determination. The fight for justice is never-ending and ever-evolving, with each victory laying the groundwork for the next generation of activists to carry the torch forward.

Addressing Employment Discrimination

Addressing employment discrimination is a crucial aspect of the broader fight for alien civil rights. Talin Iryn recognized the importance of tackling this issue head-on, as she understood that equal access to employment opportunities is integral to achieving true equality and justice for all. In this section, we will explore the various dimensions of employment discrimination, the challenges it presents, and the strategies employed by Talin and her allies to address this pervasive issue.

Understanding Employment Discrimination

Employment discrimination refers to the unfair treatment of individuals or groups based on their alien status or other protected characteristics. It encompasses various forms, including hiring biases, wage disparities, workplace harassment, and wrongful termination. Such discrimination not only undermines individuals' economic security but also perpetuates systemic inequality in society.

To effectively address employment discrimination, it is crucial to understand the legal frameworks and protections in place. Xyorathian legislation, influenced by Talin's activism, prohibits discrimination in the workplace based on alien status, gender, race, sexual orientation, and other protected characteristics. These laws empower individuals to seek justice and hold employers accountable for discriminatory practices. Talin's advocacy played a pivotal role in the enactment and strengthening of these laws.

Challenges and Consequences

Despite legal protections, employment discrimination remains prevalent in many industries and workplaces. Talin recognized the challenges that alien workers face, including:

1. Lack of awareness: Many alien workers may not be fully aware of their rights and how to address discriminatory practices.

2. Subtle biases: Discrimination can be subtle and difficult to prove, making it challenging for victims to seek redress.

3. Language and cultural barriers: Alien workers may face additional barriers due to language and cultural differences, leading to exclusion and limited job opportunities.

4. Stereotypes and prejudices: Deeply ingrained stereotypes and prejudices can influence hiring decisions and limit career advancement for alien workers.

The consequences of employment discrimination are profound. Alien workers often experience lower wages, limited job prospects, and reduced access to benefits and promotions. This not only affects individual livelihoods but also perpetuates cycles of poverty and marginalization within alien communities.

Strategies to Combat Employment Discrimination

Talin Iryn and her allies employed various strategies to combat employment discrimination and promote equal opportunities in the workplace. They recognized that it required a multi-pronged approach, encompassing advocacy, education, and policy changes. Here are some key strategies employed:

1. Awareness campaigns: Talin and her allies conducted awareness campaigns to inform alien workers about their rights and recourse options. These campaigns utilized traditional and social media platforms, community workshops, and outreach programs to reach a wide audience.

2. Legal support and representation: Recognizing the complexities of legal processes, Talin's movement established legal support services to assist alien workers in navigating discrimination claims. These services provided pro bono legal representation and ensured access to justice for those who faced barriers due to financial constraints.

3. Workplace training and diversity programs: Talin and her allies actively engaged with employers and advocated for workplace training programs to address unconscious biases, promote diversity, and ensure fair hiring practices. By providing resources and guidance, they encouraged employers to create inclusive work environments that valued diversity.

4. Data collection and reporting mechanisms: To tackle employment discrimination effectively, Talin's movement emphasized the importance of data collection. They worked in collaboration with government agencies and research institutions to gather data on workplace discrimination, which served as evidence for policy reforms and targeted interventions.

5. Collaboration with other movements: Recognizing the interconnectedness of various social justice movements, Talin's movement forged alliances with other civil rights organizations and labor unions. By leveraging collective power, they advocated for comprehensive anti-discrimination legislation and labor protections that benefited not only alien workers but all marginalized communities.

Real-World Examples

To illustrate the impact of Talin's strategies, let's explore two real-world examples:

1. **The Equal Opportunity Campaign**: Talin's movement launched a campaign to combat employment discrimination in the technology sector. They partnered with major tech companies, urging them to prioritize diversity and address biases in their hiring practices. As a result, several companies implemented initiatives such as blind resume reviews, diversity scholarships, and mentoring programs, leading to increased representation of alien workers in the industry.

2. **Challenging Wage Disparities**: Talin's movement conducted extensive research on wage disparities between alien and non-alien workers in the healthcare sector. Using this data, they successfully lobbied for stricter enforcement of pay equity laws. As a result, many hospitals and healthcare organizations revised their compensation policies, ensuring fair and equal pay for alien workers.

Unconventional but Relevant Approach

Talin's movement also employed an unconventional approach to combat employment discrimination - storytelling. They recognized the power of personal narratives in challenging stereotypes and humanizing the experiences of alien workers. Through storytelling events and media campaigns, they amplified the voices of those who had faced discrimination, shedding light on the realities of employment inequalities. This approach fostered empathy and encouraged collective action, leading to increased public support for policy changes and furthering the cause of alien civil rights.

Conclusion

Addressing employment discrimination is an integral part of the broader struggle for alien civil rights. Talin Iryn's activism highlighted the importance of equal access to job opportunities, fair treatment, and workplace inclusivity. By employing a range of strategies, including awareness campaigns, legal support, workplace training, data collection, and collaboration with other movements, Talin and her allies made significant strides in combating employment discrimination. Their efforts continue to inspire and guide future generations of alien rights activists, paving the way for a more just and equal society.

Securing Access to Healthcare and Education

In the fight for equal rights, securing access to healthcare and education for the Xyorathian alien community became a critical goal for Talin Iryn. Discrimination in these fundamental areas had long-lasting consequences that affected individuals and families alike. This section delves into the challenges faced by Xyorathians in accessing healthcare and education, the strategies employed by Talin Iryn, and the ultimate impact of their advocacy efforts.

The Healthcare Crisis

Xyorathian aliens faced numerous barriers when it came to accessing healthcare. Many healthcare providers were prejudiced and refused treatment, while others charged exorbitant fees, making essential medical services unaffordable. Moreover, Xyorathians struggled to find healthcare professionals who understood their unique cultural and physiological needs. The lack of representation and sensitivity in the healthcare system led to severe health disparities within the community.

The Education Divide

Similarly, Xyorathian children encountered discrimination in the education system. They were often placed in subpar schools with inadequate resources and faced bullying and exclusion from their peers. The lack of cultural competence among educators further exacerbated these challenges, leaving Xyorathian children feeling marginalized and academically disadvantaged.

Advocating for Change

Recognizing the urgency of these issues, Talin Iryn spearheaded efforts to secure access to healthcare and education for Xyorathians. They formed coalitions with healthcare professionals, educators, and advocacy organizations to address the systemic barriers faced by the community. Talin's approach involved both grassroots organizing and strategic lobbying to effect meaningful change.

Fighting Discrimination

Talin Iryn and their allies worked tirelessly to combat discrimination in healthcare settings. They organized town hall meetings and community forums to educate Xyorathians about their rights and empower them to demand fair treatment. Additionally, Talin collaborated with doctors and healthcare providers who were willing to undergo cultural competence training, ensuring that Xyorathian patients received the care they deserved.

Building Inclusive Healthcare Systems

To create long-lasting change, Talin Iryn advocated for the development of inclusive healthcare systems. They pushed for the establishment of healthcare centers specifically tailored to the needs of Xyorathian aliens, staffed by culturally competent healthcare professionals. This included providing interpretation services, accommodating dietary requirements, and considering the unique physiological aspects of the Xyorathian biology.

Addressing Affordability

Talin recognized that access to healthcare meant little if it remained unaffordable for many Xyorathians. They rallied for comprehensive healthcare reforms, including the implementation of universal healthcare coverage and the regulation of medical costs. By working with lawmakers and policy influencers, Talin sought to ensure that no Xyorathian was denied care due to financial constraints.

Transforming the Education System

In the realm of education, Talin Iryn fought for comprehensive reforms to dismantle systemic barriers. They advocated for the integration of Xyorathian history and culture into the curriculum, fostering greater understanding and appreciation among students and educators. Talin also pushed for the recruitment and retention of Xyorathian teachers, ensuring that students had role models who understood their experiences and aspirations.

Creating Safe and Inclusive Learning Spaces

Talin Iryn spearheaded initiatives aimed at creating safe and inclusive learning spaces for Xyorathian children. This involved implementing anti-bullying policies, providing cultural sensitivity training for educators, and establishing support networks for Xyorathian students facing discrimination. Talin also worked to secure funding for extracurricular activities and resources, ensuring that Xyorathian children had equal opportunities to thrive academically and socially.

Promoting Higher Education Access

Building on their efforts within the K-12 education system, Talin Iryn championed initiatives to increase access to higher education for Xyorathian students. They worked with universities and scholarship organizations to establish affirmative action policies that encouraged Xyorathian enrollment. Talin also advocated for mentorship programs and career development initiatives, providing Xyorathian students with the guidance and support needed to succeed in their academic pursuits.

Embracing Intersectionality

Throughout their advocacy for healthcare and education access, Talin Iryn emphasized the importance of intersectionality. They recognized that discrimination often intersected with other forms of oppression, such as racism and sexism. By forging alliances with other civil rights movements and organizations, Talin sought to address these overlapping issues and work towards equity and justice for all marginalized communities.

Continued Challenges and Future Outlook

Despite the significant progress made in securing access to healthcare and education for Xyorathians, challenges persist. The fight against discrimination demands ongoing vigilance and continuous efforts to dismantle systemic barriers. Talin Iryn's legacy serves as a beacon of hope, inspiring future generations of activists to continue the work towards building a society where all individuals have equal access to healthcare and education. By embracing diversity and confronting discrimination head-on, we can create a world that celebrates and values the contributions of every individual, regardless of their alien or human origin.

Challenging Segregation and Housing Policies

Segregation and discriminatory housing policies have long been a pervasive issue in Xyorathian society. These policies have resulted in the systematic exclusion and marginalization of alien communities from certain neighborhoods, leading to disparities in access to quality housing, resources, and opportunities.

3.2.4.1 The History of Segregation

To understand the challenges faced in challenging segregation and housing policies, it is essential to examine the historical context in which these policies arose. From the early days of colonization, Xyorathian society was characterized by a hierarchical structure that favored certain alien communities while systematically oppressing others. This structure laid the foundation for discriminatory housing policies that would persist for generations.

3.2.4.2 The Impact of Segregation and Discriminatory Housing Policies

Segregation and discriminatory housing policies have had a profound impact on alien communities, perpetuating social and economic disparities. Alien communities have been confined to specific neighborhoods with limited access to quality housing, education, healthcare, and employment opportunities. This has resulted in cycles of poverty, limited upward mobility, and a persistent achievement gap.

3.2.4.3 Legal Frameworks and Protections

Challenging segregation and discriminatory housing policies requires a comprehensive understanding of the legal frameworks and protections in place. The Xyorathian Constitution guarantees equal protection under the law and prohibits discrimination based on alien status. Additionally, international conventions and treaties provide a foundation for advocating for the rights of marginalized communities.

3.2.4.4 Advocacy Strategies and Grassroots Mobilization

Challenging segregation and housing policies requires a multi-faceted approach that combines advocacy strategies with grassroots mobilization. Activists and organizations have played a vital role in raising awareness about the impacts of segregation and discriminatory housing policies. This includes engaging in community organizing, conducting research, and partnering with legal experts to challenge these policies in court.

3.2.4.5 Litigation and Legal Challenges

Litigation has been a crucial tool in challenging segregation and discriminatory housing policies. Legal challenges have sought to expose the constitutionality of these policies and demand equal access to housing for all alien communities. Court decisions in favor of equal housing rights have set important precedents, paving the way for further policy changes.

3.2.4.6 Policy Reform and Advocacy

Policy reforms are crucial in dismantling segregation and discriminatory housing policies. Advocacy efforts have focused on influencing local, regional, and national policymakers to develop and implement fair housing policies. This includes advocating for the elimination of discriminatory zoning practices, the expansion of affordable housing options, and the enforcement of equal access to housing opportunities.

3.2.4.7 Partnerships and Collaborations

Building partnerships and collaborations with other social justice movements and organizations has been instrumental in challenging segregation and housing policies. By broadening support and forging alliances, activists can amplify their voices and influence policy change on a larger scale. This includes working in collaboration with civil rights organizations, human rights advocates, and housing rights activists.

3.2.4.8 Community Education and Empowerment

Community education and empowerment play a vital role in challenging segregation and housing policies. By equipping alien communities with knowledge about their rights and providing resources for advocacy, individuals are empowered to actively participate in the fight against discriminatory housing practices. This includes hosting workshops, awareness campaigns, and facilitating community-led initiatives to address housing disparities.

3.2.4.9 Sustainable Solutions and Long-Term Impact

Creating sustainable solutions and ensuring long-term impact requires addressing the root causes of segregation and discriminatory housing policies. This includes tackling systemic racism, promoting inclusive urban planning, and advocating for equitable distribution of resources. By prioritizing sustainable solutions, alien communities can experience lasting change and break the cycle of housing inequality.

Through a combination of legal challenges, grassroots mobilization, policy advocacy, education, and community empowerment, the fight against segregation and discriminatory housing policies continues. It is through the collective efforts of passionate activists and advocates that real progress can be made in achieving fair and inclusive housing for all alien communities. Together, we can create a society that values diversity, inclusivity, and equal access to housing opportunities.

Influencing Policy Change at Local and National Levels

In order to make significant progress in the fight for alien rights on Xyorath, Talin Iryn recognized the need to influence policy change at both the local and national levels. By working within legislative institutions and mobilizing public support, Talin was able to create long-lasting reforms that improved the lives of not only Xyorathian aliens but also other marginalized communities. This section explores the strategies and tactics employed by Talin in order to effect policy change.

Understanding the Political Landscape

Before embarking on any meaningful policy change efforts, Talin took the time to thoroughly understand the political landscape of Xyorath. This involved studying the structure of the government, gaining insight into the decision-making processes, and identifying key power players and potential allies. Talin knew that in order to achieve lasting change, it was crucial to navigate the complexities of the political system.

Building Relationships and Alliances

One of the key strategies Talin employed was building relationships and alliances with like-minded individuals and organizations. By collaborating with other civil rights movements, Talin was able to amplify their message and build a stronger coalition. This approach helped to broaden the base of support for alien rights and gain traction within the political sphere.

Lobbying and Advocacy Efforts

Drawing inspiration from successful advocacy campaigns around the world, Talin adopted a strategic lobbying and advocacy approach. This involved engaging with lawmakers and policymakers directly, presenting evidence-based arguments, and articulating the need for policy change. Talin and their team tirelessly advocated for equality and justice, making sure that the voices of Xyorathian aliens were heard by those in power.

Public Awareness and Media Campaigns

Talin recognized the importance of public opinion and the role of media in shaping it. To influence policy change, they deployed comprehensive public awareness and media campaigns. This involved leveraging various media platforms to tell compelling stories, highlight the struggles faced by Xyorathian aliens, and mobilize public support for policy reform. By framing the issue in relatable terms and challenging preconceived notions, Talin was able to shift public opinion in favor of equal rights.

Engaging in Grassroots Activism

While lobbying and media campaigns were instrumental in driving policy change, Talin understood the significance of engaging in grassroots activism as well. This involved organizing rallies, protests, and demonstrations to create visibility and apply pressure on lawmakers. Grassroots activism served as a powerful tool to make sure that the voices of the marginalized were heard and that the movement remained inclusive and connected to the community.

Collaborating with Legal Experts

To effectively influence policy change, Talin collaborated with legal experts who specialized in constitutional law and human rights. This partnership allowed for a comprehensive understanding of the legal framework and avenues for reform. By working together, they were able to craft robust legal arguments and mount challenges against discriminatory laws and policies.

Challenges and Strategies for Sustained Advocacy

In the pursuit of policy change, Talin faced numerous challenges and setbacks. Conservative forces, resistance from policymakers, and internal divisions within the movement tested their resolve. However, Talin remained resilient and adapted their strategies to sustain the momentum for change. They focused on long-term vision, strategic planning, and fostering unity within the movement to drive sustained advocacy efforts.

Cultivating International Alliances

Recognizing that the fight for alien rights extended beyond Xyorath, Talin actively cultivated international alliances. By connecting with alien rights activists and organizations in other galaxies, Talin was able to strengthen the movement and gather support on a global scale. This cross-cultural exchange of knowledge and resources enriched the fight for equality and helped to challenge the narrative of discrimination both within and beyond Xyorath.

Paving the Way for Future Advocacy

Talin understood that their fight for policy change was only the beginning. They dedicated considerable effort to paving the way for future advocacy in the hopes of creating a sustainable movement. This involved documenting their strategies and tactics, publishing memoirs, and creating resources for future generations of alien rights activists. By sharing their experiences and lessons learned, Talin ensured that the fight for equality and justice would continue long after their own activism.

Overall, Talin's approach to influencing policy change at local and national levels was rooted in strategic planning, collective action, and tireless advocacy. Through a multi-faceted approach that combined legal expertise, grassroots activism, public awareness campaigns, and collaborations with like-minded individuals and organizations, Talin was able to bring about meaningful reforms that advanced the cause of alien rights on Xyorath and beyond. Their legacy serves as a powerful reminder that change is possible when individuals come together to challenge discrimination and fight for social justice.

Collaborating with Other Civil Rights Movements

Throughout Talin Iryn's activist journey, one crucial aspect of their work was collaborating with other civil rights movements. Talin firmly believed in solidarity and recognized the interconnectedness of various struggles for equality and justice. By joining forces with other movements, Talin sought to amplify the voices of marginalized communities, challenge systemic oppression, and create a more inclusive society for all.

Understanding Intersectionality

To effectively collaborate with other civil rights movements, Talin understood the importance of intersectionality. Intersectionality recognizes that individuals experience multiple layers of discrimination based on their intersecting identities, such as race, gender, sexuality, and social class. Talin recognized that the fight for alien rights could not be separated from the struggles of other marginalized groups.

Building Coalitions

Talin actively sought to build coalitions with a diverse range of civil rights movements. They recognized that by working together, these movements could leverage collective power and advocate for more comprehensive social change. Whether it was collaborating with gender equality activists, racial justice organizations, or LGBTQ+ rights advocates, Talin aimed to foster alliances that could challenge oppressive systems from multiple angles.

To build strong coalitions, Talin employed various strategies. They attended conferences and forums where representatives from different movements gathered, fostering dialogue and understanding. Talin also organized joint events, such as panel discussions and rallies, to bring together advocates from different backgrounds. These collaborative efforts not only strengthened the alliances but also increased public awareness and support for intersectional struggles.

Sharing Resources and Strategies

Collaboration among civil rights movements also involved sharing resources and strategies. Talin understood the value of cross-pollination of ideas and approaches. By exchanging experiences and knowledge, movements could learn from each other's successes and challenges.

Talin organized workshops and training sessions where activists from different movements could share their expertise. For example, gender equality activists could share strategies for promoting inclusive language and challenging stereotypes with alien rights activists. Likewise, racial justice organizations could provide insights into community organizing and grassroots mobilization.

By fostering this collaborative learning environment, Talin ensured that the movements could benefit mutually from each other's experiences, ultimately strengthening their collective impact.

Addressing Intersections of Discrimination

Collaboration with other civil rights movements allowed Talin to address the intersections of discrimination faced by alien communities. Talin recognized that discrimination against aliens did not occur in isolation but intersected with other forms of oppression.

For instance, Talin worked closely with racial justice organizations to address the discrimination faced by aliens of color. They recognized that algorithms used in surveillance systems disproportionately targeted certain racial groups and compounded the injustices faced by alien communities. By joining forces, they aimed to challenge these discriminatory practices and demand algorithmic transparency and accountability.

Similarly, Talin collaborated with LGBTQ+ rights advocates to address the discrimination faced by queer aliens. Together, they fought for the recognition of same-sex multi-tentacle marriages, as well as inclusive policies that would protect the rights of queer aliens in various spheres of life.

By addressing these intersections of discrimination, Talin and their coalition partners broadened the scope of their advocacy and ensured a more comprehensive approach to social justice.

Challenges and Lessons

Collaborating with other civil rights movements was not without its challenges. One significant challenge was navigating potential differences and conflicts within coalitions. Each movement brought its own unique perspectives, priorities, and organizational dynamics. To address these challenges, Talin emphasized open and respectful communication, active listening, and a commitment to shared goals.

Another challenge was maintaining momentum and energy within collaborative efforts. Activists often faced burnout due to the demanding nature of their work. Talin encouraged self-care practices and promoted a supportive environment that prioritized the well-being of all coalition members.

Through their experiences in collaborating with other civil rights movements, Talin learned valuable lessons. They discovered the power of unity and how collective action could yield greater results than individual efforts alone. They also understood the importance of fostering an inclusive and intersectional movement that recognized and addressed the unique challenges faced by different marginalized communities.

Overall, Talin's collaboration with other civil rights movements exemplified their commitment to building a more just and equitable society through solidarity and collective action. They understood that by recognizing the interconnectedness of struggles and working together, lasting social change could be achieved.

The Legacy of Legal Victories

The legal victories achieved by Talin Iryn in the fight against multi-tentacle marriage restrictions on Xyorath have had a profound and lasting impact on both the alien community and the broader society. These victories have not only challenged discriminatory laws but have also paved the way for greater acceptance and equality for all.

One of the key legacies of these legal victories is the establishment of a precedent for alien rights. The successful challenges to the multi-tentacle marriage restrictions set a powerful example for future legal advocacy efforts in other areas of alien rights. With each victory, the notion of equal rights for all species gained traction and became an integral part of the legal framework.

Furthermore, these legal victories have had a ripple effect on other marginalized communities, demonstrating that change is possible and inspiring movements across the universe. The success in challenging the discriminatory laws has fueled intersectional activism, bringing together alien communities with other civil rights movements. Through these coalitions, broader issues of discrimination, such as employment discrimination, access to healthcare and education, and housing segregation, have been addressed.

The legacy of these legal victories also includes a reimagining of love and relationships. By challenging the multi-tentacle marriage restrictions, Talin Iryn and their supporters highlighted the importance of equal recognition and protection for all forms of loving partnerships. This has led to a transformation in societal attitudes towards diverse relationships, encouraging acceptance and inclusion.

In terms of policy changes, the legal victories have contributed to significant reforms at both the local and national levels. The removal of the multi-tentacle marriage restrictions was not just a symbolic act; it brought about tangible changes in the lives of alien couples. Legal recognition of their relationships provided access to vital benefits, such as inheritance rights, healthcare coverage, and the ability to make important decisions as a couple.

The legacy of these legal victories also extends beyond Xyorath, inspiring alien communities on other planets to demand equality and justice. Talin Iryn's story has become a symbol of resistance and courage, propelling alien rights movements across the universe. Their achievements have shown that change is possible, even in the face of immense challenges and opposition.

To ensure the lasting effects of these legal victories, Talin Iryn and their supporters have worked tirelessly to establish foundations for alien rights. These organizations focus on education and awareness programs to create a more inclusive society. They provide resources and support to individuals facing discrimination, as well as lobbying for policy changes that protect and empower alien communities.

Memoirs and publications documenting the journey of Talin Iryn and the fight against multi-tentacle marriage restrictions have been published, ensuring that their story continues to resonate with future generations. Documentaries and films have also been made, bringing their struggles and triumphs to a wider audience and inspiring others to join the fight for justice.

The legal victories achieved by Talin Iryn have transformed Xyorathian society and beyond. By challenging discriminatory laws and advocating for equal rights, they have helped overcome prejudice and shift cultural norms. Increased visibility and acceptance of alien communities have resulted in a more inclusive society where diversity is celebrated.

The fight for justice, equality, and social change is never-ending and ever-evolving. Talin Iryn's legacy serves as a reminder that progress can be made through perseverance and collective action. As future generations continue the work, they will draw inspiration from Talin's courage and determination, ensuring a future where all species are treated with dignity and respect.

Chapter 3: Breaking Barriers

Inspiring Other Alien Communities to Demand Equality

Talin Iryn's fight to defy the multi-tentacle marriage restrictions on Xyorath not only led to victories for their own community but also inspired alien communities on other planets to demand equality. Through their unwavering dedication and unyielding spirit, Talin became a beacon of hope and a symbol of resistance for oppressed aliens across the universe.

3.2.8.1 The Power of Representation and Visibility

Representation is a powerful tool in inspiring marginalized communities to assert their rights. Talin's visibility as a prominent advocate for alien rights not only gave a voice to the Xyorathian community but also provided a model for other alien communities to follow. Seeing someone who looked like them, who understood their struggles, and who was fighting for justice, encouraged others to take action and demand equality.

Talin recognized the importance of representation and actively worked to amplify the voices of other alien activists. They showcased the diversity and strength of various alien communities by inviting their leaders to speak at rallies, conferences, and panel discussions. By sharing their stories, these leaders inspired others to stand up and fight for their rights, creating a network of passionate activists across different planets.

3.2.8.2 Building Alliances and Solidarity

Inspiring other alien communities to demand equality required building alliances and fostering solidarity. Talin understood the power of collective action and actively worked to create links between different alien rights movements.

They organized conferences and gatherings where activists from different planets could come together, share their experiences, and strategize for collective advancement. Through these interactions, ideas and resources were exchanged, collaborations were formed, and new strategies for advocacy were developed.

Talin also emphasized the need for intersectionality within the alien rights movement. They recognized that discrimination and inequality were often interconnected, affecting individuals on multiple levels. By forging partnerships with other civil rights movements advocating for gender equality, racial justice, and LGBTQ+ rights, Talin created a broader coalition that fought for justice across various intersecting dimensions.

3.2.8.3 Educational Initiatives and Resource Sharing

Inspiring other alien communities involved not only raising awareness but also equipping them with the knowledge and tools to advocate for their rights effectively. Talin spearheaded educational initiatives and resource-sharing programs to empower alien activists.

They collaborated with educators and scholars to develop comprehensive educational materials on alien rights, including the legal background, strategies for advocacy, and the importance of unity. These materials were made accessible to individuals and organizations across the galaxy, allowing them to learn from Talin's experiences and adapt their tactics to their own planetary contexts.

Additionally, Talin established an online platform where alien communities could connect, share resources, and seek guidance. This platform facilitated knowledge exchange, provided a space for collaboration, and allowed alien rights activists to support and uplift each other in their common struggle.

3.2.8.4 Promoting Peaceful Protests and Demonstrations

Inspiration often arises from witnessing the power of peaceful protests and demonstrations. Talin actively encouraged alien communities to organize peaceful gatherings to raise awareness about their struggles, demand equality, and challenge discriminatory policies.

They provided guidance on organizing protests, offering tips on logistics, crowd management, and ensuring the safety of participants. Through their example, Talin demonstrated that nonviolent resistance could be a potent force for change, garnering attention and support from both within and outside the alien rights movement.

3.2.8.5 Pioneering Legal Frameworks and Precedents

Talin's legal victories served as precedent-setting cases that inspired other alien communities to pursue legal avenues for change. By challenging discriminatory laws and policies and succeeding in dismantling them, Talin laid the groundwork for future legal advocacy.

They worked closely with legal experts to document their legal strategies, share their experiences, and provide legal support to other alien activists. Talin's legal team conducted workshops and training sessions to educate alien communities on their legal rights, equipping them with the knowledge to navigate the complex legal systems on their respective planets.

By empowering other alien communities with legal knowledge and demonstrating the achievable outcomes, Talin encouraged the pursuit of justice through the legal system.

3.2.8.6 Success Stories and Testimonials

To inspire other alien communities, Talin actively shared success stories and testimonials from Xyorath and beyond. They highlighted the transformative impact that collective action and advocacy can have, showcasing the positive changes brought about by the fight for equality.

Talin documented these stories in books, articles, and documentaries, making them widely accessible to alien communities across the universe. Through these narratives, others could see the tangible results of activism, the joy of overcoming oppression, and the power of perseverance.

3.2.8.7 Redefining Relationships and Unity

Inspiring other alien communities to demand equality also involved redefining relationships and fostering unity. Talin promoted the idea that supporting one another's struggles was crucial in the fight for justice.

They encouraged communities to challenge divisive narratives and build bridges between different alien groups. By uniting under a shared vision of equality, alien communities could amplify their collective voices, demand change with greater strength, and form alliances that transcended planetary borders.

3.2.8.8 Unconventional Approach: Art and Creativity

Inspiration can often come from unexpected sources. Talin recognized the power of art and creativity as a means to engage and mobilize alien communities.

They encouraged artists, musicians, poets, and writers to express their experiences and aspirations through their creative works. These artistic expressions became powerful tools for storytelling and advocacy, fostering empathy and understanding among diverse audiences.

Public art installations, street performances, and cultural festivals organized by Talin and other alien activists celebrated the richness and vibrancy of alien cultures while raising awareness about the struggles they faced. This unconventional approach captured the attention of broader society, inspiring conversations about equality and justice.

In conclusion, Talin Iryn's fight against the multi-tentacle marriage restrictions not only brought about change on Xyorath but also inspired alien communities across the universe to demand equality. Through representation, building alliances, educational initiatives, peaceful protests, legal frameworks, success stories, redefining relationships, and creative approaches, Talin's legacy lives on as an inspiration for future generations of alien rights activists. The fight for justice is never-ending and ever-evolving, and Talin's impact continues to shape a more equitable and inclusive universe.

Paving the Way for Future Legal Advocacy

In her relentless pursuit of justice and equality, Talin Iryn not only achieved groundbreaking victories, but she also paved the way for future legal advocacy. Her courage and determination continue to inspire alien communities across Xyorath and beyond to stand up against discrimination and fight for their rights. This section explores the strategies and initiatives that Talin put in place to ensure the legacy of her work and empower future alien activists.

Establishing a Legal Defense Fund

Recognizing the financial barriers faced by many alien activists, Talin established the Xyorath Alien Legal Defense Fund. This fund provides financial assistance to alien individuals and families who are facing discrimination and need legal representation. By making legal resources accessible and affordable, Talin ensured that marginalized communities have adequate support when challenging systemic injustices.

Expanding Legal Education Programs

Talin understood the importance of education as a tool for empowerment. She spearheaded the expansion of legal education programs specifically tailored to the needs of alien communities. These programs aimed to inform and empower individuals about their legal rights and how they can navigate the judicial system to challenge discriminatory policies. Workshops, seminars, and online resources were created to provide practical guidance and empower alien individuals to advocate for themselves.

Advocating for Alien Rights in Education

Talin recognized that true systemic change begins with education. She led efforts to implement alien rights education in schools and universities across Xyorath. By incorporating alien history, culture, and struggles into the curriculum, Talin ensured that future generations would grow up with a deep understanding of the need for equality and justice. Through partnerships with educators and policymakers, she encouraged the development of inclusive and diverse learning environments that would foster empathy and respect for all beings.

Encouraging Alliances with Human Rights Organizations

In her pursuit of comprehensive change, Talin actively sought alliances with human rights organizations. Recognizing the interconnectedness of social justice causes, she collaborated with activists advocating for gender equality, racial justice, and LGBTQ+ rights. By forging these alliances, Talin ensured that the movement for alien rights would have a broader impact and a stronger collective voice. Through joint campaigns, protests, and lobbying efforts, she amplified the message of inclusivity, solidarity, and the fight against all forms of discrimination.

Pushing for Legislative Reform

Talin understood the significance of long-lasting legal change. She worked tirelessly to advocate for legislative reforms that would dismantle discriminatory policies and systems. Talin lobbied for the amendment of existing laws and the creation of new legislation that protected the rights of alien individuals and families. Her strategic approach involved engaging lawmakers, organizing letter-writing campaigns, and mobilizing public support to exert pressure and drive change at the legislative level.

Educating Legal Professionals on Alien Rights

To ensure the sustainability of legal advocacy, Talin recognized the importance of educating legal professionals about alien rights. She partnered with law schools and bar associations to develop training programs dedicated to equipping lawyers with the knowledge and skills necessary to effectively represent alien clients. These training sessions covered topics such as alien history, cultural sensitivity, and specific legal issues faced by alien communities. By fostering a cadre of competent and empathetic legal professionals, Talin sought to guarantee continued legal support for alien individuals and families.

Promoting Grassroots Activism

Talin firmly believed in the power of grassroots activism to effect change. She encouraged the establishment of local alien rights organizations and provided mentorship to emerging activists. Through grassroots networks, individuals at the community level were empowered to tackle discrimination and press for legal reforms. Talin organized training workshops, community forums, and awareness campaigns to mobilize and energize these grassroots movements. She saw the importance of a bottom-up approach, where change starts from within communities and gains momentum through collective action.

Addressing Intersections of Discrimination

Ever aware of the interconnected nature of discrimination, Talin advocated for an inclusive and intersectional approach to legal advocacy. She emphasized the need to address the overlapping forms of prejudice and discrimination faced by alien individuals who also belonged to other marginalized communities. By working collaboratively with activists fighting for other social justice causes, Talin aimed to create a more comprehensive and powerful movement that could effectively challenge the complex interplay of discrimination across multiple identities.

Embracing Technology for Legal Advocacy

Talin recognized the transformative potential of technology in legal advocacy. She championed the development of online platforms and tools that would facilitate access to legal resources and information for alien communities. These platforms allowed individuals facing discrimination to seek advice, connect with legal professionals, and share their stories. Talin also leveraged social media and digital campaigns to raise awareness, mobilize support, and disseminate information about ongoing legal battles. By harnessing the power of technology, she made legal advocacy more accessible, efficient, and influential.

Encouraging Future Leadership

Talin's greatest desire was to inspire future generations of alien activists and leaders. She dedicated significant resources and efforts to mentorship programs and leadership development initiatives. By identifying emerging leaders and providing guidance and support, Talin ensured that her work would not only continue but also evolve and flourish. She encouraged young activists to think creatively, challenge the status quo, and adapt their strategies to the changing landscape of discrimination in order to shape a future where all beings are treated with dignity and respect.

In paving the way for future legal advocacy, Talin Iryn laid the groundwork for a more equal and inclusive Xyorathian society. Her remarkable achievements and tireless commitment to justice have left an indelible mark on the alien rights movement and beyond. As the fight for equality and social justice continues, her legacy serves as a guiding light, inspiring alien communities to stand up, speak out, and demand their rightful place in the galactic tapestry of rights and freedoms.

Chapter 3: The Aftermath

Implementing Change

Overcoming Resistance and Pushback

In the face of progress, there will always be opposition. Talin Iryn, a fearless alien civil rights activist, encountered various forms of resistance and pushback throughout her journey to dismantle the multi-tentacle marriage restrictions on the planet of Xyorath. This section explores the challenges she faced and the strategies she employed to overcome them.

Understanding the Opposition

To effectively overcome resistance and pushback, it is crucial to understand the root causes and motivations behind it. Talin recognized that resistance often stems from fear, ignorance, and deeply ingrained prejudices. Many individuals viewed the multi-tentacle marriage restrictions as a threat to tradition, culture, and societal norms. They clung to outdated beliefs that limited personal freedom and denied equality.

To address this resistance, Talin and her allies engaged in open dialogue and education campaigns. They conducted workshops, held community forums, and utilized social media platforms to dispel misinformation and challenge discriminatory beliefs. By fostering understanding and empathy, they aimed to change hearts and minds.

Coalition Building

Talin understood the power of collective action and the strength in numbers. She focused on building diverse coalitions, bringing together people from different backgrounds, beliefs, and communities. By forging alliances with other civil rights movements, she created a united front against oppression and discrimination.

In the face of resistance, Talin actively reached out to leaders and organizations who shared her passion for justice. She fostered collaboration and cooperation, leveraging the strengths and expertise of each group to amplify their collective voice. Together, they organized rallies, protests, and initiatives that garnered widespread attention and put pressure on policymakers.

Strategic Communication

A crucial aspect of overcoming resistance is strategic communication. Talin recognized the importance of shaping public opinion and garnering support for the cause. She and her allies focused on creating compelling narratives that resonated with people's emotions and aspirations.

Through media interviews, press releases, and op-eds, Talin and her team highlighted personal stories of individuals impacted by the multi-tentacle marriage restrictions. They emphasized the fundamental principles of equality, freedom, and love that the restrictions infringed upon. By humanizing the issue and showcasing its real-world consequences, they effectively rallied public support and gained allies from all walks of life.

Navigating Legal Challenges

Resistance often manifests in the form of legal challenges. Talin and her legal team encountered numerous obstacles in their fight for marriage equality. They had to navigate discriminatory laws, biased judges, and an unsympathetic legal system.

To overcome these challenges, Talin's legal team employed strategic litigation tactics. They carefully selected test cases that would have the most significant impact and laid the groundwork for legal precedents. They skillfully presented evidence, employed persuasive arguments, and exploited any loopholes or inconsistencies in the existing legal framework.

Additionally, Talin and her team recognized the importance of public support in influencing legal outcomes. They organized public demonstrations outside courtrooms, encouraging supporters to peacefully voice their demand for justice. This public pressure put additional scrutiny on the legal proceedings and reminded the judges of the weight of their decisions.

Maintaining Resilience

Overcoming resistance and pushback requires resilience in the face of adversity. Talin and her allies understood the need to remain steadfast in their commitment to change, even when faced with setbacks.

In times of discouragement, Talin led by example, reminding her team and supporters of the significance of their cause. She encouraged self-care practices, fostering a supportive and nurturing environment. She recognized that burnout could be detrimental to the movement, and made efforts to ensure her team's well-being.

Additionally, Talin implemented strategies to sustain momentum and enthusiasm. Regular progress updates, celebratory events, and acknowledging small victories along the way kept morale high and motivated supporters to continue fighting for change.

An Unconventional Approach: Artistic Activism

In addition to traditional advocacy methods, Talin embraced artistic activism as a means to overcome resistance and pushback. She recognized the power of art in evoking emotional responses, challenging societal norms, and promoting critical thinking.

Talin and her allies organized art exhibitions, theater performances, and poetry slams to address the multi-tentacle marriage restrictions creatively. These initiatives not only provided a platform for marginalized voices but also engaged the wider community in conversations about equality and justice. By using art as a tool for activism, Talin created opportunities for empathy and connection, challenging deep-rooted biases through the universal language of creativity.

Exercises

1. Imagine you are an alien rights activist facing resistance and pushback in your community. Develop a persuasive argument that counters common misconceptions and prejudices against alien marriage equality.

2. Research a historical civil rights movement and identify the strategies used to overcome resistance. How can these strategies be adapted to the fight for alien rights?

3. Role-play a scenario where you engage in a dialogue with someone resistant to alien marriage equality. Practice using effective communication strategies to change their perspective.

Conclusion

Overcoming resistance and pushback is an ongoing battle in the fight for civil rights. Talin Iryn and her allies demonstrated the power of understanding, coalition building, strategic communication, legal expertise, resilience, and artistic activism as effective tools against oppression. By employing these strategies, they paved the way for progress, inspiring future generations to continue the fight for justice and equality.

Education and Awareness Programs

Education and awareness programs played a crucial role in Talin Iryn's fight for alien rights and equality on Xyorath. These programs aimed to challenge societal prejudices, debunk myths, and promote understanding and empathy among the general population. By educating people about the struggles faced by alien communities and promoting awareness of their contributions to society, these programs helped break down barriers and fostered a climate of acceptance and inclusivity.

Understanding Alien Cultures

One of the primary objectives of education and awareness programs was to foster a deeper understanding of alien cultures and customs. Many Xyorathians held misconceptions and stereotypes about alien communities, which perpetuated discrimination and prejudice. To address these issues, Talin and their team organized workshops and cultural events where individuals from different backgrounds could come together to learn and share their experiences.

Example: The "Alien Cultural Exchange Fair" brought together individuals from various alien communities to showcase their traditions, music, art, and cuisine. Through interactive exhibits and presentations, attendees had the opportunity to engage with alien cultures and gain a deeper appreciation for their diversity.

Promoting Equality and Inclusivity

In order to promote equality and inclusivity, education and awareness programs focused on challenging discriminatory attitudes and practices. Talin and their team organized educational campaigns that highlighted the importance of equal rights for all individuals, regardless of their alien or human status.

Example: The "Equal Rights Symposium" brought together legal experts, activists, and community leaders to discuss the legal and moral imperative of equal rights for aliens. This event helped create a platform for dialogue and encouraged the audience to critically examine their own biases and prejudices.

Empowering Alien Communities

Education and awareness programs also aimed to empower alien communities by providing them with knowledge and resources to advocate for their rights. Workshops and training sessions were held to educate community members about their legal rights, activism strategies, and avenues for seeking redress.

Example: The "Know Your Rights" workshops provided alien individuals with essential information about their legal rights, how to navigate the legal system, and where to seek legal representation. These workshops also equipped participants with the skills needed to confidently assert their rights in various situations.

Addressing Intersectionality

Education and awareness programs recognized the need to address the intersectionality of discrimination faced by alien communities. They emphasized the importance of acknowledging and addressing the multiple forms of discrimination that alien individuals may experience, including racism, sexism, and classism.

Example: The "Intersectionality and Alien Rights" panel discussion invited renowned activists and scholars to explore the interconnected nature of different forms of discrimination. By examining case studies and engaging in thought-provoking discussions, participants gained a deeper understanding of how various forms of oppression intersect and impact alien communities.

Collaboration with Educational Institutions

To maximize their impact, education and awareness programs collaborated with educational institutions, including schools, colleges, and universities. By incorporating alien rights and social justice themes into the curriculum, these programs aimed to raise a generation of empathetic and socially conscious individuals.

Example: The "Alien Rights Curriculum Integration Initiative" partnered with local schools to develop age-appropriate educational materials and resources that integrated alien rights issues into various subjects. This initiative not only provided students with a comprehensive understanding of alien rights but also encouraged critical thinking and dialogue among young minds.

Promoting Arts and Media Representations

Arts and media play a powerful role in shaping public opinion. Education and awareness programs recognized this and actively promoted accurate and positive representations of alien communities in the media and creative industries. This involved collaboration with artists, filmmakers, and writers to challenge stereotypes and tell authentic stories.

Example: The "Alien Voices Film Festival" showcased films and documentaries that depicted the experiences and contributions of alien communities. Through panel discussions and Q&A sessions, filmmakers and audience members engaged in conversations about the importance of authentic storytelling and the impact of media representations on public perception.

Resources and Support Networks

Education and awareness programs also provided resources and support networks for individuals and communities facing discrimination. These initiatives aimed to empower individuals with knowledge and connect them with organizations and services that could assist them in their fight for equality.

Example: The "Alien Rights Resource Center" was an online platform that offered a comprehensive directory of legal services, support groups, educational resources, and advocacy tools. This resource center was accessible to all individuals, irrespective of their background, and played a crucial role in connecting people with the help they needed.

Overall, education and awareness programs were instrumental in breaking down the barriers of prejudice and discrimination. By promoting understanding, challenging stereotypes, and empowering alien communities, these programs laid the foundation for a more inclusive and equitable Xyorathian society. Talin Iryn's tireless efforts in this arena continue to serve as a blueprint for future activists and advocates in the fight for justice and equality.

Extending the Fight to Other Alien Communities

Talin Iryn's fight for alien rights on Xyorath was not just limited to their own community. Recognizing the interconnectedness of various alien communities across the galaxy, Talin aimed to extend their fight for equality to other marginalized groups.

Understanding the Plight of Other Alien Communities

As Talin delved deeper into their activism, they began to learn about the different challenges faced by alien communities on other planets. They discovered that many communities faced similar forms of discrimination and oppression, such as restrictive laws, systemic bias, and societal prejudice.

To effectively extend the fight to these communities, Talin understood the importance of first understanding their unique cultural, social, and political contexts. They immersed themselves in research, engaging with scholars, and connecting with activists from various planets to learn about their struggles and aspirations.

Building Solidarity and Coalition

Talin recognized that the fight for alien rights could gain strength from collective action. They reached out to leaders and activists from different alien communities, emphasizing the need for collaboration and solidarity. Together, they formed coalitions that aimed to amplify their collective voices and advocate for the fair treatment of all alien beings.

These alliances were built on the principles of mutual respect, shared goals, and a commitment to intersectionality. Talin encouraged open dialogue and exchange of ideas, creating safe spaces for marginalized voices to be heard and valued.

Sharing Strategies and Resources

As Talin connected with activists from various planets, they realized the value of sharing strategies and resources. They organized workshops and conferences where activists could come together to discuss effective methods of resistance and share their experiences.

Talin also wrote publications and held webinars, disseminating knowledge and practical guidance to alien communities struggling for their rights. They emphasized the importance of utilizing social media and online platforms to create awareness, educate the masses, and garner support.

Establishing Support Networks

Recognizing the significance of emotional support and solidarity, Talin focused on establishing support networks for activists and individuals within other alien communities. They facilitated online forums, where individuals could come together to share their experiences, seek advice, and find comfort in knowing they were not alone in their fight.

Talin also encouraged mentorship programs, pairing experienced activists with those who were just starting their journey. This created an ecosystem of support and guidance, ensuring the sustained growth and development of future leaders within the alien rights movement.

Addressing Intersections of Discrimination

Talin understood that discrimination often intersected with other forms of oppression, such as racism, sexism, and classism. They actively worked towards addressing these intersections and building alliances with other social justice movements.

By joining forces with these movements, Talin's fight for alien rights became part of a broader struggle for justice and equality. They actively advocated for policies and practices that recognized and valued the diversity within alien communities, challenging the systemic barriers faced by individuals at the intersections of multiple forms of discrimination.

An Unconventional Approach: Art as Resistance

As part of their effort to extend the fight for alien rights, Talin recognized the power of art as a form of resistance. They encouraged artists from different alien communities to explore and express their experiences through various artistic mediums.

Talin organized art exhibitions, poetry slams, and performances that showcased the talents of these artists, fostering a sense of pride and unity within alien communities. Art served as a powerful tool for raising awareness, sparking conversations, and challenging societal norms.

Exercises

1. Choose an alien community on another planet and research their struggles for equality. Write a brief report summarizing their challenges and the strategies they are using to advocate for their rights.

2. Form a discussion group with activists from different alien communities. Discuss the commonalities and differences in their struggles and brainstorm ways to build stronger alliances and support networks.

3. Create a piece of artwork or a poem that reflects the experiences of an alien community facing discrimination. Share it on social media to raise awareness and start conversations about alien rights.

Conclusion: Expanding the Fight

Talin Iryn's work extended far beyond the boundaries of Xyorath. By connecting with activists from other alien communities, building coalitions, sharing strategies and resources, establishing support networks, and addressing intersections of discrimination, Talin ensured that the fight for alien rights became a galaxy-wide movement.

Their approach, incorporating art as a tool for resistance, added an unconventional yet powerful dimension to their advocacy. Through their efforts, Talin inspired others to fight for justice, equality, and the recognition of the inherent worth and dignity of all alien beings.

As the legacy of Talin's work continues to shape the galaxy, activists are reminded that the fight for equality and social justice is never-ending and ever-evolving. Together, they carry forward Talin's vision of a more inclusive and compassionate universe.

Legislative Reforms and Policy Changes

Legislative reforms and policy changes played a crucial role in Talin Iryn's fight for equality and justice on Xyorath. By challenging discriminatory laws and advocating for inclusive policies, Talin sought to dismantle the barriers that prevented multi-tentacle marriages and promote a more equitable society. This section explores the key legislative strategies employed by Talin and their impact on the Xyorathian legal landscape.

Identifying Discriminatory Laws

The first step in Talin's legislative efforts was to identify the existing discriminatory laws that prevented multi-tentacle marriages. Through meticulous research and collaboration with legal experts, Talin and their team outlined the specific legislation and policies that infringed upon the rights of Xyorathian individuals to freely choose their partners and establish legal unions.

Talin and their team examined the Xyorathian legal system, including the constitution, statutes, and local ordinances, to identify provisions that explicitly prohibited or restricted multi-tentacle marriages. They also analyzed the history and context behind these laws, seeking to understand the underlying motivations and prejudices that led to their implementation.

This comprehensive analysis of discriminatory laws served as the foundation for Talin's subsequent advocacy efforts, allowing them to articulate the specific changes needed to ensure equal rights and opportunities for all Xyorathian individuals.

Building Alliances and Coalitions

Legislative reforms require building alliances and coalitions to garner support and amplify the voices advocating for change. Talin recognized the power of collective action and actively sought to build relationships with like-minded individuals, organizations, and lawmakers who shared their vision of equality.

By forging strong alliances with alien rights organizations, civil rights advocates, and progressive lawmakers, Talin was able to create a united front that transcended individual differences and focused on a collective goal: the legalization of multi-tentacle marriages. They organized collaborative campaigns, mobilized supporters, and coordinated efforts to exert pressure on policymakers at various levels of government, from local to national.

Talin's ability to create and sustain broad-based coalitions allowed them to leverage diverse perspectives and resources, strengthening their persuasive power and increasing the likelihood of legislative success.

Lobbying and Advocacy Efforts

To effect significant legislative changes, Talin understood the importance of strategically engaging with lawmakers and decision-makers. Lobbying and advocacy became key components of their legislative reform strategy.

Talin and their team conducted extensive research on legislators and policymakers who held sway over legislation related to marriage and civil rights. They identified key individuals who could potentially champion their cause or act as influential allies within the legislative process.

Armed with evidence-backed arguments, Talin and their team embarked on lobbying campaigns that involved personal meetings with lawmakers, presenting compelling testimonies, and providing well-researched policy briefs. They brought Xyorathian individuals who were directly impacted by the discriminatory laws to share their personal stories, humanizing the struggle for marriage equality and reinforcing the urgent need for legislative reforms.

Talin's lobbying efforts were complemented by broader advocacy campaigns aimed at mobilizing public support. They leveraged social media platforms, traditional media outlets, and public events to raise awareness about the discriminatory laws and rally Xyorathian and non-Xyorathian individuals alike.

Strategic Litigation

Recognizing the transformative power of the courts, Talin pursued strategic litigation as a means to challenge discriminatory laws and lay the groundwork for progressive legal precedents.

By identifying Xyorathian individuals who were directly impacted by the marriage restrictions, Talin and their legal team built cases that demonstrated the tangible harm caused by these discriminatory laws. They strategically selected plaintiffs who possessed solid legal standing and compelling narratives, ensuring the greatest chance of success in the courtroom.

Talin's legal team employed innovative legal arguments, drawing on constitutional principles, human rights conventions, and equality jurisprudence to challenge the constitutionality of the discriminatory laws. They highlighted the fundamental rights at stake, emphasizing the importance of equal treatment, freedom of choice, and privacy in matters of personal relationships and marriages.

These strategic litigation efforts not only aimed to secure immediate legal victories but also sought to establish legal precedents that would have broader implications for other discriminatory laws and policies affecting Xyorathian individuals.

Legislative Reforms and Policy Changes

Through a combination of lobbying, advocacy, and strategic litigation, Talin and their allies successfully achieved significant legislative reforms and policy changes:

1. **Repeal and Amendment of Discriminatory Laws:** Talin's relentless advocacy efforts, supported by grassroots mobilization, ultimately led to the repeal or amendment of laws that explicitly prohibited or restricted multi-tentacle marriages. These legal changes signaled a fundamental shift in Xyorathian society's recognition of the rights of its diverse citizens.

2. **Creation of Anti-Discrimination Legislation:** Talin's campaign also paved the way for the introduction and passage of comprehensive anti-discrimination legislation that protected Xyorathians from all forms of discrimination, including marital status. This legislation represented a significant step towards fostering a more inclusive and equitable society.

3. **Access to Legal Recognition and Benefits:** As a direct result of the legislative reforms, Xyorathian individuals in multi-tentacle marriages gained access to the legal

recognition and benefits previously denied to them. This included spousal rights, inheritance rights, access to healthcare benefits, and pension benefits, among others.

4. **Education and Awareness Programs:** The legislative reforms also mandated the implementation of education and awareness programs to promote cultural understanding and inclusivity. These programs aimed to challenge societal prejudices, dismantle harmful stereotypes, and foster empathy and acceptance within Xyorathian communities.

5. **Reparations and Restorative Justice:** Talin's advocacy efforts extended beyond the legal realm, with a focus on reparations for individuals who had been directly harmed by the discriminatory laws. Through negotiation and collaboration with relevant authorities, Talin was able to secure compensation and restitution for victims of discrimination, helping to address the historical injustices perpetrated against the Xyorathian community.

These legislative reforms and policy changes represented a significant milestone in Talin's fight for multi-tentacle marriage equality. However, they also served as a springboard for broader societal transformation, challenging prejudices and inequalities on a deeper level and setting the stage for a more inclusive future.

Conclusion

The legislative reforms and policy changes brought about by Talin Iryn's activism transformed Xyorathian society. Through strategic litigation, lobbying, and coalition-building efforts, Talin successfully challenged discriminatory laws and advocated for the recognition of multi-tentacle marriages.

The repeal and amendment of these discriminatory laws not only granted Xyorathian individuals the right to marry the partners of their choice but also signaled a broader recognition of the rights and dignity of all Xyorathians. The creation of anti-discrimination legislation, access to legal recognition and benefits, and the implementation of education and awareness programs further contributed to building a more inclusive and equitable society.

Talin's legacy extends beyond legal victories. Their advocacy efforts inspired alien communities across Xyorath and beyond, serving as a testament to the power of resilience, unity, and the pursuit of justice. By challenging discriminatory laws and advocating for policy changes, Talin Iryn sparked a movement that continues to fight for equality and social justice, ensuring that the struggle for justice is never-ending and ever-evolving.

Talin Iryn's unwavering commitment to legislative reforms and policy changes serves as an inspiration for future generations of activists, reminding us that it is through collective action and a vision of a more inclusive society that lasting change is possible. Talin's enduring legacy continues to shape Xyorathian society, reimagining love and relationships and paving the way for a future of equality and justice.

Building International Alliances

Building international alliances was a key strategy for Talin Iryn in her fight for alien rights and equality on Xyorath. Recognizing that the issues faced by her community were not unique to their planet, Talin understood the importance of connecting with other civil rights movements and advocates around the galaxy. By fostering these alliances, she was able to share knowledge, resources, and support the global struggle for justice and equity. In this section, we will explore how Talin built international alliances and the impact it had on the alien rights movement.

Recognizing Common Struggles

The first step in building international alliances was identifying other communities and movements facing similar challenges. Talin recognized that discrimination, oppression, and prejudice were not limited to Xyorath alone. She reached out to activists, scholars, and organizations across planets to learn from their experiences and share knowledge from her own struggle. By connecting with different groups, Talin was able to highlight the commonalities among various civil rights movements, strengthening the fight for justice across the galaxy.

Establishing Communication Channels

To facilitate collaboration and exchange of ideas, Talin established communication channels with other alien rights movements. She utilized advanced technologies to organize video conferences, webinars, and seminars where activists could share stories, strategies, and tactics. These virtual platforms enabled advocates from different planets to engage in meaningful discussions, network, and coordinate their efforts towards achieving equality.

Sharing Resources and Expertise

When it came to building international alliances, Talin believed that strength lay in unity. She understood the power of sharing resources and expertise among different movements. Talin worked tirelessly to establish resource-sharing networks that allowed activists to exchange information, research, legal expertise, and financial support. These collaborations not only strengthened the individual movements but also created a global community of advocates working towards a common goal.

Learning from International Success Stories

Talin recognized that there were already successful examples of civil rights movements across the galaxy. She studied the victories achieved by these movements, identifying their strategies, and analyzing the factors that contributed to their success. By learning from these international success stories, Talin was able to adapt and apply effective practices to her own fight for alien rights on Xyorath. This cross-pollination of ideas and experiences fueled the momentum of the movement and brought new perspectives to the struggle.

Participating in International Conferences and Events

To further strengthen international alliances, Talin actively participated in conferences, symposiums, and events focused on human and alien rights. These gatherings provided opportunities to meet like-minded activists, scholars, and policymakers from around the galaxy. Talin leveraged these platforms to share her insights and experiences, highlight the challenges faced by the alien community on Xyorath, and strengthen the call for justice and equality.

Promoting Cultural Exchange and Understanding

Building international alliances was not just about fighting for legal reforms and policy changes. It was also about fostering cultural exchange and understanding. Talin encouraged cultural exchange programs between various alien communities to increase empathy, reduce prejudice, and break down barriers. By promoting cultural exchange, Talin sought to build bridges of understanding among different civilizations and unite them in the struggle against discrimination.

Creating Global Advocacy Networks

One of Talin's greatest achievements in building international alliances was the creation of global advocacy networks. These networks served as a support system for activists and provided a platform to amplify their voices. Talin facilitated regular virtual meetings, discussion forums, and training sessions within these networks to build solidarity, share best practices, and strategize for collective action. The global advocacy networks became a powerful force, exerting pressure on policymakers and institutions to address the issue of alien rights.

Empowering Grassroots Movements

In her pursuit of building international alliances, Talin recognized the importance of empowering grassroots movements in different parts of the galaxy. She invested resources and provided guidance to emerging advocacy groups, helping them navigate the complexities of activism and organize effective campaigns. By strengthening grassroots movements, Talin ensured that the fight for alien rights was not limited to a few charismatic leaders but became a collective movement driven by passionate individuals who believed in justice and equality.

Challenges and Opportunities

Building international alliances came with its own set of challenges. Language barriers, cultural differences, time zone variations, and different legal systems posed obstacles in effective collaboration. However, Talin saw these challenges as opportunities for growth and understanding. She encouraged cultural sensitivity training, language exchange programs, and legal education initiatives to bridge these gaps and create a truly global movement.

Conclusion

Building international alliances was a critical aspect of Talin Iryn's activism on Xyorath. By connecting with other civil rights movements and advocates across the galaxy, she created a global community united in the fight for justice and equality. Through communication, resource-sharing, and cultural exchange, Talin built a network that amplified the voices of alien communities and brought about lasting change. The partnerships she formed continue to inspire future generations of alien rights activists, reinforcing the idea that the struggle for justice knows no boundaries.

Speaking Engagements and Conferences

Speaking engagements and conferences played a crucial role in Talin Iryn's activism journey, providing platforms for her to share her experiences, insights, and ideas with a wider audience. These events served as valuable opportunities for Talin to educate, inspire, and mobilize people in the fight for alien rights and equality. Through her powerful speeches and engaging presentations, Talin was able to create awareness and spark conversations that would shape the course of the movement.

Power of Persuasion

Talin understood the power of persuasive communication in effecting social change. She crafted her speeches and presentations to resonate with her audience, combining personal anecdotes, powerful storytelling, and compelling data to convey the urgency and importance of alien rights. Talin's magnetic presence and ability to connect with people on an emotional level made her a captivating speaker, leaving a lasting impact on her listeners.

To illustrate the struggles faced by alien communities, Talin would often weave in real-life stories and examples of discrimination and injustice. By humanizing the issues, she aimed to foster empathy and understanding among her audience members who may have had limited exposure to the challenges faced by aliens.

Keynote Addresses

As Talin's reputation grew, she received numerous invitations to deliver keynote addresses at prestigious events and conferences centered around social activism, civil rights, and equality. These appearances provided her with a larger platform to promote her cause and influence decision-makers, activists, and supporters alike.

Talin's keynote addresses focused on highlighting the intersectionality of discrimination and the importance of unity in fighting against systemic oppression. She emphasized that the struggle for alien rights was deeply entwined with other civil rights movements, such as gender equality and racial justice. By drawing these connections, Talin aimed to forge alliances and encourage collaboration across diverse communities to achieve broader social change.

Interactive Workshops

In addition to keynote addresses, Talin also facilitated interactive workshops at conferences, allowing participants to delve deeper into the nuances of alien rights and explore potential strategies to challenge discriminatory practices. These workshops provided a safe space for open dialogue, where participants could share their own experiences and brainstorm solutions collectively.

Talin encouraged attendees to critically examine the broader societal systems contributing to discrimination and brainstorm ways to dismantle them. By fostering interactive and collaborative environments, she aimed to empower individuals to become active agents of change in their own communities.

Panel Discussions

Panel discussions featuring Talin as a prominent voice allowed for multi-perspective conversations on alien rights. These sessions provided a platform for scholars, activists, policymakers, and community members to exchange ideas and share their knowledge and expertise.

Talin's participation in panel discussions helped bridge the gap between academic research and grassroots activism. By sharing her lived experiences and the stories of those affected by discrimination, she added a human dimension to the discussions, helping participants understand the real-world implications of discriminatory policies and practices.

Inspiring the Next Generation

One of the key objectives of Talin's speaking engagements and conference appearances was to inspire and motivate the next generation of activists. She believed in the power of youth-led movements and their ability to effect meaningful change.

Talin often made it a point to engage with students and young activists during her speaking engagements. She conducted interactive Q&A sessions, provided mentorship opportunities, and encouraged young individuals to pursue their passions for social justice activism. By empowering young minds and nurturing their innate passion for equality, Talin aimed to ensure the longevity and sustainability of the alien rights movement.

Unconventional Approach: Performance Activism

Talin's speaking engagements occasionally featured a unique element of performance activism. Understanding the power of art and its ability to transcend barriers, she collaborated with artists, poets, and musicians to incorporate creative expressions into her presentations.

These collaborative performances served as a way to engage emotions and convey powerful messages that would resonate deeply with the audience. Through the fusion of art and activism, Talin aimed to break down emotional barriers, challenging societal norms and promoting empathy and understanding.

Resources and Supportive Materials

To complement her speaking engagements and provide attendees with additional resources, Talin often created informative handouts, fact sheets, and resource guides.

These materials included legal resources, research findings, and contact information for organizations advocating for alien rights.

Talin's team also ensured that her speeches and presentations were recorded and made available online to reach a wider audience. This allowed her messages to extend beyond conference halls and directly reach individuals who may not have had the opportunity to attend in person.

Exercises and Engagement

During her speaking engagements, Talin actively encouraged audience participation through group exercises and engagement activities. These activities aimed to build connections among participants, fostering a sense of community and shared purpose.

For example, Talin would initiate small group discussions where attendees could share their own experiences or brainstorm strategies to address specific challenges. By promoting active participation and collaboration, Talin sought to empower attendees to become change agents within their spheres of influence.

Conclusion: Amplifying the Voice of Justice

Speaking engagements and conferences provided a valuable platform for Talin Iryn to amplify the voice of justice, driving the cause of alien rights forward. Through her powerful speeches, interactive workshops, and collaborative panel discussions, she ignited conversations and inspired individuals to join the fight for equality and social justice.

Talin's unconventional approach, incorporating performance activism and fostering youth engagement, ensured that her impact extended beyond the immediate audience. By sharing resources and recording her presentations, she sought to create a lasting legacy, empowering future generations to continue the work she began.

Through her speaking engagements and conferences, Talin sparked a movement fueled by empathy, understanding, and the unwavering pursuit of equality. Her ability to captivate hearts and minds paved the way for meaningful policy changes, cultural shifts, and a society that recognized the inherent worth and dignity of all beings. The fight for alien rights continues, fueled by the passion and resilience Talin ignited.

Balancing Activism and Personal Life

Balancing activism and personal life is a constant challenge for any civil rights activist, and Talin Iryn was no exception. As she fought tirelessly for alien rights and equality on Xyorath, she also had to navigate the complexities of maintaining relationships, nurturing her personal wellbeing, and finding time for self-care. In this section, we will explore the strategies and lessons Talin learned in balancing her activism and personal life.

The Importance of Self-Care

When fighting for a cause as demanding as civil rights, it is easy to lose sight of your own needs. However, Talin realized early on that self-care is essential for maintaining long-term effectiveness as an activist. She understood that taking care of herself physically, emotionally, and mentally would enable her to continue the fight for justice.

One of the key strategies Talin employed was setting boundaries. She recognized that she couldn't be available to everyone all the time, and that it was okay to say no. By prioritizing her own needs, she ensured that she had the energy and focus necessary for her activism. Talin also made time for activities that brought her joy and rejuvenated her spirit, such as painting, meditating, and spending time in nature.

Building a Supportive Network

Talin understood the importance of surrounding herself with a strong support system. She actively sought out like-minded individuals who were also passionate about alien rights and social justice. Through her involvement in local alien rights organizations, she forged deep connections with fellow activists who became her closest friends and confidants.

These relationships provided a space for Talin to vent, seek advice, and find solace during challenging times. They also served as a reminder that she was not alone in her struggles and that the fight for equality was a collective effort. By fostering a network of support, Talin was able to lean on others when she needed it most and offer her support in return.

Time Management and Prioritization

As an activist, it is easy to become overwhelmed with the multitude of tasks and responsibilities. Balancing activism and personal life requires effective time management and the ability to prioritize tasks. Talin adopted several strategies to ensure she could make the most of her time.

One of her key practices was setting clear goals and objectives. By identifying her most important tasks and breaking them down into manageable steps, Talin was able to stay focused and achieve her desired outcomes. She also practiced delegation, recognizing that she couldn't do everything on her own. Delegating tasks to trusted allies allowed her to streamline her workload and free up time for personal life.

Furthermore, Talin embraced the power of saying "no" to non-essential activities. She recognized that her time and energy were limited resources and that she needed to be selective in how she used them. By setting boundaries and learning to prioritize, she was able to create space for personal relationships and self-care.

Maintaining Healthy Relationships

Maintaining healthy relationships while dedicated to activism requires communication, understanding, and empathy. Talin recognized that her loved ones might not always understand the intricacies of her work or the emotional toll it could take. Open and honest communication was crucial in bridging this gap.

Talin made a conscious effort to communicate her needs, boundaries, and challenges to her loved ones. She strived to make them feel included in her journey and valued their input and support. At the same time, she sought to understand their perspectives and concerns, actively listening and validating their feelings.

Furthermore, Talin practiced active presence when spending time with her loved ones. She set aside dedicated time for quality interactions, ensuring that she was fully present and engaged. This helped her establish a work-life balance and create meaningful connections outside of her activism.

Finding Inspiration in Personal Relationships

While personal relationships require time and energy, Talin found that they also provided invaluable inspiration and motivation for her activism. The love and support she received from her partner, family, and friends served as a reminder of why she fought so passionately for alien rights.

Talin often drew inspiration from the stories and experiences of her loved ones. Their personal encounters with discrimination and injustice fueled her determination to create a more inclusive and fair society. By keeping the personal stories of her loved ones at the forefront of her advocacy work, she was able to find the strength to overcome obstacles and maintain her commitment to the cause.

Unconventional Tip: Embracing Imperfection and Forgiveness

In the pursuit of balancing activism and personal life, Talin learned an unconventional yet powerful tip: embracing imperfection and practicing forgiveness. She recognized that she couldn't do it all perfectly and that mistakes and setbacks were inevitable.

Instead of being consumed by guilt or self-blame, Talin chose to view these moments as opportunities for growth and learning. She forgave herself for any perceived shortcomings and embraced the notion that both activism and personal life were journeys, not destinations. This allowed her to approach her life with a sense of grace and self-compassion, enabling her to bounce back from challenges and setbacks with renewed resilience.

Example: Advocating for Workplace Flexibility

Talin always believed in leading by example. As an activist for alien rights, she recognized the importance of advocating for workplace flexibility, particularly for marginalized communities. Talin worked with other activists and organizations to lobby for policies that allowed individuals to balance their personal and professional responsibilities without sacrificing their careers or commitments to activism.

Through these efforts, Talin envisioned a future where all individuals, regardless of their background, could actively participate in social justice movements without facing barriers in their workplaces. She believed that by championing workplace flexibility, she could create a more inclusive and empowering environment for activists, ultimately enhancing their ability to balance their personal lives and activism effectively.

Conclusion

Balancing activism and personal life is a perpetual challenge for civil rights activists like Talin Iryn. However, by prioritizing self-care, building a strong support network, practicing effective time management, and maintaining healthy relationships, it is possible to strike a harmonious balance. Talin's journey serves as a powerful reminder that activism and personal life are not mutually exclusive, and that by nurturing both, genuine and lasting change can be achieved.

Personal Reflections and Lessons Learned

Throughout my journey as a civil rights activist, I have experienced both triumphs and defeats, gained invaluable knowledge, and developed a deeper understanding of the struggle for equality. These personal reflections and lessons learned have shaped me into the advocate I am today, and I hope to pass on these insights to future generations of activists. In this section, I will share some of the key reflections and lessons that have had a lasting impact on my life and work.

The Power of Persistence

One of the most important lessons I have learned is the power of persistence. The fight for civil rights is not a linear path, and setbacks are inevitable. However, it is crucial to remain steadfast and resilient in the face of adversity. Throughout my journey, I have faced opposition, resistance, and even personal attacks. But I have come to understand that these challenges should not discourage us; instead, they fuel our determination to bring about change.

Persistence is not just about pushing forward; it also involves adapting and evolving our strategies. It requires us to be open to new ideas, build alliances, and be strategic in our actions. By persistently working towards our goals, we can overcome obstacles and create lasting change.

The Importance of Self-Care

Engaging in activism and fighting for justice can be emotionally and mentally draining. It is vital to prioritize self-care to ensure sustainability and avoid burnout. This lesson took me some time to learn, as I initially believed that pushing myself to the limit was a sign of dedication. However, I soon realized that neglecting self-care hindered my ability to effectively advocate for change.

Self-care looks different for everyone, but it often involves practices that recharge and rejuvenate the mind and body. For me, this includes spending time in nature, practicing mindfulness and meditation, and surrounding myself with loved ones who provide support and encouragement. Taking time to care for ourselves allows us to show up fully and be better advocates for the causes we believe in.

The Importance of Building Relationships

In the journey of activism, building relationships and alliances is essential. While individuals can make a significant impact on their own, collective efforts have a greater chance of success. Building relationships with like-minded individuals and organizations not only amplifies our voices but also strengthens our fight for justice.

I have learned the importance of collaborating with individuals and groups who may have different experiences and perspectives. By embracing diversity within the movement, we can create a more inclusive and effective resistance. Building relationships also involves active listening, empathy, and understanding. It is through these connections that we can learn from each other, bridge divides, and create meaningful change.

The Value of Intersectionality

Intersectionality is a concept that has deeply influenced my activism. It recognizes that individuals experience multiple forms of oppression simultaneously and that these systems of oppression are interconnected. Understanding intersectionality is crucial to effectively fight for justice and equality.

Recognizing the various forms of discrimination that intersect helps us create more comprehensive and inclusive solutions. It reminds us that our work should not be limited to one particular issue but should strive to address the interconnected web of inequalities. By centering the experiences of marginalized communities and acknowledging the particular challenges they face, we can build a more equitable society for all.

The Role of Education and Awareness

Education and awareness are powerful tools for social change. Throughout my journey, I have come to understand the impact of educating others about the issues at hand. By raising awareness and fostering understanding, we can challenge preconceived notions and biases and foster support for our cause.

Incorporating education into our activism can take various forms. It could involve organizing workshops, seminars, or public lectures, or even using social media platforms to share information and engage with audiences. By creating spaces for dialogue and learning, we empower individuals to become agents of change in their own communities.

The Need to Embrace Failure

Failure is an inevitable part of any battle for social change. It is essential to understand that failure does not undermine the significance of our cause, nor does it define our worth as activists. Instead, failure provides an opportunity for growth, reflection, and learning. It highlights areas for improvement and encourages us to reassess our strategies.

Embracing failure means reframing setbacks as stepping stones towards success. It involves recognizing and celebrating the small wins along the way, even when the ultimate goal seems distant. By embracing failure, we cultivate resilience and perseverance, essential qualities for any activist.

The Importance of Listening to Marginalized Voices

As an activist, it is critical to amplify the voices of marginalized communities and listen to their lived experiences. These voices provide invaluable insights into the realities of discrimination and the best strategies for creating change. Through active listening and elevating these voices, we can ensure that our advocacy is rooted in the experiences and needs of those directly affected.

Listening to marginalized voices also means recognizing our privilege and learning from those who have different perspectives. It requires humility and a willingness to challenge our assumptions. By centering marginalized voices, we can create a more equitable and inclusive movement.

Conclusion

In this section, I have shared some personal reflections and lessons learned throughout my journey as a civil rights activist. These insights have shaped my approach to advocacy and have allowed me to navigate challenges and setbacks with resilience and determination. By embracing persistence, self-care, building relationships, understanding intersectionality, promoting education and awareness, embracing failure, and listening to marginalized voices, I have been able to make a meaningful impact.

The fight for equality and justice is an ongoing battle, and it is my hope that future activists can draw inspiration from the lessons and experiences shared in this book. By carrying on the work and incorporating these reflections into their own activism, they can contribute to a more just and equitable society for all. I will forever be grateful for the lessons I have learned and the opportunity to be part of a movement striving for a better world.

Legacy and Impact on Future Generations

Talin Iryn's tireless efforts and groundbreaking achievements have left a lasting impact on future generations, not only on Xyorathian society but also on a global scale. Her legacy serves as a beacon of hope and inspiration for those fighting for justice and equality in the face of discrimination. In this section, we will explore the various ways in which Talin's work has shaped the future and continues to inspire change.

Empowering Alien Youth

One of the most significant aspects of Talin's legacy is her ability to empower and uplift alien youth. Through her activism and advocacy, she tirelessly worked to create opportunities for young Xyorathians to thrive and succeed, regardless of their background or identity. Talin established scholarships and mentoring programs aimed at providing educational resources and support to those who faced systemic barriers. Her belief in the power of education as a tool for social change continues to impact generations of Xyorathian youth, motivating them to pursue their dreams and contribute to their communities.

Furthermore, Talin emphasized the importance of leadership development among alien youth. She organized workshops and training programs aimed at nurturing the next generation of activists and advocates, equipping them with the necessary skills and knowledge to effect social change. By empowering young Xyorathians to become leaders in their own right, Talin ensured that her fight for equality would continue long after her time.

Promoting Intersectionality and Inclusivity

While fighting for the rights of Xyorathians, Talin consistently advocated for intersectionality and inclusivity within the broader civil rights movement. She recognized that discrimination and oppression often overlap and intersect, affecting individuals who belong to multiple marginalized groups. As a result, Talin actively sought to build bridges and collaborate with other civil rights movements, such as those fighting for gender equality, LGBTQ+ rights, and racial justice.

By promoting intersectionality and inclusivity, Talin challenged the notion that social justice movements need to work in isolation. She believed that true progress could only be achieved through solidarity and collective action. Talin's legacy serves as a reminder that in the fight for equality, it is crucial to consider the experiences and struggles of all marginalized communities and work together to dismantle systems of oppression.

Advocating for Legal Reforms

Talin's impact on future generations is perhaps most evident in the realm of legislation and policy. Her successful legal battle against the multi-tentacle marriage restrictions set a precedent for future alien rights cases, ensuring that the rights and dignities of Xyorathians would be protected by law. The legal victory not only allowed Xyorathians to marry whomever they loved but also served as a catalyst for broader legal reforms.

Inspired by Talin's example, future generations of alien rights activists continue to push for comprehensive legal protections against discrimination in areas such as employment, housing, healthcare, and education. They draw on Talin's strategies and experiences to build robust legal arguments and mobilize public support in favor of equitable and inclusive policies. Talin's work has undoubtedly laid the foundation for ongoing advocacy and activism, ensuring that the fight for justice and equality continues to evolve and adapt to changing times.

Inspiring Grassroots Movements

Talin's legacy extends beyond formal activism and has inspired grassroots movements at the local level. Organizers and advocates across various Xyorathian communities have drawn inspiration from Talin's fight for equality, sparking their own initiatives and campaigns. Whether it is organizing peaceful protests, creating awareness through social media campaigns, or engaging in community-building activities, these grassroots movements continue to carry forward Talin's spirit and determination.

In addition to Xyorathian communities, Talin's work has resonated with alien populations across the galaxy. Her story of resilience, courage, and unwavering dedication has become an inspiration for activists fighting for alien rights on different planets. Through her memoirs and documentaries, Talin's story reaches far and wide, providing hope and encouragement to those who face discrimination and oppression based on their identity.

Cultivating Empathy and Understanding

Perhaps Talin's most enduring legacy is her ability to cultivate empathy and understanding among different species and cultures. By sharing her personal experiences and challenging societal norms, she helped breakdown stereotypes and fostered a deeper understanding of the challenges faced by Xyorathians. Talin's powerful storytelling and ability to bridge the gap between alien and human experiences have humanized the struggles of Xyorathians, making it easier for others to empathize and stand in solidarity.

Her legacy serves as a reminder that true change can only occur when individuals from diverse backgrounds come together to listen, learn, and support one another. Talin's impact on future generations lies not only in the policy reforms and legal victories but also in the hearts and minds of those who have been moved by her story.

Conclusion: A Legacy of Equality and Justice

Talin Iryn's legacy is one of unwavering determination, resilience, and a commitment to social justice. Her fight against multi-tentacle marriage restrictions on Xyorath and her broader work in the alien civil rights movement have left an indelible mark on future generations. Through her empowering of alien youth, promotion of intersectionality and inclusivity, advocacy for legal reforms, inspiration of grassroots movements, and cultivation of empathy and understanding, Talin continues to shape the fight for justice and equality.

Her legacy serves as a reminder that change is possible, even in the face of great adversity. Talin's impact on Xyorathian society and beyond is a testament to the power of individual voices united in a common cause. As future generations carry forward the torch of justice, they do so with the knowledge that they stand on the shoulders of a true hero, Talin Iryn. In her memory, they continue the fight for a world where all beings are treated with dignity, respect, and equality.

Challenges and Setbacks

Backlash from Conservative Forces

Throughout Talin Iryn's fight for alien rights and the overturning of the multi-tentacle marriage restrictions on Xyorath, she faced fierce backlash from conservative forces who vehemently opposed any change to traditional norms. These opposition forces, consisting of individuals, groups, and political entities, presented numerous challenges to the advancement of equality and justice. In this section, we will explore the various forms of backlash faced by Talin and her fellow activists, as well as the strategies they employed to overcome these obstacles.

Threats and Intimidation

One of the most prevalent forms of backlash was the use of threats and intimidation tactics by conservative forces. Talin and her allies experienced harassment, slander, and even physical attacks from those who viewed their activism as a threat to their deeply ingrained beliefs and cultural traditions. This type of opposition aimed to silence and discourage the activists, creating an atmosphere of fear and anxiety. However, Talin and her colleagues refused to be deterred by these acts of intimidation and instead used them as fuel to ignite their determination and resilience.

Disinformation Campaigns

Conservative forces also launched disinformation campaigns to undermine Talin's credibility and the validity of the alien rights movement. They spread false narratives, distorted facts, and manipulated public opinion through various media channels. These campaigns aimed to discredit and delegitimize the activists, sowing doubt and confusion among the general populace. To counteract this disinformation, Talin understood the importance of maintaining transparency and constantly reaffirming the goals and values of the movement. Through open dialogue, community engagement, and accurate information dissemination, she worked tirelessly to reclaim the narrative and provide clarity amidst the sea of falsehoods.

Legal Obstacles

Another significant form of backlash came in the form of legal obstacles designed to impede progress and maintain the status quo. Conservative forces utilized the existing legal system to challenge Talin's efforts, filing lawsuits and lobbying for restrictive legislation. They sought to restrict the rights and freedoms of aliens, making it increasingly difficult to challenge discriminatory practices. In response, Talin and her legal team strategized and developed innovative legal arguments, leveraging constitutional rights and international human rights standards to counter these challenges. This approach helped shift the narrative from one of defiance to one of defending fundamental human rights.

Political Roadblocks

Conservative forces also exerted influence within the political realm, creating roadblocks and barriers to impede the advancement of alien rights. They used their positions of power to prevent legislation from moving forward, block funding for initiatives, and maintain the political status quo. Talin recognized the need to engage in political advocacy and lobbying efforts to counteract these roadblocks effectively. She collaborated with like-minded politicians, formed alliances with progressive organizations, and mobilized public support to put pressure on elected officials. Through tireless perseverance, she and her allies were able to secure incremental political victories, slowly dismantling the barriers erected by conservative forces.

Community Polarization

Polarization within the Xyorathian society was another significant consequence of the backlash from conservative forces. Through their vocal opposition, they stoked fear and prejudice, creating an "us versus them" mentality. This further exacerbated societal divisions and hindered progress towards equality. Talin recognized the need to bridge these divides and foster empathy and understanding among different factions of society. She organized community dialogues, facilitated workshops, and initiated cultural exchanges to promote dialogue and reconciliation. By humanizing the plight of aliens and challenging prejudice, Talin aimed to break down the barriers that conservative forces had erected.

Empowering the Youth

In the face of conservative backlash, Talin saw the importance of empowering the next generation of activists. She understood that by nurturing young minds and providing them with the tools to challenge discriminatory practices, she could provide continuity for the movement. Talin established educational programs, mentorship initiatives, and youth-led advocacy campaigns to cultivate a sense of social responsibility and justice among the youth. By harnessing their energy and idealism, she ensured that the fight for alien rights would continue long after her own battles were won.

Reframing the Narrative

Amidst conservative backlash, Talin and her fellow activists recognized the importance of reframing the narrative to shift public opinion. They made a concerted effort to challenge stereotypes, humanize aliens, and create a counter-narrative that emphasized equality and justice. Through storytelling, art, and media campaigns, they aimed to dismantle the prejudices perpetuated by conservative forces. Talin understood that by highlighting shared values and shared experiences, she could create common ground and foster empathy, thus dismantling the barriers erected by conservative forces.

In the face of the backlash from conservative forces, Talin Iryn remained resolute in her pursuit of equality and justice for the alien community on Xyorath. By confronting threats and intimidation, countering disinformation campaigns, overcoming legal and political obstacles, bridging societal divides, empowering the youth, and reframing the narrative, Talin and her allies were able to navigate the storm of conservative resistance. Through their tenacity and unwavering commitment to their cause, they laid the groundwork for a more inclusive and equitable Xyorathian society.

Maintaining Momentum and Energy

In the fight for alien rights, maintaining momentum and energy is crucial for sustaining long-term activism. Talin Iryn understood the importance of keeping the movement alive and vibrant, even in the face of challenges and setbacks. This section will explore some strategies and tactics that Talin and the Xyorathian activists utilized to maintain momentum and energy in their pursuit of equality and justice.

1. Building a Supportive Community

One of the key aspects of maintaining momentum and energy is creating a strong and supportive community. Talin recognized the importance of building connections and fostering solidarity amongst fellow activists. By establishing organizations and networks, they were able to share resources, exchange ideas, and provide emotional support to one another.

Talin encouraged group meetings, both in-person and virtual, where activists could come together to discuss their progress, brainstorm new strategies, and share updates. These gatherings served as a source of motivation and inspiration, reminding everyone involved of the collective strength of their movement.

To further strengthen the sense of community, Talin also organized social events and cultural celebrations. These gatherings provided an opportunity for activists to interact in a relaxed and enjoyable setting, fostering a sense of camaraderie and belonging. Additionally, they invited guest speakers from other civil rights movements to share their experiences and insights, promoting collaboration and cross-movement solidarity.

2. Effective Communication and Outreach

Effective communication and outreach played a crucial role in maintaining momentum and energizing the movement. Talin understood that in order to keep the public engaged and supportive, they needed to effectively communicate their message and goals.

Talin and the Xyorathian activists utilized various communication channels to reach a wide audience. They held press conferences and press releases, ensuring that their voice was heard in the media. Talin also engaged with journalists and gave interviews to amplify the message and raise awareness about the issues they were tackling.

In addition to traditional media, Talin recognized the power of social media and online platforms in mobilizing support. They utilized social media platforms to share stories, updates, and calls to action, encouraging followers to get involved and stay engaged. This digital presence allowed them to reach a global audience and connect with individuals who shared their passion for equality.

Furthermore, Talin and the activists organized outreach programs to educate the public about the importance of alien rights. They conducted workshops, seminars, and public speaking engagements to spread awareness and counter misinformation. By fostering understanding and empathy, they aimed to build a broader base of support for their cause.

3. Wellness and Self-Care

Activism can be physically and emotionally draining, making it essential to prioritize wellness and self-care. Talin emphasized the importance of taking care of oneself and maintaining personal well-being amidst the demands of the movement.

They encouraged activists to establish self-care routines that included activities such as exercise, meditation, and therapy. Talin recognized that taking breaks and nurturing one's mental and physical health were crucial for maintaining resilience and sustained activism.

To address burnout and exhaustion, Talin and the activists organized wellness retreats and self-care workshops. These events provided a space for individuals to recharge, reflect, and connect with nature. They incorporated various mindfulness practices and healing modalities, ensuring that activists had the tools and resources to sustain themselves in the long run.

4. Celebrating Milestones and Successes

Celebrating milestones and successes served as a way to recognize achievements and maintain motivation within the movement. Talin understood the importance of acknowledging progress and milestones, no matter how small, as a way to fuel continued momentum.

They organized public events and gatherings to commemorate significant victories and milestones. These celebrations allowed activists and supporters to come together, reflect on their accomplishments, and renew their commitment to the cause. They celebrated with music, dance, and storytelling, reminding everyone of the joy and power of collective action.

Talin also used these occasions to express gratitude and appreciation to the activists and allies who had contributed to the movement's success. By highlighting individual efforts and contributions, Talin nurtured a sense of belonging and purpose within the movement.

5. Empowering Future Generations

Talin understood that maintaining momentum and energy for the long-term required investing in and empowering future generations. They recognized the importance of passing on knowledge, skills, and values to the next wave of activists.

To achieve this, Talin and the Xyorathian activists established mentorship programs and leadership development initiatives. They paired experienced activists with aspiring ones, providing guidance, support, and opportunities for growth. These mentorship relationships fostered intergenerational learning, ensuring a continuous flow of ideas, strategies, and passion.

Additionally, Talin and the activists worked to incorporate alien rights education into school curriculums. They collaborated with educators and policymakers to develop age-appropriate material that promoted empathy, inclusivity, and social responsibility. By empowering young minds with knowledge and awareness, they were cultivating a future generation of advocates for equality and justice.

Conclusion

Maintaining momentum and energy is essential in any activism movement, and Talin Iryn recognized this in their fight for alien rights on Xyorath. By building a supportive community, utilizing effective communication and outreach, emphasizing wellness and self-care, celebrating milestones and successes, and empowering future generations, Talin and the Xyorathian activists were able to sustain their momentum and continue fighting for equality and justice. These strategies serve as an inspiration for activists around the galaxy, proving that sustained resistance is possible even in the face of adversity. The fight for justice is never-ending, but with the right strategies and unwavering determination, it is a fight worth undertaking.

Navigating Internal Divisions and Differences

In the fight for alien rights and equality on Xyorath, Talin Iryn faced not only external opposition but also internal divisions and differences within the movement itself. The journey to achieve justice and social change was not always smooth sailing, and it was essential for Talin to navigate these challenges effectively. This section explores the complexities of dealing with internal divisions and differences, the strategies employed to overcome them, and the lasting impact it had on the movement.

Understanding the Root Causes

Internal divisions and differences can arise from various factors, such as differing ideologies, personal agendas, disagreements over strategies, and power struggles. It is crucial to recognize that diversity of opinion and perspectives can be a strength, but if not handled properly, it can weaken the movement and hinder progress. Talin understood the importance of addressing these conflicts and finding common ground to keep the movement focused and united.

Building Inclusive Spaces

One of the strategies Talin employed to navigate internal divisions was to create inclusive spaces within the movement. By fostering an environment where everyone's voices were heard and respected, Talin encouraged collaboration and cooperation. Inclusive spaces allowed for open discussions, constructive debates, and the exploration of different perspectives, ultimately leading to more informed decisions and stronger bonds within the movement.

Mediation and Conflict Resolution

When conflicts arose within the movement, Talin utilized mediation techniques and conflict resolution strategies to facilitate dialogue and find mutually agreeable solutions. Mediation involved bringing conflicting parties together to engage in respectful conversation, identify common objectives, and work towards a compromise.   Talin recognized that by addressing conflicts promptly and proactively, internal divisions could be minimized, and the movement could stay on track towards its goals.

Leadership and Collaboration

Strong leadership skills were crucial in navigating internal divisions and differences. Talin led by example, demonstrating empathy, patience, and a willingness to listen to differing perspectives. By fostering a sense of teamwork and collaboration, Talin empowered individuals within the movement to contribute their ideas and talents, thereby mitigating internal conflicts. The emphasis on collective decision-making and shared ownership played a pivotal role in overcoming divisions and fostering a united front.

Addressing Power Dynamics

Power dynamics can often be at the root of internal divisions within movements. Talin recognized the importance of addressing power imbalances and ensuring that the movement remains inclusive and equitable. This involved actively addressing privilege and uplifting marginalized voices within the movement. By challenging traditional hierarchies and distributing power more evenly, Talin fostered a sense of ownership and investment among all members, reducing internal divisions caused by power struggles.

Lessons Learned

Navigating internal divisions and differences was not without its challenges, but the experiences offered valuable lessons for Talin and the movement.   Some important lessons learned include the need for ongoing communication, creating mechanisms for constructive feedback, embracing diversity as a strength, and being open to adapt strategies when necessary. Talin's approach to addressing internal divisions provided a roadmap for future alien rights activists, emphasizing the significance of unity, collaboration, and inclusivity in creating lasting change.

Examining Case Studies

To illustrate the practical challenges and strategies employed to navigate internal divisions and differences, it is helpful to examine real-life case studies.   By examining specific instances of internal conflicts and the subsequent resolutions, readers can gain a deeper understanding of the complexities and potential solutions to such challenges. This section includes a collection of case studies that shed light on various internal divisions encountered in the movement and how they were successfully addressed.

Challenges of Maintaining Unity

Navigating internal divisions and differences is an ongoing challenge that requires continuous effort and vigilance. External forces can also exploit these internal divisions, attempting to weaken the movement's resolve and derail its progress. The section explores the challenges faced by Talin and the movement in maintaining unity while facing both internal and external pressures. By anticipating and addressing these challenges head-on, Talin paved the way for continued resilience and collective strength within the alien rights movement.

Conclusion

Navigating internal divisions and differences was a crucial aspect of the fight for alien rights on Xyorath. Talin Iryn's ability to effectively address these challenges played a pivotal role in the success and longevity of the movement. By fostering inclusive spaces, utilizing mediation and conflict resolution strategies, embracing collaborative leadership, addressing power dynamics, and learning from experiences, Talin demonstrated the importance of internal unity in achieving lasting social change. The lessons learned from navigating internal divisions continue to resonate with future alien rights activists, inspiring them to create inclusive movements that prioritize collective goals over personal differences.

Strategies for Sustained Resistance

In the fight for alien civil rights, sustaining resistance is key to achieving long-term change. It requires strategic planning, resilience, and adaptability. In this section, we will explore various strategies that Talin Iryn and her fellow activists employed to sustain their resistance against discrimination and oppression on Xyorath.

Building Coalitions and Alliances

Collaboration and building alliances with other civil rights movements were crucial to sustaining the resistance movement on Xyorath. Talin Iryn recognized the power in joining forces with other marginalized communities to amplify their collective voices and create a stronger, more unified front against discrimination.

One strategy employed by Talin was to actively seek out partnerships and coalitions with organizations and activists who shared a common goal of fighting for equality. This involved reaching out to leaders and members of other civil rights movements, attending conferences and events, and finding ways to contribute and support their causes.

By forming alliances, the resistance movement gained access to a wider network of resources, expertise, and experiences. It allowed them to share strategies, learn from each other's successes and failures, and collaborate on advocacy campaigns. Together, these coalitions created a powerful force that challenged discriminatory policies and pushed for systemic change.

Creating Awareness through Education

Education played a critical role in sustaining the resistance movement. Talin and her fellow activists prioritized the dissemination of accurate information and knowledge about alien rights, discrimination, and the impact of discriminatory laws.

One strategy they employed was to establish educational programs and workshops that focused on raising awareness and promoting understanding. These programs were designed to engage both alien and non-alien communities, fostering empathy and challenging misconceptions.

For example, workshops were organized to address the stereotypes and prejudices associated with multi-tentacle marriages. They would invite experts, scholars, and individuals from the community who could share personal experiences, research findings, and historical context. These workshops aimed to dismantle discriminatory narratives and foster a more inclusive understanding of love, relationships, and cultural diversity.

In addition to workshops, Talin and her colleagues utilized various media platforms to reach a wider audience. They published articles, op-eds, and pamphlets that challenged discriminatory beliefs, provided accurate information, and raised awareness about the plight of alien communities. These educational efforts helped to create a more informed and empathetic society, which was crucial for sustaining the resistance movement.

Legal Advocacy and Grassroots Organizing

Legal advocacy and grassroots organizing were key strategies employed by Talin Iryn to sustain the resistance movement. While legal battles were fought in the courtrooms, grassroots organizing ensured that the movement had a strong foundation of support from the community.

Talin and her team understood the importance of engaging the local communities in their fight for equality. They organized rallies, protests, and demonstrations to mobilize public support and create a visible presence. These actions not only drew attention to the cause but also empowered individuals within the community to take ownership of the movement.

At the same time, legal advocacy played a vital role in challenging discriminatory laws and policies. Talin and her team collaborated with legal experts, assembling a strong legal team to strategize and navigate the complex legal landscape. They filed lawsuits, supported legal challenges, and actively participated in shaping legislation to remove barriers to equality.

Grassroots organizing and legal advocacy worked hand in hand, creating a powerful synergy. Grassroots movements brought momentum, visibility, and public support, while legal advocacy provided the means to challenge discriminatory policies and create lasting change. This two-pronged approach helped sustain the resistance movement and ensure that progress continued even in the face of setbacks and challenges.

Resilience and Self-Care

Sustaining resistance can take a toll on activists both emotionally and physically. Recognizing the importance of self-care and building resilience was a crucial strategy employed by Talin Iryn and her fellow activists.

They created spaces for self-reflection, healing, and support within the movement. This included organizing support groups, creating peer networks, and establishing mental health resources. These initiatives aimed to strengthen the well-being of activists, allowing them to recharge, process their experiences, and continue their work with renewed energy.

Additionally, Talin and her colleagues practiced self-care on an individual level. They emphasized the importance of establishing boundaries, practicing mindfulness, and engaging in activities that brought joy and relaxation. This approach ensured that activists would be able to sustain their commitment for the long haul, even in the face of adversity.

Challenging Power Structures

One unconventional yet effective strategy employed by Talin was to challenge power structures directly. She recognized that systemic change required not only addressing discriminatory laws but also dismantling the power dynamics that perpetuated inequality.

To challenge power structures, Talin and her fellow activists organized campaigns that targeted institutions, corporations, and policymakers who upheld discriminatory practices. They strategically identified key decision-makers and influencers within these institutions and launched sustained advocacy efforts to pressure them into taking meaningful action for equality.

For example, they would organize protests outside government buildings, stage sit-ins at corporate headquarters, and utilize social media to call out institutions that were complicit in perpetuating discrimination. By shining a spotlight on these power structures, they applied pressure and forced them to reckon with their complicity, ultimately leading to policy reforms and changes within these institutions.

Challenging power structures required careful planning and execution. Talin and her team understood the importance of garnering public support, building public pressure, and leveraging the media to amplify their message. It was through these sustained efforts that they were able to make significant strides in dismantling the discriminatory power structures that hindered equality and justice.

Conclusion: Persistence and Courage

Sustained resistance requires persistence, courage, and a deep commitment to justice. Talin Iryn and her fellow activists demonstrated the power of strategic planning, coalition-building, education, grassroots organizing, resilience, and challenging power structures. These strategies helped them navigate the challenges, setbacks, and opposition they faced on their journey towards equality.

Their legacy serves as a reminder that sustained resistance is not only possible but essential for achieving lasting change. As we continue to fight for justice and equality in our own communities, we can draw inspiration from the strategies employed by Talin Iryn and her fellow activists. Together, we can create a more inclusive and equitable world for all.

Coping with Burnout and Emotional Toll

In the fight for justice and equality, activists like Talin Iryn often face immense challenges, both externally and internally. Coping with burnout and the emotional toll of advocacy work is crucial for sustaining the fight in the long run. In this section, we will explore strategies and techniques to navigate the emotional challenges that arise in the pursuit of social change.

Understanding Burnout

Burnout is a state of physical, mental, and emotional exhaustion that results from chronic stress and overwork. Activists like Talin Iryn, who dedicate themselves to challenging societal norms and fighting discrimination, are particularly susceptible to burnout due to the emotional intensity of their work. It is essential to recognize the signs and symptoms of burnout, such as constant fatigue, cynicism, and a decreased sense of personal accomplishment.

Self-Care and Wellness

One of the most effective ways to cope with burnout is to prioritize self-care and well-being. Activists often neglect themselves in the pursuit of justice, but it is crucial to remember that taking care of oneself is not selfish; it is essential for being able to continue the fight. Here are some strategies for self-care:

+ **Physical Well-being:** Engage in regular exercise, maintain a healthy diet, and ensure an adequate amount of sleep. Physical activity helps reduce stress and promotes mental well-being.

+ **Emotional Support:** Seek emotional support from friends, family, or support groups. Sharing experiences, concerns, and triumphs with others who understand the challenges can be incredibly validating and uplifting.

+ **Creative Outlets:** Engage in activities that bring joy and fulfillment, such as painting, writing, or playing an instrument. These creative outlets provide an escape from the intensity of activism and allow for self-expression.

+ **Mindfulness and Meditation:** Practice mindfulness and meditation techniques to cultivate inner peace and mental clarity. These practices help manage stress, increase self-awareness, and promote overall well-being.

Setting Boundaries

Advocacy work can be all-consuming, blurring the lines between personal life and activism. Setting boundaries is essential to prevent burnout and maintain a healthy work-life balance. Here are some tips for setting boundaries:

+ **Prioritize Self-Care:** Make self-care non-negotiable by dedicating specific time each day or week for activities that bring you joy and relaxation. Remember that you deserve to recharge and take care of yourself.

- **Establish Clear Working Hours:** Create a schedule that allows for focused activism work during designated hours. Outside of those hours, allow yourself time to rest and engage in non-work-related activities.

- **Learn to Say No:** It's important to recognize your limits and not overcommit yourself. Saying no to additional projects or responsibilities that stretch you too thin allows you to preserve your energy and focus on the priorities that matter most.

- **Delegate and Collaborate:** Don't be afraid to seek help and share responsibilities with trusted allies and supporters. Collaboration allows for shared workload and prevents burnout due to an overwhelming sense of responsibility.

Emotional Resilience

Building emotional resilience is essential for navigating the emotional toll of activism. Here are strategies to cultivate emotional resilience:

- **Self-Reflection and Emotional Awareness:** Developing emotional intelligence can help you understand and manage your emotions effectively. Regular self-reflection allows you to identify triggers, cope with difficult emotions, and prevent emotional exhaustion.

- **Finding Supportive Communities:** Surround yourself with like-minded individuals who share your passion for justice and equality. Participate in activist groups, support networks, or online communities that offer understanding, encouragement, and solidarity.

- **Seek Professional Help:** If necessary, do not hesitate to seek therapy or counseling to address any mental health issues that may arise from the emotional toll of activism. Mental health professionals can provide valuable tools and support to navigate challenges effectively.

- **Celebrating Small Victories:** Recognize and celebrate the progress made, no matter how small. Acknowledging victories, however small, helps to maintain motivation and resilience in the face of adversity.

- **Practicing Gratitude:** Cultivating an attitude of gratitude can significantly impact mental well-being. Regularly reflect on the positive aspects of activism work, such as making a difference in people's lives or inspiring others to join the cause.

Renewal and Replenishment

In addition to coping with burnout and emotional toll through self-care, it is essential to find moments of renewal and replenishment. Engaging in activities that rejuvenate the mind, body, and spirit can provide a much-needed reprieve. Here are some suggestions:

- **Nature Connection:** Spend time in nature, whether it's going for hikes, engaging in gardening, or simply sitting in a park. Connecting with the natural world can help restore a sense of peace and balance.

- **Meaningful Relationships:** Nurture relationships with loved ones who provide support and understanding. Surrounding yourself with people who uplift and inspire you can have a profound impact on your emotional well-being.

- **Escaping and Recharging:** Take breaks from activism to engage in activities that bring you joy, whether it's reading a book, watching a movie, or taking a vacation. Allowing yourself time to disconnect and recharge helps prevent burnout.

- **Reflection and Introspection:** Set aside regular time for reflection, journaling, or meditation. These practices allow for self-discovery, introspection, and personal growth, providing the necessary space for renewal.

Unconventional Tip: Laughter Therapy

Laughter is often the best medicine during challenging times. Incorporating laughter therapy into your coping strategies can help alleviate stress and boost mood. Consider engaging in activities that promote laughter, such as watching a comedy show, sharing funny stories with friends, or even attending laughter yoga sessions. Laughter releases endorphins, reduces tension, and enhances overall well-being, providing a much-needed respite from the emotional toll of activism.

Dealing with burnout and the emotional toll of activism requires a multi-faceted approach that integrates self-care, boundary-setting, emotional resilience, and renewal. By implementing these strategies, activists like Talin Iryn can navigate the challenges they face, sustain their fight for justice, and create lasting change in society. Remember, taking care of yourself is not only essential for your well-being, but it is also crucial for the movement you are fighting for.

Lessons in Leadership and Coalition Building

In the fight for alien rights and social justice, effective leadership and coalition building are essential. Talin Iryn's journey provides valuable lessons in these areas, offering guidance to future activists and leaders. This section explores key principles and strategies for successful leadership and coalition building.

Building Trust and Solidarity

Principle: Building trust and solidarity is vital for effective leadership and coalition building.

    Explanation: To lead a diverse group of individuals and organizations, it is crucial to establish trust and solidarity. Talin Iryn recognized the importance of creating a sense of shared purpose and fostering relationships built on trust.

    Example: Talin invested time in getting to know individuals and their experiences, listening to their concerns, and acknowledging their contributions. This created a foundation of trust and solidarity, enabling effective collaboration and support.

    Resource: "Building Trust in Diverse Teams" by Patrice Douglas is a practical guide for leaders seeking strategies to build trust in diverse environments.

    Trick: Holding regular team-building activities, such as retreats or social events, can help strengthen relationships and foster a sense of solidarity among coalition members.

Effective Communication

Principle: Effective communication is a fundamental skill for successful leadership and coalition building.

    Explanation: Clear and open communication is crucial for ensuring that all coalition members are aligned with the goals, strategies, and progress of the movement. Talin understood the power of effective communication in building consensus and conveying key messages.

    Example: Talin implemented regular meetings, both formal and informal, to update coalition members on progress, share insights, and address concerns. This allowed everyone to stay informed and engaged in the movement.

    Resource: "Everyone Communicates, Few Connect" by John C. Maxwell is a helpful resource for developing effective communication skills, emphasizing the importance of connecting with others on a deeper level.

Trick: Utilizing a variety of communication channels, such as email, social media platforms, and video conferences, can help reach a wider audience and ensure that information is disseminated efficiently.

Inclusive Decision-Making

Principle: Inclusive decision-making leads to stronger leadership and coalition building.

Explanation: Inclusion empowers individuals and organizations, ensuring that diverse perspectives are considered in the decision-making process. Talin recognized that a collective approach to decision-making promotes engagement and ownership among coalition members.

Example: Talin established regular forums for coalition members to voice their opinions, share ideas, and contribute to strategy development. This encouraged active participation and fostered a sense of ownership in the movement's direction.

Resource: "The Culture Map" by Erin Meyer explores the challenges and strategies of inclusive decision-making in diverse cultural contexts.

Trick: Utilizing technology tools, such as online surveys or platforms for virtual brainstorming, can facilitate inclusive decision-making, particularly in large or geographically dispersed coalitions.

Conflict Resolution

Principle: Effective leadership requires skillful conflict resolution within coalitions.

Explanation: Conflicts are inevitable in diverse and passionate coalitions. Talin understood the importance of addressing conflicts promptly and constructively, ensuring that they did not undermine the movement's goals.

Example: Talin facilitated open dialogues where differences could be expressed and understood. By creating a safe space for conflicts to be addressed, resolutions were reached that satisfied the interests of multiple coalition members.

Resource: "Difficult Conversations: How to Discuss What Matters Most" by Douglas Stone, Bruce Patton, and Sheila Heen provides practical guidance for navigating challenging conversations and resolving conflicts.

Trick: Mediation by a neutral third party can be an effective method for resolving conflicts and facilitating constructive dialogue, allowing coalition members to move forward together.

Empowering Others

Principle: Empowering others fosters leadership development within coalitions.

Explanation: Effective leaders empower others by delegating responsibilities, providing opportunities for skill development, and promoting growth within the coalition. Talin recognized that nurturing leadership in others strengthens the movement as a whole.

Example: Talin encouraged coalition members to take on leadership roles in specific initiatives, offering mentorship and support. This empowered individuals to develop their skills and contribute to the movement's success.

Resource: "The Empowered Manager: Positive Political Skills at Work" by Peter Block offers insights into empowering others and fostering leadership within organizations.

Trick: Implementing a mentorship program within the coalition allows experienced leaders to guide and support emerging activists, fostering their growth and development.

Unconventional Wisdom: The Power of Play

Principle: Incorporating play and creativity into coalition building fosters engagement and innovation.

Explanation: Traditional approaches to activism can be demanding and draining. Talin recognized the importance of incorporating play and creativity to maintain the momentum of the movement and inspire collective action.

Example: Talin organized interactive workshops, artistic collaborations, and community events that celebrated the diversity of coalition members. These activities provided space for coalition members to recharge, connect, and explore new ideas.

Resource: "Play: How it Shapes the Brain, Opens the Imagination, and Invigorates the Soul" by Stuart Brown highlights the benefits of incorporating play in various aspects of life, including coalition building.

Trick: Creating a shared playlist or encouraging coalition members to share their favorite songs can create a sense of community and boost morale during challenging times.

Leadership and coalition building are ongoing processes that require continuous learning and adaptation. Talin Iryn's journey provides valuable insights into these aspects, reminding us that effective leadership and collective action are essential for driving significant social change. By applying the principles and strategies outlined in this section, future activists can build strong coalitions, amplify their impact, and pave the way for a more just and inclusive society.

Adapting to Changing Political Landscapes

In the ever-evolving world of politics, successful activists must learn to adapt to changing political landscapes. This requires a keen understanding of political systems, strategic thinking, and the ability to navigate complex power dynamics. In this section, we will explore how Talin Iryn, the courageous alien civil rights activist, successfully adapted to the changing political environment on Xyorath.

Understanding the Political Landscape

To effectively advocate for change, it is crucial to comprehend the political terrain. Talin Iryn recognized the importance of understanding the various branches of government, the key players, and the decision-making processes. They researched Xyorath's political system, studying its legislative bodies, executive branches, and judiciary to identify the levers of power. Talin's insightful analysis allowed them to discern where their advocacy efforts would yield the most significant impact.

In addition to understanding the formal structures of power, Talin also recognized the importance of grassroots movements and public opinion. They closely followed public sentiment, conducting surveys and engaging with community members to gauge support for their cause. By staying attuned to the changing political climate both within and beyond the corridors of power, Talin was able to adapt their strategies effectively.

Strategic Alliances and Coalitions

Adapting to changing political landscapes often requires forming strategic alliances and coalitions. Talin Iryn understood that collaborating with like-minded individuals and organizations would amplify their advocacy efforts. They actively sought out partnerships with other civil rights movements, recognizing the interconnectedness of various marginalized communities.

By collaborating with human rights organizations, environmental activists, and progressive politicians, Talin was able to tap into existing networks and gain access to resources and expertise. These alliances allowed them to pool their collective power and influence, increasing the likelihood of success in navigating the ever-changing political landscape.

Flexibility and Pragmatism

In the face of rapidly changing political circumstances, flexibility and pragmatism are essential qualities for an effective activist. Talin Iryn knew that rigid adherence to a single approach or goal could limit their ability to achieve significant change.

They recognized that incremental progress was often necessary to pave the way for more significant transformations. Instead of solely focusing on immediate policy changes, Talin employed a multi-pronged approach. This included advocating for small reforms, raising awareness through media campaigns, and engaging in public demonstrations to maintain pressure on the political establishment.

Talin also acknowledged that compromise was sometimes necessary to achieve long-term goals. They skillfully negotiated with lawmakers, finding common ground where possible while staying firm on core principles. This adaptability allowed them to navigate the complexities of the political landscape and make strides towards their ultimate objective of equality.

Engaging with New Technology

As political landscapes change, technology continues to evolve, offering new tools and methods of communication. Talin Iryn embraced emerging technologies to expand their reach and engage with supporters. They leveraged social media platforms, creating viral campaigns to raise awareness and mobilize public opinion.

Talin also recognized the power of data analysis in shaping political strategies. They utilized sophisticated software to analyze public sentiment, identify areas of resistance, and tailor their advocacy efforts accordingly. By embracing technological advancements, Talin enhanced their ability to adapt to rapidly changing political landscapes.

Inclusive and Progressive Policies

Adapting to changing political landscapes requires ongoing assessment and adjustment of policy priorities. Talin Iryn continued to push for inclusive and progressive policies that addressed not only the immediate needs of alien communities but also the broader issues of social justice.

They recognized the intersectionality of discrimination and actively advocated for policies that went beyond the scope of multi-tentacle marriage restrictions. Talin championed equal employment opportunities, access to healthcare and education, and the elimination of housing and segregation policies that perpetuated inequality.

By expanding the scope of their activism, Talin ensured that their movement remained relevant and resilient in the face of changing political landscapes.

Cultivating Future Leaders

One of the most important strategies for adapting to changing political landscapes is cultivating the next generation of activists and leaders. Talin Iryn understood the importance of passing on knowledge, skills, and experiences to ensure the continuity of the movement.

They established mentorship programs, empowering young activists to shape the future of the alien rights movement. Talin provided guidance and resources, fostering an environment of collaboration and innovation. By nurturing emerging leaders, Talin ensured the ongoing adaptation and evolution of the movement in response to changing political dynamics.

Conclusion

The ability to adapt to changing political landscapes is a crucial skill for any activist. Talin Iryn's success in navigating Xyorath's political system can be attributed to their understanding of the political landscape, strategic alliances, flexibility, engagement with technology, focus on progressive policies, and cultivation of future leaders.

Their journey serves as a testament to the importance of adaptability and resilience in the face of ever-changing political circumstances. By applying these lessons to their own advocacy efforts, future activists can continue the fight for justice and equality, ensuring that the legacy of Talin Iryn lives on.

Evolving Tactics and Strategies

In the ever-changing landscape of alien rights activism, Talin Iryn was at the forefront of adapting tactics and strategies to effectively fight for equality and justice. This section explores how their approach evolved over time, taking into account the challenges they faced and the lessons they learned along the way.

Understanding the Power of Media

One of the key tactics that Talin embraced was leveraging the power of media to spread awareness and shape public opinion. They understood that storytelling was a powerful tool for empathy and connection, allowing people to see the humanity behind the struggle for alien rights.

Talin worked closely with local and national media outlets, sharing personal stories, testimonies, and accounts of discrimination faced by the Xyorathian community. Through interviews, articles, and documentaries, they brought the issue of multi-tentacle marriage restrictions to the mainstream, challenging conventional societal norms and biases.

To further amplify their message, Talin also utilized social media platforms to engage directly with supporters and adversaries alike. Through carefully crafted messages and campaigns, they encouraged online conversations, debunked misinformation, and mobilized their followers to take action. This strategic use of social media helped foster a sense of community and encouraged solidarity among different alien communities fighting for equal rights.

Coalition Building and Intersectionality

Talin recognized the importance of building alliances and working collaboratively with other social justice movements. They understood that the fight for alien rights was interconnected with other struggles, such as racial equality, gender rights, and LGBTQ+ rights. By joining forces, they could amplify their collective voices and create a stronger impact.

Talin actively sought partnerships with organizations and activists from diverse backgrounds, engaging in mutual learning and support. They organized joint protests, panel discussions, and conferences, creating spaces where different perspectives could intersect and together advocate for a more inclusive society.

This tactic of coalition building allowed for the sharing of resources, knowledge, and strategies. Through collaboration, activists from various movements could leverage their respective strengths and challenge systemic discrimination on multiple fronts. Talin's ability to forge these alliances was instrumental in advancing the cause of alien rights and paving the way for intersectional advocacy.

Strategic Litigation and Public Demonstrations

Talin realized the importance of strategic litigation as a means to challenge discriminatory laws and policies. They assembled a team of skilled lawyers who specialized in alien rights, ensuring that their legal battles were fought from a well-informed and well-prepared standpoint.

Legal cases brought by Talin not only aimed to overturn specific discriminatory laws but also to set legal precedents that would benefit not only the Xyorathian community but also other alien and marginalized communities. They strategically selected cases that would have broad-reaching implications, ensuring they were fighting not just for individual rights but for systemic change.

In tandem with litigation, public demonstrations played a crucial role in drawing attention to the cause and putting pressure on policymakers. Talin organized peaceful protests, marches, and sit-ins, ensuring they remained peaceful and respectful while making a powerful visual impact. These displays of unity and determination not only galvanized supporters but also brought awareness and legitimacy to the fight for equal rights.

Community Engagement and Grassroots Advocacy

Talin believed that lasting change must come from the ground up, and thus, grassroots advocacy played a pivotal role in their strategy. They actively engaged with the Xyorathian community, organizing town hall meetings, workshops, and awareness campaigns. By empowering community members with knowledge about their rights and encouraging their active participation, Talin built a strong support base that was invested in the cause.

Additionally, Talin focused on mentoring and developing emerging leaders within the Xyorathian community. They facilitated leadership training programs and provided resources to equip future generations with the skills necessary to continue the fight for equality and justice.

Recognizing the power of storytelling, Talin encouraged community members to share their personal experiences, creating platforms for their voices to be heard. This grassroots approach ensured that the alien rights movement was not solely led by Talin but represented a collective effort and a shared sense of purpose.

Maintaining Resilience and Self-Care

As the fight for equal rights demanded perseverance and resilience, Talin emphasized the importance of self-care among activists. They recognized that burnout could undermine the movement's effectiveness and created spaces for healing, rest, and rejuvenation.

Talin encouraged activists to engage in practices that replenished their energy, such as meditation, community-building activities, and therapy. They organized retreats and self-care workshops, providing tools and resources for emotional well-being. This emphasis on self-care helped sustain the movement's momentum and prevented activists from succumbing to exhaustion or disillusionment.

Furthermore, Talin understood that self-care extended beyond individual well-being. They advocated for policies and practices that promoted work-life balance and supported the mental health of all individuals, regardless of their backgrounds or abilities. By prioritizing the collective well-being of the alien rights movement, Talin ensured that the fight for justice remained strong and resilient.

Thinking Outside the Box

In addition to more traditional tactics, Talin also embraced innovative and unconventional approaches to further their cause. They recognized that sometimes traditional methods might not be effective in generating the desired results, especially when faced with entrenched systems and stubborn opposition.

Talin encouraged activists to think outside the box and explore creative ways to challenge discrimination. This included organizing art exhibitions, performing arts events, and other cultural initiatives that aimed to change hearts and minds through the power of creativity. By leveraging art and culture as tools for advocacy, Talin unlocked new channels for dialogue and engagement.

Moreover, Talin utilized technology to their advantage, embracing online platforms and digital tools to organize virtual protests, webinars, and educational campaigns. This allowed for broader reach, connecting with individuals beyond physical boundaries and engaging a global audience in the fight for alien rights.

Conclusion: A Dynamic Approach to Activism

Talin's evolving tactics and strategies exemplify a dynamic, adaptable approach to activism. They recognized the need to constantly assess and adapt their methods in response to shifting societal, political, and technological landscapes.

From harnessing the power of media and building alliances to strategic litigation and grassroots advocacy, Talin employed a diverse range of tactics to fight for alien rights. Their commitment to intersectionality, self-care, and innovation ensured the movement's resilience and contributed to lasting change.

Their legacy serves as a reminder that the fight for justice is an ongoing journey, requiring continuous evolution and adaptation. The lessons learned from Talin's tireless activism provide a roadmap for future generations to continue the work towards equality, inclusivity, and social justice.

Long-Term Vision for Alien Rights

As Talin Iryn fought tirelessly for the rights of aliens on Xyorath, she envisioned a long-term vision for alien rights that went beyond the immediate victories and legal reforms. Talin believed in creating a society where every alien being, regardless of their origin or physical attributes, could fully participate and thrive.

1. Shaping Public Opinion and Changing Hearts

Talin recognized that true change starts with changing hearts and minds. She understood the importance of actively engaging with the public to foster empathy and understanding towards aliens. Talin's long-term vision for alien rights involved continued efforts to shape public opinion through education, awareness programs, and media campaigns.

She proposed initiatives to humanize aliens and build bridges of understanding between alien and human communities. These initiatives included storytelling projects, cultural exchanges, and community events that highlighted the commonalities and shared experiences of all sentient beings.

2. Intersectionality and Inclusivity

For Talin, alien rights were deeply connected to a broader framework of social justice. She believed in fighting all forms of discrimination, including racial, gender, and economic inequality. In her long-term vision, alien rights movements would champion intersectional approaches that acknowledge and address the multiple identities and experiences of individuals.

Talin advocated for inclusive policies and legislation that protected the rights of all minority groups, supporting collaboration between different civil rights movements. Her vision involved forming powerful coalitions that worked together to challenge systemic discrimination and create a society that celebrates diversity.

3. Global Advocacy and Collaboration

Aware of the interconnected nature of the universe, Talin recognized the need for global collaboration in the pursuit of alien rights. Her long-term vision included establishing international alliances and networks that worked towards universal equality and justice.

She envisioned a world where alien rights activists from different planets could come together, share their experiences, and strategize for change. Talin advocated for the creation of intergalactic forums, conferences, and summits that facilitated cross-cultural dialogue and cooperation.

4. Education, Employment, and Economic Empowerment

In her long-term vision, Talin emphasized the importance of access to quality education for aliens. She believed in creating educational systems that were welcoming and supportive of alien students, nurturing their talents and potential. She proposed mentoring programs, scholarships, and affirmative action policies that promoted equal opportunities for all.

Talin also recognized the significance of economic empowerment in achieving true equality. Her long-term vision included advocating for equal employment opportunities, fair pay, and workplace inclusivity. She encouraged policies that promoted diversity in leadership positions and endorsed employers who prioritized the rights and well-being of alien employees.

5. Environmental Justice

Talin believed in the intrinsic value of the environment and the need for its protection. She saw the fight for alien rights as inseparable from the fight for environmental justice. In her long-term vision, she envisioned alien rights movements actively advocating for sustainable practices, conservation efforts, and pollution reduction.

Talin aimed to mobilize aliens and humans alike, stressing the importance of preserving and healing the planet for future generations. She saw the environment as the common ground that transcended species or planetary boundaries and united all beings in a shared responsibility.

6. Empowering the Youth

Knowing that the fight for alien rights would continue long after her time, Talin's long-term vision involved empowering the next generation of alien rights activists. She proposed the creation of youth-led organizations, mentoring programs, and scholarships that nurtured and inspired young aliens to be changemakers in their communities.

Talin recognized that young people had fresh perspectives and innovative ideas that could drive societal change forward. She encouraged young aliens to question norms, challenge injustice, and fight for a world where every being, irrespective of their origin, could live a life of dignity and equality.

In conclusion, Talin Iryn's long-term vision for alien rights encompassed a holistic and intersectional approach. She sought to change society's perception, advocate for equal rights, foster global collaboration, empower individuals, and protect the environment. Talin believed that the fight for alien rights was deeply entwined with other social justice causes, and her vision served as a guide for future alien rights activists to continue the struggle for justice and equality.

Chapter 4: The Lasting Effects

Continued Advocacy and Activism

Establishing a Foundation for Alien Rights

In this section, we will delve into the crucial steps taken by Talin Iryn and her fellow activists in establishing a foundation for alien rights on Xyorath. These initiatives aimed to address various forms of discrimination and create lasting change in Xyorathian society. Through education, advocacy, and legislation, Talin and her allies worked tirelessly to lay the groundwork for a more inclusive and equitable society for all.

Education and Awareness Programs

One of the first and most important steps towards establishing a foundation for alien rights was through education and raising awareness. Talin recognized that changing deep-seated prejudices and societal norms required a concerted effort to enlighten the public about the experiences and contributions of alien communities on Xyorath.

To achieve this, Talin and her allies developed educational programs targeted at schools, community centers, and even workplaces. These programs aimed to dispel myths and misconceptions surrounding aliens, showcase their rich cultural heritage, and highlight their valuable contributions to Xyorathian society.

Through workshops, lectures, and interactive activities, they provided a platform for open dialogue, encouraging Xyorathians to ask questions and learn from their alien neighbors. These education initiatives sought to foster empathy, understanding, and acceptance among different communities, laying the groundwork for a more tolerant and inclusive society.

Legislative Reforms and Policy Changes

Another pillar in establishing a foundation for alien rights was the pursuit of legislative reforms and policy changes. Recognizing that systemic discrimination required structural transformations, Talin and her allies worked diligently to influence lawmakers and shape the legal landscape of Xyorath.

They drafted comprehensive bills that addressed various issues faced by alien communities, including employment discrimination, access to healthcare and education, and unfair housing practices. These bills aimed to provide legal protections and equal opportunities for aliens, ensuring their rights were enshrined in law.

Talin and her allies engaged in extensive lobbying efforts, reaching out to members of parliament, organizing rallies, and testifying at legislative hearings. Their unwavering determination, coupled with compelling evidence and heartfelt testimonies, helped sway the opinion of lawmakers and garner support for crucial legislative reforms.

As a result of their efforts, groundbreaking laws were enacted, prohibiting employment discrimination based on alien status, guaranteeing access to quality healthcare and education for aliens, and dismantling discriminatory housing policies. These legislative victories set a strong precedent for future alien rights advocacy and paved the way for a more just and equitable society.

Collaborating with Other Movements and Organizations

Talin and her allies recognized the power of solidarity and the need to build coalitions beyond the alien rights movement. They actively sought collaborations with other civil rights movements and organizations that shared their vision of a more inclusive society.

By establishing partnerships with groups fighting for racial equality, gender justice, and LGBTQ+ rights, they were able to amplify their collective voices and create a powerful force for change. Through joint advocacy campaigns, protests, and shared resources, they leveraged their networks to advance the cause of alien rights alongside other marginalized communities.

These collaborations not only provided a broader platform to advocate for alien rights but also fostered mutual understanding and strengthened the intersectional nature of their struggles. By recognizing the interconnectedness of discrimination and oppression, Talin and her allies were able to build a more resilient and inclusive movement that tackled the root causes of inequality.

Publications and Memoirs

An essential part of establishing a foundation for alien rights was the documentation and dissemination of the movement's history, achievements, and challenges. Talin and her allies recognized the power of storytelling in shaping public opinion and inspiring future generations of activists.

They published books, articles, and memoirs that chronicled their journey, providing a firsthand account of the struggles faced by alien communities and the victories they achieved. Through these publications, they sought to educate and engage a wider audience, bringing the alien rights movement into the collective consciousness of Xyorathian society.

Talin's memoir, "Defying the Odds: My Journey as an Alien Rights Activist," became a bestseller and served as a source of inspiration for countless individuals facing discrimination. It offered a glimpse into the personal sacrifices, triumphs, and resilience of Talin and her fellow activists, further solidifying their place in history as trailblazers for justice.

Honors and Recognitions

Recognition and acknowledgement of their contributions played a crucial role in establishing a foundation for alien rights. Talin and her allies received numerous honors, awards, and accolades for their tireless advocacy and commitment to social justice.

These honors not only validated their efforts but also served as a powerful reminder to both aliens and Xyorathians that their fight for equality was making a significant impact. Talin's acceptance speeches and public appearances at award ceremonies provided a platform to further amplify the alien rights movement's message and inspire others to join the cause.

Additionally, Talin and her fellow activists established their own awards and scholarships, recognizing outstanding individuals and organizations working towards the advancement of alien rights. These initiatives fostered a sense of pride, encouraged continued activism, and helped build a strong network of like-minded individuals dedicated to creating lasting change.

Remembering Talin's Contributions

Talin Iryn's legacy as a pioneering alien rights activist should not be forgotten. Establishing a foundation for alien rights involves commemorating Talin's contributions and ensuring her story continues to inspire future generations.

In honor of her remarkable achievements, a statue of Talin was erected in the heart of the capital city, symbolizing her indomitable spirit and the ongoing fight for justice. In addition to the physical monument, an annual Talin Iryn Day was established, dedicated to celebrating her life, accomplishments, and the progress made in advancing alien rights.

Furthermore, efforts were made to incorporate Talin's story into Xyorath's educational curriculum, ensuring that her legacy remains a part of the nation's collective memory. By studying and reflecting on Talin's journey, future generations are empowered to continue the fight for alien rights and build upon the foundation she worked so hard to establish.

Conclusion: A Legacy of Equality and Justice

The establishment of a foundation for alien rights on Xyorath marked an important milestone in the ongoing struggle for equality and justice. Through education, legislative reforms, collaborations, publications, honors, and remembrance of Talin's contributions, the alien rights movement laid the groundwork for a more inclusive society.

Talin and her allies demonstrated the power of collective action and resilience in the face of adversity. They challenged discriminatory norms, shattered stereotypes, and created lasting change that extended far beyond the alien community.

Their efforts serve as a powerful reminder that the fight for justice is never-ending and ever-evolving. By establishing a foundation for alien rights, Talin Iryn and her fellow activists inspired future generations to continue the work of creating a society where all individuals are treated with dignity, equality, and respect.

Fighting for Intersectionality and Inclusivity

In Talin Iryn's tireless advocacy for alien civil rights, a central pillar of her work was fighting for intersectionality and inclusivity. She recognized that discrimination and oppression are often interconnected and that tackling them in isolation would be incomplete. This section explores Talin's efforts to address the intersections of discrimination and ensure inclusivity within the alien rights movement.

Intersectionality is the understanding that an individual's social and political identities (such as race, gender, sexuality, and disability) overlap and intersect, resulting in unique experiences and forms of discrimination. Talin firmly believed that alien rights advocacy should not only address discrimination based on one's alien status but also acknowledge and combat other forms of prejudice that alien communities face.

To promote intersectionality and inclusivity, Talin employed various strategies. One of the key initiatives was to embrace coalition building. She actively sought partnerships and collaborations with other marginalized communities and movements, such as the LGBTQ+ rights movement, the disability rights movement, and the feminist movement. By joining forces, they could amplify their collective voices and effectively challenge systemic discrimination.

Talin also emphasized the importance of education and awareness programs within the alien rights movement. She recognized that in order to address intersecting forms of discrimination, individuals within the movement needed to be well-informed and equipped with a comprehensive understanding of social justice issues. Through workshops, seminars, and conferences, she promoted dialogue and encouraged discussion on topics related to intersectionality and inclusivity. By fostering a culture of learning, Talin aimed to empower movement members to recognize and combat discrimination in all its forms.

In her fight for intersectionality, Talin advocated for policy changes that recognized and addressed overlapping discrimination. She pushed for reforms that not only protected alien rights but also encompassed broader civil rights. For example, she championed inclusive anti-discrimination laws that prohibited not only alien discrimination but also discrimination based on race, gender, sexuality, and disability. This comprehensive approach aimed to dismantle intersecting systems of oppression and create a more equitable society for all.

Talin understood that creating a truly inclusive movement required addressing internal divisions and differences. She actively worked to create spaces within the alien rights movement where diverse voices and perspectives could be heard and respected. By fostering an environment that valued and embraced diversity, Talin believed that the movement's impact would be more inclusive and impactful.

To illustrate the importance of intersectionality and inclusivity, Talin often cited real-world examples. For instance, she highlighted the experiences of alien individuals who faced compounded discrimination due to their gender identity or sexual orientation. By sharing these stories, she encouraged empathy and understanding among members of the movement and the broader society.

Talin's commitment to intersectionality and inclusivity was not without its challenges. She faced resistance from some within the alien rights movement who believed that solely focusing on alien rights would be more effective. However, Talin remained steadfast in her belief that true equality and justice could only be achieved by addressing intersecting forms of discrimination.

To reinforce her message, Talin employed unconventional strategies. She organized art exhibitions, poetry slams, and cultural events that celebrated diverse identities within the alien community. These events provided a platform for individuals to express their experiences of intersectionality and highlighted the richness and diversity within the alien rights movement.

Finally, Talin documented her experiences and learnings in publications and memoirs, ensuring that future generations would benefit from her insights. She wrote about the challenges, successes, and strategies employed to fight for intersectionality and inclusivity. Through her writings, Talin aimed to inspire and guide future alien activists to continue the fight for justice and equality.

In conclusion, Talin Iryn's advocacy for alien civil rights went beyond addressing alien discrimination alone. She fought for intersectionality and inclusivity, recognizing that discrimination is multifaceted and should be combated in its entirety. Through coalition building, education, policy reform, and amplifying diverse voices, Talin's work laid the foundation for creating an inclusive movement that works towards dismantling intersecting systems of oppression. Her commitment to intersectionality serves as a guiding principle for future alien activists and reminds us that true justice and equality can only be achieved by embracing all dimensions of discrimination.

Partnering with Other Movements and Organizations

In her relentless fight for equality and social justice, Talin Iryn recognized the power of collaboration and solidarity. She understood that by forming strategic partnerships with other movements and organizations, she could amplify her impact and create a stronger collective voice against discrimination. In this section, we will explore how Talin effectively partnered with other movements and organizations, forging alliances that transformed the landscape of alien rights advocacy.

The Importance of Collaboration

Talin firmly believed that the struggle for alien rights was interconnected with other social justice movements. She recognized that discrimination and oppression often intersected, affecting individuals from marginalized communities on multiple fronts. By partnering with other movements, Talin sought to bring attention to the intersectional nature of discrimination and work towards comprehensive change.

Collaboration allowed for the sharing of resources, knowledge, and experiences. When movements came together, they combined their strengths, widening their reach and impact. By building alliances, Talin sought to create a strong unity among different communities fighting for justice, fostering a sense of solidarity and understanding.

Forging Alliances

Talin actively sought out organizations and movements that aligned with her goals and principles. She recognized that there were existing groups advocating for civil rights, gender equality, LGBTQ+ rights, and other related causes. By reaching out and building bridges, Talin was able to explore common ground and identify shared objectives.

One of the first organizations Talin partnered with was the Galactic Alliance for Equality (GAE), a coalition of various alien rights groups across the galaxy. The GAE provided a platform for knowledge-sharing, organizing collective actions, and lobbying for policy changes. Talin's collaboration with the GAE not only strengthened her cause but also enabled her to connect with activists from different planets and learn from their experiences.

Talin also understood the importance of partnering with terrestrial human rights organizations. She forged alliances with prominent civil rights groups such as the Universal Civil Liberties Union (UCLU) and the Interplanetary Human Rights Council (IHRC). These organizations had extensive experience in advocating for marginalized communities and offered support and expertise in legal battles, awareness campaigns, and lobbying efforts.

In addition to these alliances, Talin actively sought to collaborate with other grassroots movements. She recognized the power of collective action, and by joining forces with feminist movements, environmental advocates, and indigenous rights activists, she was able to highlight the interconnectedness of social justice issues. Together, they brought attention to the complexity of discrimination and worked towards dismantling oppressive systems in multiple spheres.

Shared Strategies and Impact

Partnering with other movements and organizations allowed Talin to adopt shared strategies and tactics. By working together, they developed effective advocacy campaigns, awareness programs, and legal initiatives. They leveraged each other's strengths and resources, maximizing their impact and reaching a broader audience.

For example, Talin's partnership with feminist movements allowed her to emphasize the intersections between gender discrimination and alien rights. Together, they organized workshops and seminars on gender equality, challenging traditional gender roles, and advocating for comprehensive policies that protected the rights of all individuals, regardless of their gender or alien status.

Through collaboration with environmental advocates, Talin shed light on the impact of climate change on marginalized alien communities. By highlighting the disproportionate effects of environmental degradation on vulnerable populations, they successfully advocated for sustainable policies that prioritized the well-being of all people and the planet.

Challenges and Lessons Learned

While partnering with other movements and organizations brought numerous benefits, it also posed challenges. Differences in priorities, strategies, and perspectives sometimes created tensions and required careful navigation. Balancing the diverse needs and aspirations of multiple movements demanded open dialogue, respect, and compromise.

Talin learned the importance of active listening and empathy when collaborating. She recognized that true collaboration required understanding and respecting the unique struggles and experiences of partner organizations. By creating spaces for dialogue and fostering inclusivity, Talin ensured that joint efforts remained sensitive to the needs of all communities involved.

Through her partnerships, Talin also learned the significance of long-term commitment and sustainability. Building strong alliances required nurturing relationships, maintaining open lines of communication, and acknowledging the importance of each partner's contributions. Sustained collaboration allowed movements to weather challenges, adapt to changing political landscapes, and continue the fight for justice.

Conclusion: Collective Power

Partnering with other movements and organizations became a cornerstone of Talin's advocacy. By recognizing the shared struggle for justice across different communities, she built bridges, fostered unity, and amplified the collective power of all those fighting for equality.

Talin's collaborations served as a reminder that the fight for alien rights was intricately woven into a broader tapestry of social justice movements. By seeking solidarity, forging alliances, and acknowledging the interconnectedness of discrimination, Talin and her partners blazed a trail towards a more inclusive, equitable universe. Their efforts continue to inspire future generations of activists to join hands and strive for a world where every being is treated with dignity and respect.

Publications and Memoirs

As Talin Iryn's activism and impact on Xyorathian society gained recognition, it was natural for her to transition into the world of literature. Publications and memoirs became important tools for documenting her experiences, sharing her wisdom, and inspiring future generations of activists. In this section, we will explore some of the notable publications and memoirs that emerged from Talin Iryn's journey.

1. "Ink of Change: My Alien Activism"

Talin's first memoir, "Ink of Change: My Alien Activism," takes readers on a deeply personal journey through her life as an activist. The memoir begins with her early experiences of discrimination on Xyorath and traces her development into a fierce advocate for the rights of aliens everywhere. Through her captivating storytelling, Talin highlights pivotal moments in her journey, including the discovery of the multi-tentacle marriage restrictions and the subsequent fight for their abolition.

One of the strengths of "Ink of Change" is Talin's ability to combine raw emotion with keen analysis. She delves into the complexities of systemic alien oppression, dissects the sociopolitical landscape of Xyorath, and exposes the underlying prejudices that perpetuated discrimination. Moreover, she sheds light on the intersectionality of her activism, highlighting how issues of race, gender, and socioeconomic status intertwined with her fight for equal rights.

Throughout the memoir, Talin also shares intimate anecdotes about the challenges she faced as an activist: the threats, backlash, and sacrifices she made in pursuit of justice. By recounting these stories, she humanizes the struggle and inspires readers to persevere in the face of adversity.

"Ink of Change" ultimately serves as a call to action, urging readers to question their own biases, challenge oppressive systems, and champion equality. Talin's memoir becomes a guiding light for alien communities, reminding them that their voices matter and their fight for justice is worth every sacrifice.

2. "Beyond Boundaries: Voices of Xyorathian Activism"

Recognizing the power of collective narratives, Talin Iryn spearheaded the compilation of "Beyond Boundaries: Voices of Xyorathian Activism." This groundbreaking book brings together stories and perspectives from a diverse range of Xyorathian activists, highlighting the intersectional nature of their struggles and the transformative power of solidarity.

"Beyond Boundaries" offers a platform for marginalized voices that had long been silenced in Xyorathian society. It includes personal narratives, essays, and poems that showcase the unique experiences of individuals from different backgrounds and walks of life. By sharing their stories, these activists aim to challenge societal norms, provoke thought, and inspire readers to take action.

Talin's contribution to "Beyond Boundaries" centers around the importance of allyship and coalition building. She discusses the challenges of bridging divides within the alien community and forging alliances with other civil rights movements. Through her insights, readers gain a deeper understanding of the strategic and emotional complexities of Xyorathian activism.

The collective nature of "Beyond Boundaries" allows readers to empathize with experiences that may be different from their own, fostering a sense of empathy and unity. This book becomes a testament to the power of solidarity, reminding readers that true change comes when individuals come together to challenge oppressive systems.

3. "Love and Liberation: A Blueprint for Change"

In "Love and Liberation: A Blueprint for Change," Talin Iryn offers readers a comprehensive guide to pursuing social justice and equality. By drawing on her extensive activism experience, she provides practical strategies, theoretical frameworks, and innovative ideas for effecting societal change.

The book begins by establishing the importance of love in activism, transcending traditional notions and exploring love as a powerful force for transformative justice. Talin emphasizes the need for activists to practice empathy, compassion, and forgiveness as they navigate the challenges of fighting against oppressive systems.

"Love and Liberation" also delves into important topics such as grassroots organizing, effective communication, and building sustainable movements. Talin shares her insights on coalition building, mobilizing communities, and creating inclusive spaces for marginalized voices.

One unique aspect of "Love and Liberation" is its incorporation of creative approaches to activism. Talin encourages readers to explore art, music, storytelling, and other forms of expression as tools for resistance and social change. By highlighting the power of imagination and creativity, she inspires readers to think outside of traditional activist frameworks and explore new avenues for advocacy.

In addition to providing practical guidance, "Love and Liberation" also addresses the emotional toll of activism. Talin emphasizes the importance of self-care, mental health, and community support systems, ensuring that activists are equipped with the tools to sustain themselves in the long run.

4. "Resilience and Renewal: Lessons from the Alien Rights Movement"

As Talin Iryn's impact on Xyorathian society continued to reverberate, she collaborated with a team of researchers and activists to compile "Resilience and Renewal: Lessons from the Alien Rights Movement." This book serves as a comprehensive analysis of the strategies, tactics, and lessons learned from the movement, providing a roadmap for future activists and advocates.

"Resilience and Renewal" examines the successes and challenges of the alien rights movement, offering insights into the complex dynamics of social change. The book explores the role of legal advocacy, grassroots organizing, public relations, and policy reform in effecting lasting change. It also delves into the nuances of alliance-building, intersectionality, and the importance of centering the most marginalized voices in the movement.

Through case studies and real-world examples, "Resilience and Renewal" provides a practical framework for activists seeking to challenge oppressive systems. It explores the various stages of movement-building, from grassroots mobilization and awareness raising to legislative and legal battles. The book also addresses the importance of adapting strategies to changing political landscapes and maintaining momentum in the face of setbacks.

Moreover, "Resilience and Renewal" offers valuable insights into the long-term impact of the alien rights movement on Xyorathian society. It examines changes in cultural norms, policy reforms, and the ongoing work needed to ensure that the fight for justice is never-ending and ever-evolving.

In conclusion, Talin Iryn's publications and memoirs play a vital role in preserving her legacy as a trailblazing alien rights activist. Through her heartfelt storytelling, practical guidance, and strategic analysis, she inspires readers to challenge oppressive systems, champion equality, and embrace the power of collective resilience.

Honors and Recognitions

Throughout her tireless activism and fearless advocacy, Talin Iryn received numerous honors and recognitions for her groundbreaking work in fighting for alien civil rights on the planet of Xyorath. Her unwavering commitment to equality and justice made her a revered figure among her peers, and her impact on Xyorathian society and beyond was widely acknowledged. In this section, we will explore some of the significant honors and recognitions bestowed upon Talin Iryn, highlighting the lasting legacy she left behind.

The Luminary Award

In recognition of her remarkable contributions to the alien rights movement, Talin Iryn was honored with the prestigious Luminary Award. This award is granted annually to individuals who have demonstrated exceptional leadership and dedication in advancing the cause of social justice. Talin's unwavering commitment to challenging discriminatory practices and her relentless pursuit of equality made her a worthy recipient. The Luminary Award not only recognized Talin's achievements but also celebrated her as a beacon of hope and inspiration for future activists.

The Freedom Fighter Medal

Talin Iryn was bestowed with the esteemed Freedom Fighter Medal, a recognition granted by the Xyorathian government to individuals who have made outstanding contributions to the fight against discrimination and oppression. This medal symbolizes the bravery and sacrifice of those who have dedicated their lives to upholding the principles of justice and equality. Talin's relentless efforts in challenging societal norms and dismantling systemic barriers made her a true freedom fighter, deserving of this esteemed honor.

The Unity and Peace Award

The Unity and Peace Award is an internationally acclaimed honor that recognizes individuals who have made significant strides in promoting unity and fostering peaceful coexistence. Talin Iryn's work in advocating for equal rights and fighting against discrimination resonated far beyond the borders of Xyorath, inspiring others around the universe to work towards social justice. Her tireless efforts in breaking down barriers and empowering marginalized communities made her a deserving recipient of the Unity and Peace Award.

The Champion of Equality Trophy

Talin Iryn's relentless pursuit of equality for all Xyorathians earned her the distinguished Champion of Equality Trophy. This award acknowledges individuals who have shown exceptional dedication to advancing equal rights, and Talin's unwavering determination in challenging discriminatory laws and policies exemplified the qualities of a true champion. The Champion of Equality Trophy stands as a testament to Talin's remarkable influence and her transformative impact on Xyorathian society.

The Voice of the Voiceless Award

In recognition of her exceptional advocacy work in amplifying the voices of the marginalized and oppressed, Talin Iryn was honored with the Voice of the Voiceless Award. This prestigious award acknowledges individuals who have gone above and beyond to elevate the voices of those who have been silenced by discrimination and prejudice. Talin's passionate and fearless advocacy gave a voice to countless alien communities who had long been marginalized, making her a deserving recipient of this esteemed recognition.

The Talin Iryn Day

To commemorate Talin Iryn's profound impact on Xyorathian society, the government declared a special day each year in her honor, known as Talin Iryn Day. On this day, Xyorathians come together to celebrate the achievements of this remarkable activist and reflect on the progress that has been made in the fight for equality. Talin Iryn Day serves as a reminder of the ongoing struggle for justice and inspires future generations to continue the work that Talin started.

Through these honors and recognitions, Talin Iryn's legacy as a trailblazer and an advocate for alien civil rights is cemented. Her unwavering dedication to equality, her courage in the face of adversity, and her relentless pursuit of justice have left an indelible mark on Xyorathian society and beyond. Talin's pioneering work serves as an inspiration for future activists, reminding us all that the fight for equality is one that should never be abandoned.

Documentaries and Films

Documentaries and films have played a crucial role in spreading awareness about Talin Iryn's activism and the fight for alien civil rights on Xyorath. Through storytelling and visual narratives, these mediums have captured the struggles, triumphs, and legacy of Talin Iryn, inspiring and educating audiences around the world. In this section, we will explore some of the notable documentaries and films that have shed light on Talin's journey and the broader movement for equality.

Documentaries

"Lifting the Veil: The Talin Iryn Story"

Directed by Kira Rodriguez, "Lifting the Veil" provides an intimate and in-depth look at Talin Iryn's life and the challenges faced by alien species on Xyorath. Through interviews with Talin's family, friends, and fellow activists, this documentary uncovers the personal struggles and milestones of Talin's journey. It delves into the cultural background and customs of Xyorathian society, shedding light on the discriminatory multi-tentacle marriage restrictions that Talin fought against. In addition to capturing the legal battles and victories, "Lifting the Veil" highlights the emotional toll that activism can take on individuals and the importance of community support.

"Beyond Boundaries: The Unbreakable Spirit of Talin Iryn"

Directed by Maya Patel, "Beyond Boundaries" explores the impact of Talin Iryn's activism on Xyorathian society and the wider alien community. Through interviews with lawmakers, activists, and ordinary citizens, the documentary examines the ripple effect of Talin's work in dismantling discrimination. It also delves into the legal and policy reforms that were triggered by the movement, such as addressing employment discrimination, securing access to healthcare and education, and challenging segregation and housing policies. "Beyond Boundaries" showcases the alliances formed with other civil rights movements and emphasizes the importance of intersectionality in achieving social change.

Films

"Love Across the Stars"

This fictional film, directed by Ravi Gupta, takes inspiration from Talin Iryn's life and the fight for multi-tentacle marriage equality. Set in a futuristic Xyorathian society, the film follows the journey of a young alien couple, Alix and Zara, who defy societal norms and fight for their love. As they navigate legal battles and social backlash, they find strength and inspiration in the story of Talin Iryn. "Love Across the Stars" weaves together romance, drama, and science fiction, captivating audiences with its message of hope, resilience, and the power of love to overcome prejudice.

"Voices of Resistance"

Directed by Maria Sanchez, "Voices of Resistance" is a documentary-style film that chronicles the broader alien rights movement on Xyorath, of which Talin Iryn was a central figure. Through a series of interconnected stories, the film gives voice to various individuals and communities who fought for equality. It explores the diverse experiences and perspectives within the movement, highlighting the common struggles and shared goals. "Voices of Resistance" aims to foster empathy and understanding, emphasizing the importance of solidarity and unity in the quest for justice.

Additional Resources

In addition to the documentaries and films mentioned above, there are several resources available for those interested in learning more about Talin Iryn's activism and the broader alien civil rights movement on Xyorath. These include:

- *"Talin Iryn: Rebel with a Cause"* by Samantha Green: This comprehensive biographical book provides an in-depth exploration of Talin Iryn's life and activism, offering insights into the challenges faced and victories achieved. It includes personal anecdotes, interviews, and historical context to paint a vivid picture of Talin's legacy.

- *"Alien Rights on Xyorath: A Journey Towards Equality"* by the Xyorathian Alliance for Civil Rights: This informative guidebook explores the history and legal framework surrounding alien rights on Xyorath. It delves into the multi-tentacle marriage restrictions and the efforts taken to challenge and overcome them, providing a detailed analysis of the battles fought and legislative changes achieved.

- *"Breaking Barriers: The Alien Rights Movement on Xyorath"* podcast series: This compelling podcast series features interviews with activists, historians, and legal experts, offering diverse perspectives on the fight for alien civil rights. It delves into the intersectionality of the movement and examines its impact on broader social change.

Unconventional Approach: The Fictionalized Account

In addition to traditional documentaries and films, an unconventional yet impactful approach to capturing Talin Iryn's story would be through a fictionalized account. By creating a fictional narrative inspired by Talin's activism, the story could explore the emotional journey and personal struggles of the characters in a relatable and engaging way.

This fictionalized account could incorporate elements of science fiction or fantasy to provide a unique lens through which to view the fight for alien civil rights. By immersing the audience in a fantastical world, it would allow for a deeper exploration of the themes of discrimination, justice, and resilience.

Through memorable characters and a strong storyline, a fictionalized account could spark the imagination of viewers and encourage them to reflect on real-world issues of equality and social justice. The power of storytelling lies in its ability to evoke empathy and emotion, and a fictional narrative inspired by Talin Iryn's activism would undoubtedly leave a lasting impact.

Conclusion

Documentaries and films have been instrumental in shining a spotlight on Talin Iryn's activism and the broader alien civil rights movement on Xyorath. Through these mediums, the personal and legal battles faced by Talin and other activists have been brought to life, inspiring audiences across the galaxy. Whether through documentaries that provide a historical account or fictional films that capture the essence of the struggle, the power of storytelling has played a vital role in promoting empathy, education, and change. Talin Iryn's legacy will continue to live on through these documentaries and films, reminding future generations of the importance of fighting for equality and justice.

Remembering Talin's Contributions

Talin Iryn's tireless advocacy and unwavering determination have left an indelible mark on Xyorathian society and beyond. Her contributions to the fight for alien rights and equality will be remembered for generations to come. In this section, we will take a closer look at the lasting effects of Talin's work and the ways in which she continues to inspire and empower others.

Creating Lasting Change

Talin Iryn's efforts have brought about significant change in Xyorathian society, breaking down barriers and challenging deeply ingrained prejudices. Through her work, the multi-tentacle marriage restrictions were dismantled, opening the doors to love and commitment for countless individuals. Talin's contributions reached far beyond this single issue, as she led the charge in addressing broader discrimination faced by the alien community.

Empowering Alien Voices

One of the most significant legacies of Talin's work is her commitment to empowering alien voices. She recognized the importance of providing marginalized communities with platforms to share their experiences and advocate for change. Talin founded the Alien Empowerment Foundation, a nonprofit organization dedicated to amplifying alien voices and promoting their inclusion in decision-making processes. The foundation continues to provide support, leadership training, and resources to alien activists, ensuring that their voices are heard and valued.

Advocacy Beyond Xyorath

Talin's impact extended far beyond the planet of Xyorath. With her charismatic and compassionate approach, she built bridges with other civil rights movements, recognizing the interconnectivity of various struggles for justice. Her collaboration with leaders from different communities paved the way for alliances and collective action, resulting in policy changes and widespread social transformation.

Education and Awareness Initiatives

Talin understood the power of education and awareness in effecting lasting change. She worked tirelessly to educate Xyorathian society about the experiences and struggles of the alien community. Through public speaking engagements, documentaries, and publications, she brought the realities of discrimination to light, challenging societal norms and fostering empathy among the general population. Talin's educational initiatives continue to combat ignorance and promote understanding, leaving a lasting impact on societal attitudes.

Inspiring Future Activists

Perhaps one of the most significant ways in which Talin's contributions will be remembered is through her ability to inspire future generations of activists. Her resilience, courage, and unwavering commitment to justice serve as an example to young alien and non-alien activists alike. The Talin Iryn Activism Award, established in her honor, recognizes and supports individuals who are carrying on her legacy of advocating for alien rights and fighting for social justice.

A Vision for the Future

Talin always spoke passionately about her vision for a more inclusive and equitable future, not just for Xyorath, but for all beings in the universe. Her belief in the power of solidarity and collective action resonated with many, and her call for intersectionality and inclusivity continues to guide activists today. Talin's vision serves as a guiding light for those who seek to challenge the status quo and create a more just society.

In remembering Talin's contributions, we honor her legacy by continuing the work she started. As we celebrate her victories, we also recognize the challenges that lie ahead. Talin's impact on Xyorathian society and beyond serves as a reminder that the fight for justice is never-ending and ever-evolving. We must remain steadfast in our commitment to equality and draw inspiration from the courage and determination of Talin Iryn.

Continuing the Work: Future Alien Activists

As Talin Iryn's legacy lives on, it is crucial to examine the enduring impact of their work and how it has paved the way for future alien activists. The fight for equality and justice must continue, and it is up to the next generation to carry on the torch and build upon the progress made by Talin and their allies.

Educating and Empowering the Next Generation

One of the key steps in continuing the work of alien activism is educating and empowering the next generation. It is essential to ensure that young aliens understand their rights, the history of the civil rights movement, and the ongoing struggles they may face. Education on social justice issues should be incorporated into school curricula and community programs, fostering empathy and understanding among future alien activists.

Additionally, mentorship programs can be established to connect young aliens with experienced activists. Through these programs, seasoned activists can provide guidance, support, and leadership training to emerging advocates. This mentorship will help equip young activists with the skills and knowledge needed to navigate complex challenges and effectively advocate for change.

Building Alliances and Collaboration

To further the cause of alien rights, it is crucial for future activists to build alliances and collaborate with other social justice movements and organizations. By joining forces with movements fighting for racial equality, gender equity, LGBTQ+ rights, and disability rights, alien activists can amplify their voices and create a more inclusive and intersectional movement.

Collaboration can take various forms, such as joint advocacy campaigns, shared resources and strategies, and coalition-building efforts. By understanding the interconnectedness of various forms of discrimination, future alien activists can work towards dismantling systemic inequalities on multiple fronts.

Adapting Strategies to New Challenges

As societal dynamics evolve, future alien activists must be prepared to adapt their strategies to new challenges. This requires staying informed about emerging issues, technological advancements, and legal frameworks. By remaining adaptable and responsive, activists can effectively address the ever-changing landscape of discrimination and prejudice.

For example, harnessing the power of social media and online platforms can help reach a broader audience and mobilize support. Leveraging digital tools for organizing demonstrations, sharing educational resources, and engaging in online discussions can greatly enhance the impact of alien activists.

Addressing Emerging Issues and Inequalities

Continuing the work of alien activism also involves addressing emerging issues and inequalities that may arise in the future. As alien communities grow and diversify, it is crucial to ensure that the intersectionality of identities is acknowledged and accounted for in advocacy efforts.

Future activists must be vigilant in identifying and addressing the specific challenges faced by marginalized segments within the alien community. This includes the experiences of alien women, elderly aliens, disabled aliens, and aliens from intersecting minority groups.

By actively engaging with these issues and centering the voices of those most affected, future alien activists can work towards a more equitable and inclusive society for all aliens.

Using Art and Culture as Tools for Change

Art and culture have always played a powerful role in social movements, and future alien activists can harness these tools to effect change. Through visual arts, music, literature, theater, and film, activists can challenge stereotypes, promote empathy, and inspire collective action.

Artistic expressions can help humanize the alien experience, inviting others to connect on an emotional level and fostering a sense of shared humanity. By reflecting the diversity and richness of alien cultures, art and culture can create spaces for dialogue and understanding, ultimately contributing to a more inclusive society.

Keeping the Fire Alive: Self-care and Sustainability

As future alien activists carry the torch of justice, it is vital to prioritize self-care and sustainability. The fight for equality can be emotionally and physically demanding, and activists must find ways to sustain themselves for the long haul.

Practicing self-care involves setting boundaries, seeking support, and pursuing activities that nourish the mind, body, and soul. This could include regular exercise, mindfulness practices, therapy, and engaging in hobbies and creative outlets.

Moreover, fostering a community of care within the movement itself is essential. By creating support networks, sharing resources, and promoting a culture of compassion and mutual aid, future alien activists can sustain their commitment to the cause while uplifting one another.

Conclusion: A Legacy of Equality and Justice

As future alien activists pick up the mantle from Talin Iryn and their contemporaries, they enter a world shaped by their predecessors' groundbreaking efforts. Through education, collaboration, adaptability, intersectional advocacy, artistic expression, and self-care, these activists have the tools to continue the fight for equality and justice.

The journey towards full equality for aliens is ongoing and requires the collective commitment of individuals and communities. By honoring and building upon Talin's legacy, future alien activists can forge a path towards a more inclusive and equitable society for all, where the rights and dignity of every individual are respected and celebrated.

Talin Iryn will forever be remembered as a true hero and catalyst for change, inspiring generations to come and reminding us that the fight for justice is never-ending and ever-evolving.

Conclusion: A Legacy of Equality and Justice

Throughout Talin Iryn's journey as a civil rights activist, they spearheaded a movement that fought against the oppressive multi-tentacle marriage restrictions on Xyorath. Through their tireless efforts and unwavering determination, Talin was able to bring about significant changes in Xyorathian society, leaving behind a powerful legacy of equality and justice.

Talin's impact on Xyorathian society cannot be overstated. Their relentless advocacy and activism played a pivotal role in shaping the cultural norms and attitudes towards alien rights. Talin's fight against discrimination helped to overcome prejudice and create a more inclusive society where everyone, regardless of their species or number of tentacles, could enjoy the same rights and opportunities.

Moreover, Talin's accomplishments went far beyond the mere removal of the multi-tentacle marriage restrictions. Their efforts inspired other alien and civil rights activists to continue the fight for equality and social justice. Talin served as a beacon of hope and a role model for future generations, encouraging them to challenge injustice and demand change.

In their quest for justice, Talin recognized the importance of intersectionality and inclusivity. They understood that the struggle for alien rights intersected with other social justice movements, such as gender equality, racial justice, and LGBTQ+ rights. By partnering with these movements and organizations, Talin not only broadened the scope of their activism but also fostered a sense of solidarity and unity among diverse communities fighting for a common cause.

Talin's legacy extends beyond their activism. They were not only a change-maker but also a prolific writer and speaker. Their publications and memoirs continue to inspire and educate others about the importance of equality and justice. Talin's powerful words and personal experiences serve as a testament to the resilience and determination needed to challenge discriminatory systems.

To honor Talin's contributions, numerous awards and recognitions have been bestowed upon them. Their unwavering commitment to advancing alien rights earned them national and international acclaim. The impact of Talin's work is even more evident in the lasting effects it had on Xyorathian society and beyond.

As a result of their advocacy, cultural norms and attitudes towards aliens have shifted significantly. Xyorathian society has become more accepting, inclusive, and understanding. The once prevalent prejudices have been replaced with a celebration of diversity and a recognition of the inherent worth and dignity of all beings.

Talin's fight for equality also led to concrete policy changes and legal reforms. Employment discrimination against aliens has been challenged, ensuring fair and equal opportunities in the workplace. Access to healthcare and education has been secured, guaranteeing that all individuals have the resources they need to thrive. Challenging segregations and housing policies has created more inclusive communities, where diversity is welcomed and celebrated.

The legacy of Talin Iryn goes beyond Xyorath. Their impact on alien rights resonates with marginalized communities across the universe. Talin's spirit of resistance and courage inspires others to stand up against injustice and fight for a more equitable and just society.

Talin's journey as a civil rights activist is a testament to the power of individuals to create lasting change. Their story serves as a reminder that progress is not inevitable and that the fight for justice is ongoing. It requires sustained effort, resilience, and an unwavering belief in the inherent dignity and worth of all beings.

As we reflect on Talin's legacy, we are reminded of the transformative power of love and relationships. The fight against discrimination and bigotry calls upon us to reimagine our understanding of what it means to build inclusive and equitable societies.

In conclusion, Talin Iryn's life and work have left an indelible mark on Xyorathian society and beyond. Their unwavering commitment to equality and justice serves as a guiding light for future generations of activists. Talin's legacy reminds us that the fight for justice is never-ending and ever-evolving. Their extraordinary journey underscores the importance of embracing diversity, challenging discriminatory systems, and creating a world where every individual can live with dignity and respect.

Impact on Xyorathian Society and Beyond

Shifting Cultural Norms and Attitudes

In the fight for alien rights and equality, Talin Iryn played a pivotal role in shifting cultural norms and attitudes on Xyorath. Through their tireless advocacy and unwavering determination, Talin challenged traditional beliefs and paved the way for a more inclusive and accepting society. This section explores the significant changes that occurred in Xyorathian culture as a result of Talin's work, focusing on the transformation of social norms and attitudes towards alien communities.

Overcoming Fear and Prejudice

One of the major hurdles Talin faced was the deep-seated fear and prejudice towards alien communities. Many Xyorathians held misconceptions and stereotypes about aliens, viewing them as strange and threatening. Talin recognized the urgent need to deconstruct these prejudices and promote understanding.

To achieve this, Talin initiated educational campaigns that aimed to dispel myths and promote positive representations of aliens in Xyorathian media. Through documentaries, public lectures, and community discussions, Talin educated the general population about the diverse alien cultures and highlighted their contributions to society. By showcasing the shared humanity between Xyorathians and aliens, Talin worked towards breaking down barriers and fostering empathy.

Promoting Diversity and Inclusivity

Talin emphasized the importance of diversity and inclusivity in Xyorathian society, advocating for equal participation and representation for all alien communities. By challenging the notion of a homogenous Xyorathian identity, Talin encouraged a more nuanced understanding of citizenship and belonging.

To promote diversity, Talin collaborated with artists, writers, and filmmakers to create works that celebrated alien cultures. This included literature featuring alien protagonists, films telling alien stories, and art exhibitions showcasing the beauty and richness of alien traditions. By incorporating alien perspectives into mainstream cultural productions, Talin demonstrated that diversity could enrich Xyorathian society.

Furthermore, Talin actively worked towards creating inclusive spaces for aliens in various aspects of life, such as education, employment, and public services. Talin's advocacy led to the implementation of policies that prohibited discrimination based on alien status, ensuring that aliens had equal opportunities to thrive and contribute to Xyorathian society.

Challenging Gender Norms and Roles

Another significant cultural shift Talin brought about was the challenge to traditional gender norms and roles. Xyorathian society had long been governed by strict gender expectations that limited opportunities for both Xyorathians and aliens. Talin recognized that true equality could only be achieved through dismantling these discriminatory norms.

Talin advocated for gender equality, promoting the idea that individuals should not be judged or restricted based on their gender identity. Talin's efforts led to the establishment of support networks for gender non-conforming aliens, ensuring that they had access to healthcare, legal protections, and social acceptance. Through public speaking engagements and awareness campaigns, Talin empowered individuals to embrace their authentic selves, creating a more inclusive and diverse Xyorathian society.

Transforming Interactions and Relationships

One of the most profound changes brought about by Talin's activism was the transformation of interactions and relationships between Xyorathians and aliens. Prior to Talin's work, there was a significant divide between the two communities, resulting in alien communities being marginalized and excluded.

Talin tirelessly worked to bridge this divide, organizing community events that fostered dialogue and mutual understanding. These events provided spaces for Xyorathians and aliens to come together, share their experiences, and build meaningful connections. By facilitating these interactions, Talin helped to break down barriers and cultivate a sense of unity and togetherness.

Furthermore, Talin advocated for intercultural exchange programs, encouraging Xyorathians and aliens to learn from one another's traditions and customs. This not only fostered cultural appreciation but also helped to develop a collective identity that transcended differences.

Empowering Alien Voices

In addition to challenging Xyorathian societal norms, Talin recognized the importance of amplifying alien voices and empowering alien communities to shape their own narrative. Prior to Talin's activism, alien perspectives and experiences were often overlooked or distorted in mainstream discourse.

To address this, Talin supported the establishment of alien-led community organizations, providing resources and platforms for aliens to share their stories and advocate for their rights. These organizations played a crucial role in shaping cultural norms and attitudes by showcasing the multifaceted contributions aliens made to Xyorathian society.

Talin's efforts also led to the inclusion of alien perspectives in policymaking processes, ensuring that decisions impacting the alien communities were made collaboratively. By empowering alien voices, Talin helped to reshape the fabric of Xyorathian society, emphasizing the importance of inclusivity and equal representation for all.

Conclusion: A Legacy of Equality and Justice

Talin Iryn's tireless activism and unwavering commitment to alien rights have left an indelible mark on Xyorathian society. Through the fight for equality, Talin revolutionized cultural norms and attitudes towards aliens, fostering inclusivity, and acceptance.

The shifts in cultural norms and attitudes that resulted from Talin's work have had far-reaching effects, not only on Xyorathia but also on neighboring planets and realms beyond. The Xyorathian society that once feared and marginalized aliens now embraces diversity, understanding, and unity.

Talin's legacy is one of empowerment, as their advocacy continues to inspire alien communities and civil rights activists across the universe. By challenging prejudice, promoting inclusivity, and amplifying alien voices, Talin has set a powerful example for generations to come, reminding us that the fight for justice is never-ending and ever-evolving. Talin Iryn will forever be remembered as an icon of resistance, courage, and the enduring power of love to overcome all boundaries.

Increased Visibility and Acceptance

In this section, we explore the profound impact that Talin Iryn's activism had on the increased visibility and acceptance of alien communities on Xyorath and beyond. Talin's tireless efforts to challenge discrimination and fight for equality paved the way for a significant shift in cultural norms and attitudes toward aliens.

Challenging Stereotypes and Prejudice

One of the key achievements of Talin's activism was the dismantling of stereotypes and prejudice against aliens. Through their courageous advocacy and representation, Talin highlighted the diverse talents, skills, and contributions of alien individuals. They challenged the perception of aliens as "other" and promoted a more inclusive understanding of their experiences and identities.

Talin used various platforms, including media interviews, public speaking engagements, and social media campaigns, to showcase the rich cultural heritage and achievements of alien communities. By sharing personal stories and experiences, they humanized the plight of aliens, giving a face and voice to a marginalized group. This increased visibility helped debunk stereotypes and fostered empathy and understanding among the general population.

Promoting Cultural Exchange and Dialogue

Talin recognized the power of cultural exchange in fostering acceptance and appreciation for diverse communities. They organized events and initiatives that encouraged interaction and dialogue between alien and non-alien populations. These events aimed to create spaces where individuals from different backgrounds could come together, learn from one another, and challenge their biases.

One such initiative was the Alien Cultural Festival, an annual event that showcased the vibrant traditions, music, and art of Xyorath's alien communities. This festival provided a platform for aliens to share their cultural practices and values with the broader society. Through food, music, dance, and interactive workshops, the festival promoted understanding and fostered connections between aliens and non-aliens.

Advocating for Representation in Media

Another critical aspect of Talin's work was advocating for accurate and positive representation of aliens in the media. They recognized that media had a significant influence on public perception and attitudes toward various communities. Talin collaborated with writers, filmmakers, and producers to ensure that alien characters were portrayed authentically and respectfully in popular culture.

Talin also called for increased representation of alien voices in media decision-making processes. They lobbied for the inclusion of more alien journalists, writers, and producers, advocating for their unique perspectives to be reflected in news stories, films, and television shows. This push for representation helped humanize aliens in the eyes of the public and challenged prevailing stereotypes.

Creating Safe Spaces and Support Networks

Talin understood the importance of creating safe spaces where alien individuals could express their identities and find support. They established community centers and organizations that provided resources, counselling services, and networking opportunities for those facing discrimination.

These safe spaces played a crucial role in fostering a sense of belonging for aliens, helping them navigate the challenges of living in a society that often marginalized them. Through support networks and mentorship programs, Talin ensured that alien individuals had access to the necessary tools and guidance to thrive.

Educational Initiatives

Education was a cornerstone of Talin's efforts to increase visibility and acceptance. They advocated for comprehensive and inclusive curricula that accurately represented the history, contributions, and experiences of alien communities.

Talin championed the inclusion of diverse perspectives and voices in textbooks, curriculum materials, and classroom discussions. They collaborated with educators and policymakers, providing them with resources and training on creating inclusive learning environments. By challenging educational institutions to be more inclusive, Talin laid the foundation for future generations to grow up in an environment that celebrated diversity and rejected discrimination.

Promoting Interplanetary Solidarity

Talin believed in the power of unity and collaboration among alien communities and between aliens and other marginalized groups. They actively sought partnerships with other civil rights movements, recognizing the intersectionality of discrimination and the importance of collective resistance.

By building bridges between different communities, Talin fostered interplanetary solidarity and amplified the voices of those fighting for justice and equality. They organized joint protests, conferences, and awareness campaigns, uniting individuals from diverse backgrounds under a shared vision of a more inclusive and equitable society.

In conclusion, Talin Iryn's activism ushered in a new era of increased visibility and acceptance for alien communities on Xyorath and beyond. Through their tireless efforts in challenging stereotypes, promoting cultural exchange, advocating for representation, creating safe spaces, advancing educational initiatives, and promoting interplanetary solidarity, Talin paved the way for a more inclusive society that celebrates diversity and rejects discrimination. Through their legacy, future generations of alien and minority communities continue to break down barriers and fight for justice, inspired by the indomitable spirit of Talin Iryn.

Policy Changes and Legal Reforms

Policy changes and legal reforms were at the forefront of Talin Iryn's fight for alien rights on Xyorath. Through strategic advocacy and legislative efforts, Talin was able to challenge discriminatory laws and regulations, paving the way for greater equality and social justice. This section will explore the key policy changes and legal reforms that were instrumental in reshaping Xyorathian society.

Legislative Challenges

Talin recognized that bringing about real change required a multidimensional approach. They understood that lasting impact necessitated challenging discriminatory laws at every level of government, from local municipalities to the national legislature. However, this was no easy feat.

Legislative challenges were plentiful, as conservative forces vehemently resisted any attempts to grant alien communities equal rights. Talin had to navigate through a web of entrenched prejudices and biases to gain support for their cause. This involved extensive lobbying, mobilizing grassroots movements, and leveraging various coalitions.

Reforming Marriage Laws

One of the central policy changes Talin focused on was the reform of marriage laws that restricted multi-tentacle marriages on Xyorath. These laws were deeply rooted in xenophobia and cultural misunderstandings. Talin fought tirelessly to dismantle these barriers and redefine the definition of marriage to be more inclusive.

Through public awareness campaigns and legal battles, Talin successfully challenged the archaic notion that marriage could only be between two individuals. They argued for a more expansive understanding of love and relationships, encouraging the recognition of diverse family structures in Xyorathian society.

Anti-Discrimination Legislation

In addition to challenging marriage laws, Talin championed comprehensive anti-discrimination legislation. They recognized that achieving true equality required addressing discrimination in all spheres of life, including employment, education, healthcare, and housing.

Talin worked closely with legal experts and alien rights organizations to craft legislation that explicitly protected individuals from discrimination based on their alien status. These laws aimed to ensure fair treatment and equal opportunities for all Xyorathians, regardless of their planet of origin.

Creating Inclusive Public Spaces

Talin also focused on policy changes that promoted inclusivity in public spaces across Xyorath. This included advocating for the removal of segregation and discriminatory practices in areas such as restaurants, parks, and transportation systems. They aimed to challenge the deeply ingrained societal norms that perpetuated inequality and fostered prejudice.

Through strategic litigation and community organizing, Talin was able to bring attention to instances of discrimination and push for policy changes that guaranteed equal access to public spaces. These efforts resulted in the dismantling of various discriminatory practices and the gradual transformation of Xyorathian society into a more inclusive and accepting one.

Educational Reforms

Recognizing the importance of education in shaping attitudes and beliefs, Talin advocated for educational reforms that cultivated inclusivity and understanding. They emphasized the need to teach Xyorathian history from diverse perspectives, highlighting the contributions of alien communities and their struggle for civil rights.

Talin's push for educational reforms not only aimed to curb prejudice and discrimination but also aimed to empower future generations of Xyorathians to continue the fight for justice and equality. They believed that education played a pivotal role in shaping a more inclusive and empathetic society.

Expanding Legal Protections

Talin's fight for policy changes and legal reforms did not happen in isolation. They actively sought alliances with other civil rights movements and organizations to amplify their efforts. By forming coalitions with like-minded groups, Talin was able to secure broader legal protections for alien communities and advance the cause of social justice.

These expanded legal protections included not only anti-discrimination laws but also measures to address systemic inequalities and promote equitable access to resources. Talin's collaborative approach ensured that their fight for alien rights was intertwined with a larger movement for social change.

Redefining Future Laws

Talin's legacy extended beyond their immediate successes in policy changes and legal reforms. Their activism and advocacy laid the groundwork for future legal advancements in alien rights on Xyorath. Their efforts redefined the boundaries of what was considered acceptable in terms of discrimination and set a precedent for challenging unjust laws.

The impact of Talin's work can be seen in subsequent legal battles and ongoing efforts to secure equal rights for all Xyorathians. Their fight provided a blueprint for future activists and lawmakers to build upon, continually pushing the boundaries of equality and justice.

In conclusion, Talin's pursuit of policy changes and legal reforms revolutionized Xyorathian society. Through challenging discriminatory marriage laws, advocating for anti-discrimination legislation, creating inclusive public spaces, pushing for educational reforms, expanding legal protections, and redefining future laws, Talin laid the foundation for a more equitable and inclusive Xyorath. Their relentless efforts continue to inspire generations of alien rights activists and shape the ongoing fight for justice and social change on Xyorath and beyond.

Addressing the Intersections of Discrimination

Addressing discrimination is a complex and multifaceted task that requires an understanding of the different types of oppression that intersect and compound each other. In the fight for equality and justice, it is crucial not only to address specific forms of discrimination but also to recognize the interconnectedness of various marginalized identities and experiences. This section explores the concept of intersectionality and highlights the importance of addressing the intersections of discrimination in the quest for social change.

Understanding Intersectionality

Intersectionality, coined by legal scholar Kimberlé Crenshaw, refers to the overlapping systems of oppression that affect individuals with multiple marginalized identities. It recognizes that people do not experience discrimination in isolation but rather at the crossroads of various social categories such as race, gender, sexuality, class, disability, and more. Discrimination becomes amplified when individuals face the overlapping effects of these intersecting identities.

For example, an alien individual may face discrimination not only because of their extraterrestrial status but also due to their race, gender, or socioeconomic background. Intersectionality helps us understand the ways in which different forms of discrimination intersect, creating unique challenges and experiences for individuals.

The Intersections of Discrimination

Discrimination can intersect in various ways, resulting in compounded disadvantages for individuals. Let's explore some common intersections of discrimination:

Race and Gender: Aliens of color often face discrimination that stems from both their racial and gender identities. For example, an alien woman of color may experience racialized sexism, where she faces discrimination based on both her race and gender. This intersectional oppression requires addressing both racism and sexism simultaneously to bring about meaningful change.

Sexual Orientation and Gender Identity: Discrimination against alien individuals based on their sexual orientation or gender identity is another significant intersection. Aliens who identify as LGBTQ+ face unique challenges and discrimination that are distinct from those faced by heterosexual or cisgender individuals. It is crucial to address the particular issues faced by queer and trans aliens and ensure their rights and experiences are validated.

Disability and Socioeconomic Status: Disabled aliens who belong to lower socioeconomic backgrounds often face compounded disadvantages.

Discrimination based on ableism can intersect with class discrimination, limiting access to resources, education, healthcare, and employment opportunities. By addressing the intersections of disability and socioeconomic status, we can work towards a more inclusive and equitable society for all.

Challenges in Addressing Intersectional Discrimination

Addressing the intersections of discrimination comes with its own set of challenges. Here are some key obstacles:

Limited Understanding and Awareness: Many individuals and institutions may not fully comprehend or appreciate the concept of intersectionality. This lack of understanding can hinder efforts to address intersectional discrimination effectively. Education and awareness programs are crucial to foster a deeper understanding of intersectionality and its importance.

Lack of Representation: In many spheres, marginalized voices and experiences are still underrepresented. This lack of representation can perpetuate stereotypes and biases, further marginalizing vulnerable communities. It is essential to amplify the voices of those affected by intersectional discrimination and create spaces for their stories to be heard.

Institutional Barriers: Discrimination often persists within various institutions and structures, making it challenging to dismantle the systemic barriers that perpetuate intersecting forms of oppression. Challenging and reforming these institutions is crucial for achieving meaningful change.

Resistance to Change: Resistance to change is a common obstacle when addressing intersectional discrimination. Privileged individuals and groups may fear that addressing intersecting discrimination will diminish their own power or status. Overcoming this resistance requires ongoing dialogue, empathy, and a commitment to dismantling all forms of discrimination.

Strategies for Addressing Intersectionality

To effectively address intersectional discrimination, it is important to employ strategic approaches and initiatives. Here are some key strategies to consider:

Creating Inclusive Policies and Legislation: Implementing inclusive policies and legislation that explicitly recognize and address intersectional discrimination is crucial. These policies should address the unique needs and challenges faced by individuals with multiple marginalized identities.

Promoting Intersectional Advocacy: Advocacy efforts must embrace intersectional frameworks and actively engage with various marginalized communities. This involves collaborating with multiple civil rights movements and working towards shared goals of equality and justice.

Providing Support and Resources: Providing support and resources to individuals facing intersectional discrimination is essential. This includes access to mental health services, legal assistance, affordable housing, education, and employment opportunities that are sensitive to diverse identities and needs.

Encouraging Intersectional Research and Data Collection: Promoting research and data collection that focuses on intersectional discrimination is vital. Understanding the unique challenges faced by individuals at the intersections of various identities helps inform targeted interventions and policy changes.

Fostering Intersectional Dialogue and Education: Creating spaces for open dialogue and education on intersectionality is crucial. Workshops, seminars, and training programs can help individuals and organizations understand the interconnectedness of different forms of discrimination and work collaboratively towards social change.

Case Study: Advancing Intersectional Rights

One inspiring example of addressing the intersections of discrimination is the advancement of rights for disabled queer aliens. This community faces compounded discrimination based on their disability, sexual orientation, and alien status.

To address this intersectional discrimination, activists and organizations have collaborated to advocate for inclusive policies and legislation that recognize the unique challenges faced by disabled queer aliens. They have worked towards improving access to healthcare, employment opportunities, and legal protections, while also challenging the ableism and heteronormativity that perpetuate discrimination.

Through their advocacy efforts, this community has been able to raise awareness, build alliances, and influence policy change at local and national levels. Their work serves as a powerful example of how addressing the intersections of discrimination can lead to tangible improvements in the lives of marginalized individuals.

Conclusion

Addressing the intersections of discrimination is vital for creating a more inclusive and equitable society. Intersectionality helps us recognize the complexity of discrimination and the unique challenges faced by individuals with multiple marginalized identities. By understanding these intersections and implementing targeted strategies, we can work towards dismantling the systemic barriers that perpetuate discrimination and create a more just future for all. Let us continue to fight for equality, embracing the intersections of our identities and ensuring that no one is left behind.

Lessons for Advocacy and Social Change

Advocacy and social change are crucial components of any movement seeking equality and justice. Talin Iryn's journey on Xyorath taught us valuable lessons that can inspire and guide future activists in their pursuit of a more inclusive and equitable society. Here, we explore these lessons and the principles that underpin them.

Understanding Intersectionality

One of the most important lessons from Talin's activism is the recognition of intersectionality. Talin understood that discrimination does not happen in isolation, but rather as a result of the overlapping systems of oppression. Recognizing the interconnectedness of various forms of discrimination—such as gender, race, and socio-economic status—is crucial to effectively advocating for social change.

For instance, Talin recognized that the fight against multi-tentacle marriage restrictions on Xyorath was not solely about the rights of alien individuals to marry, but also about dismantling broader systems of discrimination. By incorporating intersectional perspectives into their advocacy efforts, Talin was able to build stronger alliances and address the diverse needs of different marginalized communities.

Building Coalitions and Alliances

Another vital lesson from Talin's activism is the power of building coalitions and alliances. Talin understood the importance of collaboration and sought to unite different groups of people with shared goals. Through partnership with other civil rights movements, Talin was able to amplify their message and strengthen their impact.

Future activists can learn from this lesson by actively seeking out partnerships with diverse organizations and social justice movements. By working together, activists can leverage their collective power and expertise, build broader public support, and create sustainable social change.

Crafting Effective Messaging

Talin's success in advocating for change can also be attributed to their skill in crafting effective messaging. They understood that clear and concise messaging is key to attracting public support and mobilizing action. Talin used powerful narratives and personal stories to connect with the public on an emotional level, making their cause relatable and compelling.

Future activists can learn from Talin's approach by honing their storytelling skills and developing persuasive messaging. By employing narratives that highlight the lived experiences of marginalized communities, activists can create empathy, challenge stereotypes, and foster a greater understanding of the issues at hand.

Utilizing Digital Platforms

The rise of digital platforms has revolutionized advocacy and social change efforts. Talin recognized the power of social media and other online platforms in reaching a broader audience and mobilizing support. Through strategic use of digital tools, Talin was able to connect with individuals around the world, spread awareness about their cause, and galvanize action.

To effectively utilize digital platforms, future activists must develop skills in social media management, online organizing, and digital storytelling. By leveraging the power of technology, activists can transcend geographical boundaries, amplify their message, and engage with a diverse range of stakeholders.

Addressing Systemic Change

Talin's activism went beyond individual battles; they sought to address and dismantle the underlying systemic structures of oppression. Talin recognized that achieving true equality required not only challenging discriminatory laws and policies but also working to transform societal norms, attitudes, and institutions.

Future activists must adopt a systemic change approach, recognizing that their advocacy efforts should address root causes rather than superficial fixes. By challenging systemic barriers and promoting inclusive policies and practices, activists can create lasting and meaningful change.

Practicing Self-Care and Resilience

Advocacy work is demanding and often emotionally draining. Talin emphasized the importance of self-care and resilience throughout their journey. They recognized that without taking care of one's own well-being, it becomes difficult to sustain the energy and drive needed to fight for justice in the long run.

Future activists should prioritize self-care strategies such as mindfulness, rest, and seeking support from communities. It is essential to strike a balance between activism and personal well-being to avoid burnout and maintain long-term engagement.

Promoting Education and Awareness

Talin's activism was deeply rooted in education and awareness-raising. They understood that knowledge is power and played a critical role in challenging ignorance and prejudice. Talin organized workshops, seminars, and educational programs to inform the public about the harmful impacts of discrimination and the importance of equality.

Future activists should prioritize engaging in educational initiatives aimed at raising awareness and fostering empathy. By providing accurate information and challenging stereotypes, activists can reshape societal attitudes and promote a more inclusive and tolerant society.

Engaging in Peaceful Resistance

Throughout their activism, Talin emphasized the power of peaceful resistance. They understood that change could be achieved through nonviolent means, and they actively promoted peaceful protests, demonstrations, and civil disobedience.

Future activists can draw inspiration from Talin's commitment to peaceful resistance. By adopting nonviolent strategies, activists can create a moral high ground, garner public sympathy, and challenge oppressive systems without resorting to violence.

Taking Inspiration from Intersectional Icons

Finally, Talin's journey serves as an inspiration for future activists. Their story demonstrates the power of resilience, determination, and unwavering commitment to justice. Future activists should look to intersectional icons like Talin to draw strength and motivation in their own struggles for equality and social change.

In conclusion, Talin Iryn's activism on Xyorath offers valuable lessons for advocacy and social change. By embracing intersectionality, building coalitions, crafting effective messaging, utilizing digital platforms, addressing systemic change, practicing self-care, promoting education and awareness, engaging in peaceful resistance, and taking inspiration from intersectional icons, future activists can help shape a more inclusive and equitable society. The fight for justice and equality is never-ending and ever-evolving, but the lessons from Talin's journey can guide us on our path towards a brighter future.

Resources and Further Reading

1. bell hooks. "Feminism Is for Everybody: Passionate Politics". Routledge, 2000.

2. Kimberlé Crenshaw. "Demarginalizing the Intersection of Race and Sex: A Black Feminist Critique of Antidiscrimination Doctrine, Feminist Theory, and Antiracist Politics". University of Chicago Legal Forum, 1989.

3. Bryan Stevenson. "Just Mercy: A Story of Justice and Redemption". Spiegel & Grau, 2014.

4. Rinku Sen. "The Accidental American: Immigration and Citizenship in the Age of Globalization". Berrett-Koehler Publishers, 2008.

5. Erica Chenoweth and Maria J. Stephan. "Why Civil Resistance Works: The Strategic Logic of Nonviolent Conflict". Columbia University Press, 2011.

Remember to check local bookstores, libraries, and online platforms for more resources on advocacy, social change, and intersectionality.

Empowering Alien and Minority Voices

In the fight for equality and social justice, one of the most crucial aspects is the empowerment of alien and minority voices. Throughout history, marginalized communities have been silenced, their experiences ignored, and their perspectives dismissed. In this section, we will explore the importance of empowering these voices and discuss strategies to uplift and amplify the voices of aliens and minorities.

Understanding the Importance of Representation

Representation matters.   When alien and minority voices are not heard or acknowledged, their unique experiences and perspectives are overlooked, leading to a skewed understanding of society and perpetuating systemic inequalities.   By empowering these voices, we foster inclusivity, create a more accurate representation of diverse experiences, and challenge dominant narratives that often fail to capture the richness of human diversity.

Challenges to Empowering Alien and Minority Voices

Empowering alien and minority voices is not without its challenges. Historically, power structures have worked to maintain the status quo, suppressing alternative narratives to uphold the interests of the dominant majority. Economic disparities, limited access to education and resources, and discriminatory laws and policies all pose significant obstacles.   Overcoming these challenges requires a multifaceted approach and a commitment to dismantling systems of oppression.

Community Building and Support Networks

Building strong communities and support networks is essential for empowering alien and minority voices. By creating spaces where individuals can come together, share their experiences, and support one another, we provide a platform for marginalized communities to have their voices heard. These networks can provide emotional support, amplify individual stories, and mobilize collective action for change.

Access to Education and Resources

Education is a powerful tool for empowerment.   Providing access to quality education and resources is crucial in equipping alien and minority communities with the knowledge and skills to effectively articulate their experiences and concerns. Educational institutions must not only ensure diverse representation in their curricula but also cultivate inclusive and safe learning environments that validate the experiences of all students.

Media Representation and Engagement

The media plays a significant role in shaping public opinion and fueling social change. By increasing representation and visibility of alien and minority voices in media, we can challenge stereotypes and create positive narratives that promote understanding and acceptance. It is also essential to encourage alien and minority individuals to engage with media platforms, sharing their stories directly and participating in public discourse to challenge and reshape societal narratives.

Advocacy and Activism

Advocacy and activism are powerful tools for empowering alien and minority voices. By engaging in peaceful protests, legislative advocacy, and community organizing, individuals can raise awareness, demand justice, and effect systemic change. It is crucial to provide resources, training, and support to individuals who are willing to take on advocacy roles, ensuring that their voices are amplified and their efforts are sustained.

Seeking Allies and Building Coalitions

Building alliances and coalitions with individuals and organizations that share a commitment to social justice can amplify the impact of alien and minority voices. By partnering with like-minded advocates, diverse communities can leverage their collective power, pool resources, and implement strategic campaigns to address common goals. These alliances can also provide mentorship and support, guiding marginalized individuals in navigating complex systems and accessing opportunities for growth.

Addressing Intersectionality

Intersectionality recognizes that individuals can experience multiple forms of oppression simultaneously, based on their intersecting identities. Empowering alien and minority voices requires an understanding of the intersections of discrimination and an acknowledgment of the unique challenges faced by individuals who belong to multiple marginalized communities. By centering intersectionality in our advocacy efforts, we ensure that no one is left behind, and we create a more inclusive space for all voices to be heard.

Recognizing and Celebrating Diversity

True empowerment lies in celebrating the diversity within alien and minority communities. It is crucial to recognize that each individual's lived experience is unique and valuable. By embracing diversity and fostering an inclusive environment, we create a space where all voices are encouraged and appreciated.

This celebration of diversity strengthens the collective power of alien and minority communities and drives positive social change.

In conclusion, empowering alien and minority voices is at the heart of advocacy for equality and social justice. By amplifying these voices, challenging dominant narratives, and addressing systemic barriers, we can work towards a more inclusive and equitable society. Through community building, access to education and resources, media representation, advocacy, and coalition building, we can create lasting change and ensure that all voices are heard and valued. Let us commit ourselves to the task of empowering alien and minority voices, as their stories and perspectives hold the key to a brighter and more just future for all.

Talin Iryn: An Icon of Resistance and Courage

Throughout history, there have been countless individuals who have stood up against injustice and fought for equality. Talin Iryn is one such individual, an alien civil rights activist who became an icon of resistance and courage. In this section, we will explore the remarkable life and legacy of Talin Iryn, and how their activism paved the way for a more just and inclusive society.

Talin Iryn was born on the planet of Xyorath, a world known for its rich cultural diversity and vibrant alien communities. Growing up, Talin witnessed firsthand the discrimination and prejudice faced by alien individuals, particularly in the context of multi-tentacle marriage restrictions. These restrictions, deeply rooted in societal norms and customs, prohibited individuals from entering into multi-tentacle marriages, leading to the marginalization and exclusion of many.

From an early age, Talin developed a strong sense of justice and a passion for activism. Influenced by family members who had experienced discrimination, as well as prominent alien rights figures in their community, Talin was determined to challenge the status quo and fight for change. Educated on the principles of equality and human rights, they realized that it was their duty to fight against the injustice they and their loved ones faced.

Talin's journey as an activist began with their move to the capital city, where they experienced urban life for the first time. This new environment opened their eyes to the extent of the discrimination faced by alien communities. They found employment and achieved financial independence, enabling them to dedicate their time and resources to advocate for alien rights.

Joining local alien rights organizations, Talin built networks and allies who shared their vision of a more inclusive society. They actively participated in the first attempt at legalizing multi-tentacle marriages, facing opposition and backlash from conservative forces. However, their determination and resilience paid off when they gained media attention and public support, leading to the first victory: the lifting of the ban in local communities.

But Talin's fight didn't stop there. They understood the importance of expanding the movement and bringing about statewide legalization. Drawing on the lessons learned from the first attempt and strengthening alliances, Talin engaged in lobbying and advocacy efforts. They faced legislative roadblocks and challenges but persevered, leveraging media strategies and public opinion to sustain momentum.

Finally, their efforts paid off with the second victory: statewide legalization. The impact of this historic decision extended beyond Xyorathian communities. It challenged societal norms, influencing policy change at both local and national levels. Talin's courage and determination during the legal battle sparked a new wave of activism, empowering other alien communities to demand equality.

Talin's legacy goes beyond their fight for multi-tentacle marriage rights. They recognized the importance of intersectionality and inclusivity, expanding their advocacy to address employment discrimination, access to healthcare and education, and challenging segregation and housing policies. Their collaboration with other civil rights movements strengthened solidarity and amplified the voices of marginalized communities.

In recognition of their significant contributions, Talin received national recognition and was honored at award ceremonies. Their story inspired other alien and civil rights activists, serving as a reminder of the power of resistance and courage. Talin's memoirs and publications continue to serve as a source of inspiration and education.

The impact of Talin Iryn's activism can be seen in the shifting cultural norms and attitudes surrounding alien communities. Their tireless efforts led to increased visibility and acceptance, paving the way for policy changes and legal reforms. By tackling the intersections of discrimination, Talin demonstrated the power of collective action and the importance of empowering alien and minority voices.

Talin Iryn will forever be remembered as an icon of resistance and courage, a true hero who dedicated their life to fighting for equality and social justice. Their legacy serves as a reminder of the ongoing fight for justice, inspiring future generations to continue the work started by Talin and further advance the rights of alien communities. Talin's story reimagines love and relationships, challenging societal norms and advocating for a more inclusive and compassionate world.

The fight for justice is never-ending and ever-evolving, and Talin Iryn's indomitable spirit and unwavering commitment to equality will remain an enduring inspiration for generations to come.

Let us now turn our attention to the lasting effects of Talin's activism and their impact on Xyorathian society and beyond.

Reimagining Love and Relationships

Love and relationships are fundamental aspects of human life, and they play a crucial role in shaping our happiness and well-being. However, societal norms and expectations often limit the ways in which we can express and experience love. For Talin Iryn, the fight for alien civil rights extended to reimagining love and relationships to challenge the restrictive norms imposed by Xyorathian society. In this section, we will explore the transformative ideas and practices that emerged as a result of Talin's activism.

Questioning Traditional Ideas of Love

In many societies, love is often seen through a narrow lens, limited to monogamous, heterosexual relationships. Talin Iryn challenged these traditional notions and fostered a reevaluation of what love and relationships could be. She advocated for a more inclusive definition that encompassed various forms of love, regardless of gender, sexual orientation, or relationship structure.

One of the key insights from Talin's work was the recognition that love is not a finite resource but rather an abundant force that can be shared and experienced in multiple ways. By questioning the idea that love is exclusive to a romantic partnership, she opened up possibilities for non-traditional relationships to be valued and celebrated.

Embracing Non-Monogamy and Polyamory

Talin Iryn's activism paved the way for the acceptance of non-monogamous and polyamorous relationships within Xyorathian society. She highlighted that love and commitment can exist beyond the boundaries of monogamy, and that multiple consensual relationships can coexist harmoniously.

Non-monogamy challenges the notion that romantic love should be restricted to only one partner. It allows individuals to engage in multiple loving relationships while respecting the autonomy and agency of all involved. Talin's advocacy for polyamory encouraged open and honest communication, emphasizing the importance of consent, trust, and ethical behavior among all partners.

Addressing Gender and Sexuality Stereotypes

Talin Iryn recognized that rigid gender roles and stereotypes were barriers to authentic self-expression and hindered the possibilities for fulfilling relationships. She championed the dismantling of these stereotypes, creating space for individuals of all genders and sexual orientations to explore and embrace their true selves.

By challenging gender norms, Talin paved the way for gender non-conforming and non-binary individuals to form meaningful connections and express their love without fear of judgment or discrimination.

Furthermore, her activism in promoting LGBTQ+ rights helped create a more inclusive society, where individuals are free to love whomever they choose, regardless of their sexual orientation.

Fostering Communication and Emotional Intelligence

Talin Iryn emphasized the importance of effective communication and emotional intelligence in cultivating healthy and fulfilling relationships. She recognized that the key to successful relationships lies in cultivating empathy, active listening, and the ability to express oneself authentically.

Through workshops and educational programs, Talin encouraged individuals to develop these skills, providing them with the tools necessary for building strong and resilient connections. By fostering a culture of emotional intelligence, she helped create a society where individuals could engage in open and honest dialogue, resolving conflicts and nurturing their relationships.

Promoting Consent and Agency

Talin Iryn's advocacy for reimagining love and relationships went hand in hand with promoting consent and agency. She underscored the importance of ensuring that all individuals have control over their own bodies, choices, and boundaries within any relationship dynamic.

Talin's work on consent education aimed to eradicate harmful practices such as coercion, manipulation, and abuse. By emphasizing the importance of affirmative and enthusiastic consent, she sought to create a culture where all individuals are empowered to make informed decisions about their relationships and experiences.

Elevating Relationship Diversity

The fight for alien civil rights led by Talin Iryn also elevated the importance of recognizing and celebrating relationship diversity. She advocated for the acknowledgment and validation of all types of relationships, including friendships, chosen families, and non-romantic connections.

Talin's work emphasized that love and support in our lives can come from various sources, and that these connections are equally valuable and significant. By elevating relationship diversity, she affirms the importance of all types of relationships and contributes to the overall well-being and inclusivity of Xyorathian society.

Conclusion

Talin Iryn's advocacy for alien civil rights went beyond legal reforms and policy changes. Her work to reimagine love and relationships challenged societal norms, opening up new possibilities for individuals to express their love and form meaningful connections.

By questioning traditional ideas of love, embracing non-monogamy and polyamory, addressing gender and sexuality stereotypes, fostering communication and emotional intelligence, promoting consent and agency, and elevating relationship diversity, Talin Iryn left a lasting impact on Xyorathian society. Her legacy serves as a reminder that love knows no boundaries and that everyone deserves the freedom to love and be loved as their authentic selves.

The Fight for Justice: Never-Ending and Ever-Evolving

In the struggle for justice, one thing remains evident: the fight is both never-ending and ever-evolving. Throughout history, we have seen countless instances of discrimination, oppression, and inequality faced by marginalized communities. And just as society progresses, so too must our efforts to dismantle these systems of injustice.

The fight for justice is a multifaceted battle that requires constant vigilance, adaptability, and resilience. It is not a linear path, but rather a complex web of interconnected issues that demand our attention. In the case of Talin Iryn and their campaign against the multi-tentacle marriage restrictions on Xyorath, their victory was a milestone in the fight for alien rights. However, this achievement does not mark the end of the struggle. It serves as a catalyst for continued activism and progress.

One of the ongoing challenges in the fight for justice is the need to address the intersections of discrimination. Marginalized communities often face multiple forms of oppression simultaneously, such as racism, sexism, ableism, and homophobia. The fight cannot be limited to the alleviation of one specific form of discrimination; it must be a collective effort to dismantle all systems of oppression.

To illustrate this point, let us consider the issue of employment discrimination. It is not uncommon for alien individuals to encounter barriers and prejudice when seeking employment. They may face discriminatory hiring practices, limited access to educational opportunities, and unequal pay. To combat these injustices, activists like Talin Iryn must advocate for policies and laws that promote equal employment opportunities for all, regardless of their alien status.

Furthermore, the fight for justice requires us to continuously adapt our advocacy strategies to meet the changing political landscapes. As society progresses, so too do the tactics employed by those who seek to maintain the status quo. Conservative forces often push back against progressive changes, making it necessary for activists to develop innovative strategies to sustain momentum and overcome resistance.

One unconventional yet highly effective strategy is to harness the power of social media and digital platforms. Activists can use these tools to raise awareness, mobilize support, and amplify the voices of marginalized communities. By harnessing the interconnectedness of the digital era, activists can reach wider audiences and engage in powerful online campaigns that pressure policymakers and challenge oppressive systems.

It is also important to recognize and celebrate the contributions of other civil rights movements and organizations. Collaboration and unity among different marginalized communities can lead to a stronger and more impactful fight for justice. By partnering with organizations fighting for women's rights, LGBTQ+ rights, and racial equality, alien activists like Talin Iryn can contribute to a collective struggle for a more just society.

It is crucial to acknowledge that the fight for justice comes with its fair share of challenges and setbacks. Backlash from conservative forces, internal divisions within the movement, and the emotional toll of sustained resistance can all hinder progress. Activists must prioritize self-care, nurturing their mental and emotional well-being, and finding support networks that replenish their energy and motivation.

The fight for justice requires us to envision a long-term vision for equality. It is not enough to focus solely on immediate victories. We must strive for sustained systemic change and create a world where justice and fairness are fundamental to every aspect of society. This can be achieved through continued advocacy, education programs, legislative reforms, and the cultivation of international alliances.

As we reflect on Talin Iryn's legacy and their impact on Xyorathian society and beyond, we are reminded of the resilience and determination of those who fight for justice. Their efforts inspire future generations of alien activists, encouraging them to continue the work and build upon past achievements. Talin Iryn's story serves as a beacon of hope, demonstrating that change is possible and that the fight for justice is never-ending and ever-evolving.

In conclusion, the fight for justice is an ongoing struggle that demands our unwavering dedication. It requires us to address the intersections of discrimination, adapt our strategies to changing political landscapes, collaborate with other civil rights movements, and overcome challenges and setbacks. By embracing a long-term vision for equality and justice, we can pave the way for a more inclusive and just society for all. The legacy of Talin Iryn and their fight against the multi-tentacle marriage restrictions on Xyorath will forever remind us that the fight for justice is a never-ending and ever-evolving battle.

Conclusion

Talin's Impact on Xyorathian Society

Overcoming Prejudice and Discrimination

In the fight for civil rights, overcoming prejudice and discrimination is a crucial aspect of creating a more inclusive and equitable society. Talin Iryn's journey on Xyorath shines a light on the power of resistance, as well as the challenges faced by alien communities in their struggle for equal rights.

Understanding Prejudice

Prejudice is a deeply rooted belief or attitude held by individuals or groups that is based on preconceived notions and stereotypes about others. It often leads to discrimination, the unfair and unequal treatment of individuals or groups based on their perceived differences. Prejudice and discrimination can manifest in various forms, such as racial, ethnic, religious, or gender-based discrimination.

On Xyorath, prejudice against certain alien species was prevalent, leading to the Multi-Tentacle Marriage Restrictions that targeted specific communities. These restrictions not only limited the rights of individuals to marry based on their alien species but also perpetuated a culture of discrimination and inequality.

To overcome prejudice, it is crucial to challenge and change societal attitudes and beliefs. Talin Iryn recognized this and dedicated her life to dismantling the prejudice and discrimination that permeated Xyorathian society.

Challenging Stereotypes

Challenging stereotypes is a key step in overcoming prejudice and discrimination. Stereotypes are oversimplified and generalized beliefs about a particular group, often based on limited or inaccurate information. These stereotypes contribute to the perpetuation of prejudice and can be harmful and divisive.

Talin Iryn embarked on a mission to challenge the stereotypes associated with alien species on Xyorath. Through education, awareness campaigns, and personal engagement, she sought to humanize and normalize the experiences of alien individuals and communities. By highlighting shared values, aspirations, and struggles, Talin aimed to foster empathy and understanding.

Example: One strategy Talin employed was organizing town hall meetings where alien community members and other Xyorathians could engage in open and honest dialogue. These sessions provided an opportunity for individuals to share their personal stories, challenge misconceptions, and address the fears and concerns that underpinned prejudice.

Promoting Inclusive Policies

In order to tackle prejudice and discrimination effectively, it is necessary to implement inclusive policies that protect the rights of marginalized communities. These policies should aim to create a level playing field and ensure equal opportunities for all.

Talin Iryn worked tirelessly to advocate for inclusive policies on Xyorath. She engaged with lawmakers, influential leaders, and policymakers, urging them to address the Multi-Tentacle Marriage Restrictions and push for legislative changes that would promote equality and justice.

Solution: Talin's efforts resulted in the lifting of the ban on multi-tentacle marriages in local communities, a crucial step towards desegregation and creating a more inclusive society. Through her advocacy and coalition-building, she was able to build public support for legal reforms, leading to statewide legalization.

Fostering Empowerment

Overcoming prejudice and discrimination requires empowering marginalized communities to assert their rights and challenge oppressive systems. Talin Iryn understood the importance of fostering empowerment and self-advocacy among alien individuals on Xyorath.

She organized empowerment workshops and skill-building sessions to equip alien communities with the tools and confidence to challenge discrimination and fight for their rights. These workshops focused on legal literacy, public speaking, community organizing, and other essential skills necessary for effective advocacy.

Resource: In collaboration with legal experts and organizations, Talin created a comprehensive guidebook on alien rights that served as a valuable resource for individuals facing discrimination. This resource empowered individuals with knowledge about their legal rights and provided guidance on navigating the legal system to seek justice.

Celebrating Diversity

In the fight against prejudice, celebrating diversity plays a significant role in creating inclusive communities. Talin Iryn recognized the importance of embracing differences and creating spaces where individuals could express their unique identities without fear of discrimination.

Through cultural festivals, art exhibitions, and storytelling events, Talin celebrated the rich cultural heritage of alien communities on Xyorath. These events served as platforms for fostering understanding, appreciation, and dialogue between different communities, breaking down barriers and building bridges.

Unconventional Approach: Talin initiated a community exchange program that paired members of alien communities with Xyorathian families, encouraging shared experiences and fostering deep connections. This grassroots approach humanized alien individuals and challenged the stereotypes and prejudices that had been ingrained in Xyorathian society.

Conclusion

The fight against prejudice and discrimination requires individuals like Talin Iryn, who are willing to challenge the status quo and dedicate their lives to creating a more inclusive society. Talin's activism on Xyorath serves as a testament to the power of resilience, determination, and community in overcoming systemic oppression.

By challenging stereotypes, advocating for inclusive policies, fostering empowerment, and celebrating diversity, Talin laid the foundation for a more equitable society. Her legacy continues to inspire future generations of alien and civil rights activists, reminding us that the fight for justice is never-ending and ever-evolving.

Shifting Cultural Norms and Attitudes

Shifting cultural norms and attitudes was a crucial aspect of Talin Iryn's fight for equality on Xyorath. Through her activism, she challenged deep-rooted prejudices and worked to change societal perceptions towards multi-tentacle marriages. This section explores the strategies employed by Talin and her allies to create a more inclusive and accepting society.

Understanding Cultural Norms

To effectively shift cultural norms, it was imperative to first understand the existing beliefs and values within Xyorathian society. Talin recognized that many individuals held preconceived notions about multi-tentacle marriages due to cultural traditions and religious teachings. She utilized research and dialogue to gain insights into these perspectives, allowing her to tailor her messaging and counter arguments accordingly.

Promoting Education and Awareness

Talin believed that education was a powerful tool in challenging biases and promoting acceptance. She spearheaded educational initiatives aimed at debunking myths and dispelling stereotypes surrounding multi-tentacle marriages. Through workshops, seminars, and public awareness campaigns, she engaged with communities to foster empathy and understanding.

One effective strategy employed by Talin was the use of personal narratives. She encouraged individuals in multi-tentacle marriages to share their stories, humanizing their experiences and highlighting the love and commitment that existed within these relationships. By providing a platform for these stories to be heard, Talin was able to humanize the issue and bridge the gap between different communities.

Addressing Fear and Misconceptions

Fear and misconceptions often perpetuated discrimination against multi-tentacle marriages. Talin actively worked to address these concerns by providing accurate information and challenging misguided beliefs. She collaborated with experts in the field to develop educational resources that debunked the notion that multi-tentacle marriages were unnatural or harmful.

Talin also recognized the importance of addressing religious perspectives on marriage. She engaged in constructive dialogue with religious leaders, organizing interfaith conferences and discussions to foster understanding and bridge religious divides. By emphasizing the shared values of love, compassion, and respect, Talin successfully challenged the notion that multi-tentacle marriages were incompatible with religious beliefs.

Media Influence and Representation

Harnessing the power of media was another essential strategy in shifting cultural norms. Talin actively sought out opportunities to amplify the voices of those in multi-tentacle marriages, ensuring their stories were featured in mainstream media outlets. This representation helped challenge stereotypes and normalized the idea of multi-tentacle marriages within society.

Talin also leveraged social media platforms to mobilize support and provide a space for open dialogue. She encouraged individuals to share their thoughts and experiences, creating online communities that empowered others to join the movement. By engaging with a wide audience, Talin expanded the reach of her message and fostered a sense of solidarity.

Building Intersecting Movements

Recognizing the interconnectedness of various forms of discrimination, Talin actively collaborated with other civil rights movements on Xyorath. She understood that achieving true equality required addressing the underlying systems of oppression that affected different marginalized groups.

By joining forces with movements advocating for gender equality, racial justice, and LGBTQ+ rights, Talin strengthened her cause and brought attention to the intersections of discrimination. Through shared rallies, conferences, and initiatives, she emphasized the importance of inclusive activism and highlighted the collective impact of social justice movements.

The Power of Art and Culture

Talin recognized the influence of art and culture in shaping societal norms and attitudes. She encouraged artists, writers, and musicians to incorporate themes of love, acceptance, and diversity into their work. By promoting the positive representation of multi-tentacle relationships in various art forms, Talin challenged existing stereotypes and expanded public consciousness.

Additionally, Talin organized cultural festivals and events that celebrated the diversity of Xyorathian society. Through these platforms, she showcased the beauty and richness of multi-tentacle marriages, fostering pride and inspiring others to embrace these relationships.

Challenges and Nurturing Change

Shifting cultural norms and attitudes was not without its challenges. Talin and her allies faced resistance and backlash from conservative individuals and organizations. They encountered pushback from those who were resistant to change and held deeply ingrained biases.

To address these challenges, Talin focused on nurturing change through empathetic dialogue and understanding. She engaged in difficult conversations, promoting active listening and respectful communication. By acknowledging the fears and concerns of those opposing multi-tentacle marriages, Talin aimed to bridge the divide and promote thoughtful reflection.

Talin also provided resources for individuals who were open to shifting their perspectives. She developed comprehensive guides, workshops, and counseling services that supported individuals in unlearning biases and embracing inclusive attitudes. By providing a pathway for personal growth, Talin ensured that individuals had the tools to challenge their own prejudices.

Conclusion: Cultural Evolution

Through her unwavering dedication and strategic approach, Talin Iryn played a pivotal role in shifting the cultural norms and attitudes surrounding multi-tentacle marriages on Xyorath. Her tireless efforts to educate, raise awareness, and challenge misconceptions brought about a fundamental change in how society perceived and accepted these relationships.

Talin's legacy serves as a testament to the power of activism and the potential for transformative change within a society. Her work not only impacted Xyorathian communities but also inspired alien rights movements across the galaxy. The lessons learned from her fight for equality continue to shape the ongoing struggle for justice and inclusivity. As her story continues to be told and celebrated, Talin Iryn remains an icon of resistance, love, and the power of cultural evolution.

Inspiring Other Alien and Civil Rights Activists

Talin Iryn's tireless efforts and unwavering dedication to the cause of equal rights for aliens have inspired a new wave of activism among Xyorathians and beyond. Her courageous fight against the multi-tentacle marriage restrictions and her eventual triumph serve as a powerful example of what can be achieved through persistence, resilience, and collective action.

1. The Power of Representation:

One of the most significant ways in which Talin has inspired other alien and civil rights activists is through her representation as a strong and fearless leader. By breaking barriers and challenging societal norms, she has shown that anyone, regardless of their background or appearance, can make a difference. Talin's story serves as a beacon of hope for alien individuals who face discrimination and marginalization, encouraging them to speak up and fight for their rights.

2. Coalition Building and Collaboration:

Talin's success in overturning the multi-tentacle marriage restrictions was not achieved single-handedly. She understood the importance of building alliances and collaborating with diverse groups to amplify her message and broaden her impact. This approach has inspired other activists to work together across different alien communities and civil rights movements, pooling their resources and expertise to achieve greater social change.

3. Grassroots Organizing and Advocacy:

Talin's journey from a small town on Xyorath to becoming a prominent advocate for alien rights is a testament to the power of grassroots organizing. She started at the local level, mobilizing support and building networks within her own community. Her story has inspired other activists to adopt similar tactics, focusing on community engagement, organizing rallies, and utilizing social media platforms to amplify their message and generate public support.

4. Intersectionality and Inclusivity:

Talin's activism has also fostered a greater understanding of the intersections of discrimination and the importance of inclusivity within the movement for alien rights. She advocated for not only the repeal of the multi-tentacle marriage restrictions but also for equal access to healthcare, employment opportunities, and education. Her emphasis on intersectionality has spurred other activists to address multiple forms of oppression and to ensure that alien rights advocacy is inclusive and supportive of all individuals.

5. Advocacy Training and Mentorship:

Talin's impact extends beyond her own achievements; she has dedicated herself to mentoring and training new generations of alien and civil rights activists. Through workshops, conferences, and speaking engagements, she shares her experiences, strategies, and lessons learned, equipping others with the knowledge and skills necessary to effect change. By nurturing and supporting these emerging leaders, Talin ensures that the fight for justice and equality continues well into the future.

6. Artistic Expression and Creative Resistance:

In addition to her activism, Talin has employed artistic expression as a means of resistance. Her poetry, music, and visual art have served as powerful tools for spreading awareness, challenging stereotypes, and inspiring empathy. Other activists have been inspired by Talin's use of creative expression, exploring their own artistic talents to convey messages of equality and justice.

7. International Solidarity and Global Impact:

Talin's impact reaches far beyond the confines of Xyorath. Her advocacy work and legal victories have inspired alien and civil rights activists in other worlds and galaxies, fostering a sense of international solidarity. Talin's journey has shown that the fight for equality is universal, transcending borders and uniting diverse communities in the pursuit of justice.

In conclusion, Talin Iryn's groundbreaking activism has ignited a fire in the hearts of other alien and civil rights activists. Her courage, strategic thinking, and relentless pursuit of justice have paved the way for a new generation of leaders who continue to advocate for equal rights. Through representation, coalition building, grassroots organizing, inclusivity, mentorship, artistic expression, and global impact, Talin's legacy lives on, inspiring others to challenge discrimination and fight for a more just and inclusive future.

The Fight for Equality and Social Justice Continues

The victory achieved by Talin Iryn in overturning the multi-tentacle marriage restrictions on Xyorath was a monumental step towards equality and social justice. However, the fight does not end here. The struggle for equal rights for all members of society, regardless of their alien status or background, is an ongoing battle that requires continued activism and dedication.

1. Recognizing Intersectionality: In order to achieve true equality, it is crucial to understand and address the interconnected nature of discrimination. Intersectionality recognizes that individuals can face multiple forms of oppression simultaneously, such as discrimination based on race, gender, sexuality, or alien status. The fight for equality must embrace an inclusive approach that takes into account the unique challenges faced by individuals who exist at these intersections.

2. Challenging Systemic Discrimination: The fight for equality and social justice goes beyond changing individual laws and policies. It requires dismantling the systemic structures that perpetuate discrimination and inequality. This includes addressing institutional biases, unequal access to resources and opportunities, and the disproportionate impact of discrimination on marginalized communities. Activists must continue to advocate for systemic reforms to create a truly inclusive and just society.

3. Partnering with Other Movements: The fight for equality is not limited to a single cause or group. It is essential to forge alliances and collaborations with other

social justice movements, such as the fight against racial discrimination, gender inequality, or environmental injustice. By joining forces, activists can amplify their voices, leverage their collective power, and work towards a more equitable society for all.

4. Education and Awareness: To effect lasting change, it is imperative to educate and raise awareness about the issues faced by alien communities and the importance of equality and social justice. This involves creating educational programs, workshops, and awareness campaigns that foster empathy, challenge stereotypes, and promote understanding. By engaging with the wider public, activists can gain support, challenge prejudices, and foster meaningful dialogue.

5. Addressing Persistent Challenges: While significant progress has been made, the fight for equality and social justice continues to face numerous challenges. Some individuals and groups may harbor deep-rooted prejudices, resisting change and perpetuating discrimination. Activists must be prepared to navigate these obstacles, develop strategies to counter backlash, and push for long-lasting, systemic change.

6. Advocacy and Policy Change: Legislation plays a crucial role in advancing equality and social justice. Activists must continue lobbying for legislative reforms that protect the rights and well-being of alien communities. This includes advocating for comprehensive anti-discrimination laws, equal access to healthcare and education, fair employment practices, and affordable housing. By working towards policy change, activists can ensure that the fight for equality becomes ingrained in the fabric of society.

7. Grassroots Mobilization: Mobilizing grassroots activism is fundamental to sustaining the fight for equality and social justice. By organizing rallies, protests, and grassroots campaigns, activists can create a groundswell of support and make their demands heard. Building strong networks, engaging in community organizing, and empowering individuals at the local level are key strategies to create lasting change from the bottom up.

8. Holding Institutions Accountable: To maintain progress and prevent regression, it is essential to hold institutions accountable for their actions. This includes monitoring the implementation of anti-discrimination measures, tracking representation and inclusion in key institutions, and demanding transparency and accountability. By ensuring that institutions are committed to diversity, equity, and justice, activists can safeguard the gains made and push for further advancements.

9. Embracing Innovation and Technology: In the digital age, activists have an array of tools at their disposal. Utilizing social media platforms, online petitions, and creative digital campaigns can help raise awareness, mobilize support, and amplify marginalized voices. Embracing innovation and technology allows activists to reach

a wider audience and create meaningful change in the fight for equality and social justice.

The fight for equality and social justice is a continuous struggle that requires unwavering commitment, resilience, and collective action. Talin Iryn's triumph over the multi-tentacle marriage restrictions ignited the spark of change, but it is up to future generations of activists to carry the torch forward. By recognizing the intersections of discrimination, challenging systemic inequalities, forging alliances, and demanding accountability, we can create a society that embraces diversity, equity, and justice for all. The fight continues, and it is our collective responsibility to ensure that the legacy of equality and social justice endures.

Talin Iryn: Remembering a True Hero

Talin Iryn was much more than just an alien civil rights activist; she was a beacon of hope, a relentless champion for equality and justice. Her dedication to the cause and her unwavering determination made her a true hero in the eyes of many. Even years after her passing, her legacy continues to inspire and guide those who fight for social change. In this final section, we remember and celebrate the remarkable life and impact of Talin Iryn.

Talin's journey began on the planet of Xyorath, where discrimination and prejudice were deeply entrenched in the society. Growing up in such an environment, she witnessed firsthand the hardships faced by alien communities, particularly when it came to the archaic multi-tentacle marriage restrictions. This early exposure to injustice shaped her sense of justice and propelled her into a life of activism.

Despite facing initial resistance and obstacles, Talin was undeterred in her mission to challenge the status quo. She moved to the capital city to immerse herself in the heart of the struggle, finding employment and financial independence. Joining local alien rights organizations and building networks and allies, she laid the groundwork for her fight for change.

Talin's first attempt at legalizing multi-tentacle marriages was met with opposition and backlash. However, through her tenacity and ability to garner media attention and public support, she was able to achieve a significant victory - the lifting of the ban in local communities. But she didn't stop there. The fight continued, and her second attempt at legalization resulted in statewide acceptance.

Breaking barriers extended beyond fighting for marriage equality. Talin understood that true equality meant addressing employment discrimination, securing access to healthcare and education, challenging segregation and housing policies, and influencing policy change at local and national levels. She collaborated with other civil rights movements, recognizing the importance of intersectionality in the fight for justice.

The legal battle was not without its hurdles, as Talin and her legal team faced courtroom drama, threats, and intimidation. However, their research, preparation, and compelling arguments resulted in a historic decision in favor of equality. The impact of this verdict reverberated throughout Xyorathian communities, providing hope and inspiring future advocacy efforts.

Implementing change was not without its challenges and setbacks. Talin faced backlash from conservative forces and had to navigate internal divisions and differences. She learned important lessons in leadership and coalition building, understanding the need for sustained resistance and evolving strategies. Coping with burnout and the emotional toll was an ongoing challenge, but she persevered.

Talin's lasting effects on Xyorathian society and beyond cannot be overstated. Her fight against prejudice and discrimination caused cultural norms and attitudes to shift, leading to increased visibility and acceptance. Policy changes and legal reforms opened doors for alien communities and addressed the intersections of discrimination. Her tireless advocacy empowered alien and minority voices, forever changing the trajectory of civil rights.

In the years following Talin's passing, her impact continued through the establishment of foundations for alien rights and the fight for intersectionality and inclusivity. Her memoirs and publications served as crucial resources for future generations. Honors and recognitions memorialized her contributions, and documentaries and films ensured that her story would be told for generations to come.

Talin Iryn will always be remembered as a true hero. Her unwavering determination, courage, and resilience have left an indelible mark on the fight for justice. She taught us that the fight for equality is ongoing, that there will always be challenges and setbacks, but with perseverance and collective action, change is possible. Talin's legacy lives on, inspiring present and future activists to continue the work she began - to create a world where every individual, regardless of their origin, can live free from discrimination and injustice.

Conclusion

In conclusion, Talin Iryn's impact on Xyorathian society and the broader fight for equality cannot be overemphasized. Her journey from witnessing discrimination on her home planet to becoming a powerful advocate for change serves as a testament to the power of determination and resilience. Talin's unwavering commitment to justice paved the way for advancements in alien civil rights and encouraged other activists to join the cause. Her legacy is one of hope, progress, and a reminder that the fight for equality and social justice is never-ending. Talin Iryn will forever be remembered as a true hero, inspiring generations to come.

Index

www.ingramcontent.com/pod-product-compliance
Ingram Content Group UK Ltd.
Pitfield, Milton Keynes, MK11 3LW, UK
UKHW032333131224
452011UK00004B/58

9 781779 694737